Ice Sculpting
The Modern Way

Ice Sculpting
The Modern Way

ROBERT GARLOUGH

RANDY FINCH

DEREK MAXFIELD

DELMAR
CENGAGE Learning™

Australia • Brazil • Japan • Korea • Mexico • Singapore • Spain • United Kingdom • United States

Ice Sculpting The Modern Way
Robert Garlough, Randy Finch, and
Derek Maxfield

Vice President, Career Education Strategic
Business Unit: Dawn Gerrain

Director of Editorial: Sherry Gomoll

Senior Acquisitions Editor: Joan M. Gill

Editorial Assistant: Lisa Flatley

Director of Production: Wendy A. Troeger

Production Manager: Carolyn Miller

Production Editor: Matthew J. Williams

Director of Marketing: Donna J. Lewis

Channel Manager: Wendy E. Mapstone

For product information and technology assistance, contact us at
Cengage Learning Customer & Sales Support, 1-800-354-9706

For permission to use material from this text or product,
submit all requests online at **www.cengage.com/permissions**
Further permissions questions can be emailed to
permissionrequest@cengage.com

Library of Congress Control Number: 2003046768

ISBN-13: 978-1-4018-0405-3

ISBN-10: 1-4018-0405-5

Delmar
Executive Woods
5 Maxwell Drive
Clifton Park, NY 12065
USA

Cengage Learning is a leading provider of customized learning solutions with office
locations around the globe, including Singapore, the United Kingdom, Australia,
Mexico, Brazil, and Japan. Locate your local office at **www.cengage.com/global**

Cengage Learning products are represented in Canada by Nelson Education, Ltd.

To learn more about Delmar, visit **www.cengage.com/delmar**

Purchase any of our products at your local bookstore or at our preferred online store
www.cengagebrain.com

Notice to the Reader

Printed in the United States of America
5 6 7 15 14 13 12 11

For Jenny, whose beauty, art, and love of life transcend her time on this earth.

Contents

Foreword

Sculptors have used ice as a medium to produce a range of ethereal, and ephemeral, pieces for centuries. Over 300 years ago in China, near the city of present day Harbin, fishermen hollowed out blocks of ice to shield their candles from the wind; it is possible that these practical pieces were the basis for ice carving, as we know it today. Around 1740, Empress Anna of Russia ordered a palace made completely of ice to be built along the Neva as a conspicuous and ostentatious show of power and wealth. Today, the Ice Hotel in Jukkasjärvi, Sweden, draws tourists each year from all over the world who pay for the pleasure of sitting, dining, and sleeping on ice.

Ice is a challenging medium for the sculptor and makes special demands. Unlike marble, stone, or clay, ice carvings eventually melt. The costs of acquiring and storing the ice, the skills to carve it into an attractive three-dimensional sculpture or display piece, transporting it, and setting it up are significant. Yet ice carvings remain a powerful tool for setting the tone at any event. The fleeting life span of an ice carving, coupled with its high demands in terms of skill and artistry, sends out subtle and not so subtle messages about who we, as culinarians, actually are. Properly done, ice carvings convey an aura of elegance, attention to detail, artistry, and mastery of the craft. They indeed help to send a signal to our guests, assuring them that they are in good hands.

Ice Sculpting the Modern Way heralds the resurgence of this historic art form, bringing it from the 18th century into the 21st by providing its readers with a comprehensive look at ice carving as an art form, but also a business. The techniques presented by the authors may in some cases break with "tradition" but they are tested and proven. *Ice Sculpting the Modern Way* calls our attention to the imagination and skills necessary to conceive a piece and bring it to life. It does this by discussing not just the actual sculpting process, but also the important issues of safety, storage, transportation, and the financial aspects of sculpting for hire.

As a compendium of useful information about ice, *Ice Sculpting the Modern Way* is a giant step into the future. Well organized, well researched, and well written, the book provides a chapter structure prepared with education and training in mind, a glossary filled with over two hundred relevant terms, comprehensive listings offering readers access to a host of suppliers and organizations, as well as photographs and design templates. The book's three authors, professional chefs all, collaborated to produce a cutting edge book, certain to be an important reference for aspiring sculptors, practicing ice artists, and educators for years to come.

L. Timothy Ryan
President, The Culinary Institute of America

Preface

Ice Sculpting the Modern Way: For Beginning and Advanced Ice Artists can be used either as a reference text for a multi-day ice sculpting course or as a guide for anyone wishing to advance his or her skills without an instructor. Written with both the beginning sculptor and the practicing ice artist in mind, this book is also intended to be a reference for those teaching garde manger or buffet catering courses.

Technology drives the ice sculpting industry today. Born from the tools and knowledge of stone carvers, ice sculpting, with the added impetus of technology, has quickly evolved into its own discipline. Modern power tools and chain saws challenge the chisels, chippers, and handsaws of the not-too-distant past. Computer-aided design and cutting machines introduced in the late 1990s, such as the Iceculture 5200 used by the authors, utilize the unsurpassed accuracy of computers. This applied technology allows for consistent production of precise ice components, which can be assembled to form both large, multi-block displays, or small serving pieces.

The team at Ice Sculptures, Ltd. has long been on the cutting edge of ice sculpting technology, researching and developing various methods to efficiently produce ice works for all occasions. The company's total focus and full-time occupation is the artful creation of ice sculptures and ice serving pieces.

For those wishing to use the text in a classroom situation, an *Instructor's Guide* with instructional strategies, test questions, form masters, and lesson plans is available to accompany *Ice Sculpting the Modern Way*.

The Making of this Text

Over the years, we honed skills and gained knowledge under the tutelage of many outstanding ice sculptors. Throughout the 1970s, 80s, and into the 90s, we learned under those ice-sculpting masters, who generously shared their experience and the knowledge available at the time. We were inspired by their passion for the art to pursue our own understanding of the medium and to develop our own styles of ice sculpting.

As our skill levels increased through practice and experience, we were given opportunities to teach this craft to aspiring culinarians. Initially we used what references were readily available on the market at the time, as all instructors do, but as our understanding progressed, we began to look beyond the available reference tools.

Our knowledge of ice and of efficient and consistent methods of sculpting were greatly enhanced when we went into the ice sculpting business on a full-time basis. We developed our own procedures and discovered improved methods of producing quality works in less time. We introduced greater and broader use of power tools into our daily work, and our production quality and quantity grew substantially. In an industry that values productivity, that translates well.

As our use of power tools in ice competitions and daily production became routine, we deviated even more from the techniques described in older publications on the subject. We began developing our own handouts for our ice sculpting demonstrations, garde manger, and ice sculpting classes. And we addressed teaching from a different perspective—that of a traditional sculptor, but using power tools.

Our combined 60 years' experience in ice sculpting and culinary education brings a wealth of new knowledge not offered in other books on this subject. For example, we suggest new methods of sculpting and fusing ice never before described in other sculpting references. Our methods sometimes conflict with traditional methods of doing various tasks. Our methods are included in this book because they work well and are a dependable and preferred method for use in our daily occupation.

The Organization of this Text

We have structured this book as a comprehensive, learner-oriented text that can serve as a foundation for a course in ice sculpting. One of the primary motivations for producing this text was to develop a reference book on ice sculpting that could easily be used in a classroom setting. Our combined backgrounds in occupational education and culinary arts formed the organization of a text that we believe to be both user-friendly and instructive.

The book is divided into four distinct sections, each with several supporting chapters, plus numerous step-by-step photographs, various appendices, and a comprehensive glossary. The text is divided into four parts:

- Learning About Sculpting in Ice
- Working with Ice
- Managing the Ice
- Advanced Skills with Ice

Part I, "Learning About Sculpting in Ice," provides a necessary foundation for students in the fundamentals of sculpting, the science of ice, tools and equipment, and safe practices and procedures. We believe that before a student is allowed to handle valuable tools or ice, he needs to gain an appreciation for the practice of sculpting. Coupled with an understanding of the fragile nature of ice and the proper use and care of tools, this foreknowledge will greatly increase the student's likelihood of success in ice sculpting. And since safety is paramount in any business operation, we stress methods that insure the sculptor's protection.

After the student understands the basics of shape, form, and dimension, Part II, "Working with Ice," teaches the student how to make his own guiding patterns, called "design templates." The student learns how to take a suitable photograph or line drawing and translate it into a working template. Using the template and applying the skills learned up to this point, the student is then guided through the actual sculpting process. Additionally, this section teaches the student how to extend a sculpture beyond the limiting dimensions of an ice block by mastering the different fusing techniques illustrated in the text.

Part III, "Managing the Ice," focuses on the proper care, transportation, and display of ice sculptures. The ice artist must address these important aspects of managing the ice to ensure that the sculpture arrives safely at the display location and is viewed in its best form. Different display pans are featured, including a lighted sculpture cart created by one of the authors. Additionally, we describe how to safely transport ice sculptures over long distances.

Part IV, "Advanced Skills with Ice," is intended for practicing ice artists, exceptional students, and entrepreneurial sculptors; this section provides insights on designing original works and special event pieces. Here, the reader will uncover "tricks of the trade" never before published in ice carving books. This portion also provides the reader with useful information on planning for, and competing in, different ice sculpting competitions and festivals. The book ends with a discussion of the business aspects of creating sculptures on a full-time basis. The business-minded sculptor must wear many hats, and this section explores those responsibilities and the financial tools needed for managing the business.

In addition to the main text, we have incorporated a section of appendices with detailed templates and photographs. We feel this unique feature of *Ice Sculpting the Modern Way* sets this text above all other ice sculpting references. Included are three sections of sculptures, intended to provide instruction to ice artists at all levels: beginning, practicing, and advanced. Each section contains detailed templates, sized to scale, for the learner to photocopy and enlarge. A generous series of carefully photographed, step-by-step photos accompanies each design template, detailing the sculpting process.

Also included in the back matter of the book is a useful collection of additional design templates and reference addresses, including suppliers, organizations, and competitions, complete with many corresponding URLs. The glossary contains a comprehensive lexicon of ice sculpting terminology, providing the student with a useful reference to expand his understanding of this sub-zero art form. All terms appearing in bold in each chapter are in the glossary. We have also provided a selected bibliography of texts that we have used over the years to learn about the art and business of ice, sculpting, and ice sculpting. Each reference has elements that have proven extremely valuable in our learning, and, ultimately, to the development of this text.

Organization of the Chapters

In an attempt to meet the needs of students, instructors, and chefs interested in learning this sub-zero art form, we have chosen a chapter format that includes many pedagogical features. The chapters all begin with a detailed **Chapter Outline** which provides a sequential listing of headings and sub-headings. An **Objectives** section follows, which identifies the key elements the student will learn. This is followed by a list of **Key Terms and Concepts**, and the words are highlighted throughout the chapter text. Each chapter is concluded with an **Ask the Artist** section that features comments from a member of our ice sculpting industry.

After many years in culinary education, we understand that students' talents and abilities are varied. But we also know that anyone can learn to create ice sculptures when given appropriate direction and tools. It is our hope that *Ice Sculpting the Modern Way* will become the definitive reference book for today's ice artists, as the title suggests, just as we hope to bridge the gap between the art of sculpting and the medium of ice. We know from experience that the methods in this book work.

The practice of sculpting ice remains our quest for a greater understanding of the medium and the tools. We know that readers of this text will use the information contained herein to expand their personal boundaries and that of the entire industry. Today's students of modern ice sculpting are destined to be tomorrow's innovators; we expect our readers will be among those leading the ice sculpting industry of the future.

> *"We believed that anything worth doing was worth overdoing."*
> Steven Tyler—*Aerosmith*

Acknowledgements

We would like to thank and to acknowledge the many individuals who collectively wrote this book along with us. It has been said that it takes a village to raise a child; we would like to gratefully acknowledge the following family, friends, and professionals who contributed to this book's growth and development, as well as our own.

Joan Gill, our Acquisitions Editor at Delmar, who saw the potential in the book and supported our efforts to make it a reality. Thank you for allowing this text to become what it was meant to be.

Erin Connaughton, Project Manager at nSight, Inc., who guided the book from its infancy as a manuscript into a finished textbook. Your care for the project was incredible.

Lisa Flately, our Editorial Assistant at Delmar, who provided us with the liaison support necessary to produce the text. Thank you for guiding us through the production process.

Gary Finch, whose patience and skill in photography has produced some of the best step-by-step photographs of ice art ever published. Thank you for being an integral part of this book; through your eyes others will learn about *Ice Sculpting the Modern Way*.

Mary Ellen Finch, who came to the rescue at Ice Sculptures, Ltd. and provided much-needed computer and research assistance. Thank you for your belief in the project and your eagerness to lend a talented hand and caring heart to make it work.

From Grand Rapids Community College, Nick Antonakis, Visual Arts Department Head, who became our mentor in sculpture. Thank you for helping us learn the language of art and how to properly communicate it to our readers. Elaine Kampmueller, Geology Professor, and Tom Neils, Chemistry Professor, from the Physical Sciences Department, who validated and improved the science-related materials contained in Chapter 2.

Julian Bayley, President of Iceculture, who so generously provided us with photographs to illustrate the text. Thank you for your support of our project and your contributions to the ice industry.

Susan Walters, William Garlough, and Julie and Pete Metsker for their careful review of the manuscript. The final product is a better document because of your deliberate and careful study of the text.

Tim Ryan, President of The Culinary Institute of America, who wrote the Foreword. Thank you for continued visionary leadership in foodservice and culinary education and your willingness to validate and introduce our work.

Andrea Jacques and Diana Riley, ice-sculpting students from Schoolcraft College. Thank you for helping to develop and test some of the advanced designs featured in this text.

Robert Garlough would like to express grateful appreciation to his wife, Nancy, for her unselfish love and continued support of his career. He also extends his deepest appreciation to his children Jeremy, Kristen, Jon, and Melissa for their love and willingness to share their father with others, allowing him the countless hours he has spent in pursuit of this goal, among many. He recognizes the love, guidance, values, and friendship provided by his parents Bill and Charlotte, mother-in-law Ruth, brother Bill and sister-in-law Karen, brother-in-law Jeff and sister-in-law Natalie. He thanks all his remaining family for their contributions to his sense of family values. Robert would also like to acknowledge the outstanding faculty and staff at Grand Rapids Community College, in particular those in the Hospitality Education Department, for their friendship and support over the years. They are an incredible group of talented and dedicated professionals. Robert appreciates the efforts of his mentors and teachers, in particular the faculty at the Culinary Institute of America. He also recognizes the special opportunity made available to him by Richard Calkins, Till Peters, and Robert Partridge at Grand Rapids Community College. Finally, he would like to acknowledge the thousands of culinary students he has had the privilege to know and teach. Their quest for knowledge has been a true joy in which to share; they continue to educate him as they learn.

Randy Finch would like to acknowledge the following influences in his life. Chef Joseph Yezbick for introducing him to the world of ice sculpting. A structure is only as strong as its base. Chef Joseph's patience and his ability to teach are the cornerstones of Randy's foundation. He wishes to thank Dan Hugelier, CMC, for his guidance, both personally and professionally; Chef Dan's devotion to his family as well as to his artistic endeavors is a balance Randy will always admire. Randy is also grateful for the education he has received from his instructors at Oakland Community College, and from his students who are constantly teaching him new tricks in sculpture. He would like to recognize his business partner, Derek Maxfield, for continually striving for personal and professional perfection. He also wishes to acknowledge Jim Phipps for sharing his refined approach to the business of ice sculpting. Most importantly, Randy wishes to express enormous gratitude to his family for their support over the years, especially to his parents, Pat and Mary Ellen Finch.

Derek Maxfield would like to acknowledge his parents John and Cathy Maxfield, grandparents Joanne Johns, Helen and John Maxfield, and Susan Walters for providing love and support throughout the years. He is appreciative of Dan Hugelier, CMC, and Chef Michael Green for introducing him to ice sculpting. Derek also thanks Joshua Eickelberg, Stuart Eickelberg, and Joshua Goote as key staff members at Ice Sculptures, Ltd., who managed daily production throughout this project, and Randy Finch, as a great friend and business partner who shares an equal interest in the promotion and progression of ice sculpture.

About the Authors

Ice Sculpting the Modern Way was a collaborative effort of three professional chefs who have extensive but varied experiences in culinary education and the foodservice industry. Robert Garlough is the voice of the project; his understanding of occupational education brings the considerable sculpting talents of Randy Finch and Derek Maxfield to the classroom learner.

Robert Garlough, MS, AAC

Chef Emeritus, Grand Rapids Community College

Chef Garlough has over 33 years experience in the foodservice industry and more than 25 years in culinary education as founding director of the Hospitality Education Department at Grand Rapids Community College (GRCC) in Grand Rapids, Michigan. In addition to the courses and seminars that he teaches at the college, Robert leads students and industry executives on culinary study tours to destinations around the globe. He is a partner in the catering corporation of My Chef, Inc., located in Naperville, Illinois, and Principal of his consulting company, The Culinary Group.

Chef Garlough is certified as a Foodservice Management Professional by the Educational Foundation of the National Restaurant Association, and is a member of the American Academy of Chefs and The Honorable Order of the Golden Toque. He holds an Associate's degree in Occupational Studies in Culinary Arts from the Culinary Institute of America, a Bachelor of Business Administration degree in Restaurant and Lodging Management from Davenport University, and a Master of Science degree in Occupational Education from Ferris State University.

Robert personally earned silver and bronze medals at the 1988 Internationale Kochkunst Ausstellung (considered the "Culinary Olympics") in Frankfurt, Germany, while managing a six-member team of GRCC faculty and graduates. He served as manager for the 1993 Pastry Team USA that represented the United States at the 1993 Coupe du Monde de la Patisserie (World Pastry Cup) in Lyon, France. Chef Garlough also served as manager for Team USA 1998, a culinary student team representing America at the Malta International Students Culinary Salon in St. Julian's Bay, Malta. In 1984, Chef Garlough was awarded the Chef Herman Breithaupt Memorial Award by the Council on Hotel, Restaurant, and Institutional Education, naming him their national chef-instructor of the year. The American Culinary Federation (ACF) Educational Institute honored him as their National Educator of the Year in 1992.

His professional affiliations include having served as president of the Michigan Council on Hotel, Restaurant, and Institutional Education; president of the ACF Greater Grand Rapids Chapter; chairman of the ACF Educational Institute Accrediting Commission; and executive director of the International Consortium of Hospitality and Tourism Institutes.

RANDY FINCH

Co-Owner, Ice Sculptures, Ltd.

Chef Finch has more than 20 years experience in the foodservice industry, most recently working as Department Head and Chef in garde manger departments and fine dining restaurants at prestigious hotels. Randy has also taught beginning and advanced courses in ice sculpture for Grand Rapids Community College, Oakland Community College, and Schoolcraft College.

Chef Finch holds an Associate in Applied Science degree in Culinary Arts from Oakland Community College, where he received two gold medals in culinary shows and a Best of Pastries award.

In 1994, Randy co-founded Ice Sculptures, Ltd. The company has produced sculptures for a wide range of celebrities. Musicians such as Aerosmith, AC/DC, Bruce Springsteen, ZZ Top, Van Halen, Hootie and the Blowfish, Patti La Belle, and John Tesh have incorporated Randy's sculptures into their acts and after-parties. Corporations, including Absolut, A & W Root Beer, Meijer Inc., Rogers Department Store, and Grolsch Beer, have promoted their products using carvings from Ice Sculptures, Ltd. Still other clients, such as former President Gerald R. Ford, attorney Johnny Cochran, Michigan Governors John Engler and Jennifer M. Granholm, the Detroit Lions NFL Football Team and the US Culinary Olympic Team, have used the ice sculpting talents of Chef Finch and his partner Derek Maxfield.

Randy began sculpting more than18 years ago and became an avid culinary competitor soon afterwards. In addition to his many National Ice Carving Association (NICA) competition accolades, Chef Finch has earned first place awards in team and individual professional competitions at such prestigious events as the National Restaurant Association Chicago Food Show and the Plymouth International Ice Spectacular. He has judged both NICA and ACF-sanctioned ice-sculpting competitions.

DEREK MAXFIELD

Co-Owner, Ice Sculptures, Ltd.

Chef Maxfield began his culinary career in the late 1980s at the highly regarded Amway Grand Plaza Hotel where he had the good fortune to work under several very talented ice sculptors, one of whom would become his future business partner at Ice Sculptures, Ltd. While continuing to work as the sous chef at the Kent Country Club in Grand Rapids, Michigan, until 1996, Derek co-founded Ice Sculptures, Ltd. with Randy Finch in 1994.

Chef Maxfield received his Associate in Applied Arts and Sciences degree in Culinary Arts from Grand Rapids Community College in 1992. He is also a founding member of World Ice Sculptor's Alliance (WISA). Derek continues his education by regularly participating in ice carving seminars and various art classes to hone his craft.

While a student at Grand Rapids Community College, Derek earned first-place in the college-level division at the 1990 Plymouth International Ice

Spectacular. At that same competition, he served as an apprentice to the team of Dan Hugelier, CMC; Mac Winker, CCM; and Randy Finch that took first place in the team event. Also that year, Derek served as an apprentice to Culinary Olympic Certified Master Chef James Hanyzeski. That training has helped Derek to earn many awards at NICA-certified and other ice sculpting competitions.

Derek and Randy were recently featured on a televised episode of *Ripley's Believe It or Not,* where their talents were nationally showcased sculpting a working double Ferris wheel and full-sized pool table from ice. They have also produced sculptures for the *Discovery Channel* and have made appearances on many affiliates of NBC, ABC, CBS, and FOX. Additionally, their work has been featured in *Chef* magazine, the National Restaurant Association's *Fork in the Road, MBA Jungle, The Wall Street Journal,* and numerous other trade and daily press publications.

I

Learning About Sculpting in Ice

The Art of Sculpting

OBJECTIVES

After reading this chapter, you will be able to:

- Explain how nature uses erosive forces to create art
- Explain how technology has impacted the production of ice sculptures
- Discuss the global evolution of ice sculpting
- Discuss the evolution of modern ice sculpting in North America
- Discuss the similarities and differences of sculpting ice versus other media
- Define composition as it relates to sculpture
- Discuss the rules on composition
- Discuss the rules on unity
- Describe basic sculpting exercises
- Discuss the lessons in design and sculpting basics
- Describe the sculptor's passion and challenge

Key Terms and Concepts

three-dimensional vision	composition	proximity
erosive forces	ice-friendly	lost perspective
balance	visualization	contours
medium	unity	continuation
artisan	texture	temporary medium
movement	proportion	passion
dimension	scope	unity with variety
borrowed technology	repetition	visual unity
sub-zero art	symmetry	intellectual unity
	negative space	
	primary lines	

Figure 1-1. The Grand Canyon

Figure 1-2. Red rock formations in Monument Valley

Figure 1-3. Ice-covered branches

Sculpted art is as timeless as the earth itself. Those etched faces of the great stone monoliths of Monument Valley, Colorado, and the windswept trees of Anastasia Island, Florida, are examples of true artistic merit. The magnitude of the Grand Canyon's deep, twisting, stone walls and the delicate smooth shapes of ordinary creek stones, polished to geometric perfection, are nature's forces at play. And the shimmer of ice crystals enveloping frozen tree branches after a winter's ice storm is yet another illustration of nature's glory.

Nature regularly uses its tools to carve these very common, yet extraordinary, works. The forces of heat and cold, mixed with wind and water, are sufficient to create these most memorable sculptures.

Man's art is generally less ancient and usually less grandiose. Yet, man has learned to harness the tools of nature to produce his own memorable works. With the gifts of creativity, **three-dimensional vision**, and physical stamina, man is capable of producing works that rival those of nature in beauty and drama.

FROM PAST TO PRESENT

Sculpture has been a vehicle of human expression since the beginning of mankind. The history of many civilizations is told by sculpted works that have survived even centuries longer than their people. The ability to artfully sculpt ice requires knowledge and skill in several distinct and important areas. The artist must understand his **medium**: ice. Although this appears simplistic, ice can pose a formidable challenge to the uninformed sculptor. Ice varies in **dimension**, **composition**, and **texture**. Each block is unique and must be addressed according to its condition and characteristics.

Equally important to the sculptor are his tools. Nature uses **erosive forces** to carve, etch, and smooth its medium, and temperature variations to fuse pieces together. So it is with ice sculpting. The **artisan** wields tools and devices to systematically, yet artistically, cut, etch, and polish the ice until his vision is realized.

Early ice carvers used the tools of the wood carver to cut, shave, and smooth their creations. These axes, wood saws, and chisels were reasonably effective, but left the finished works rough in appearance after several hours of painstaking effort. Eventually, specially designed handsaws and chisels were developed for specific use by ice carvers. These later modifications allowed for finer cuts and different angles, and helped to produce better and more precise finished pieces.

As ice carving evolved, the carver again **borrowed** the **technology** of the woodsman. Chain saws were introduced into ice carving in the 1970s. At first they were only used as a timesaving device to rough out the sculptures, leaving the detail work to be finished with hand chisels. However, as carvers became more adept with the saws and as the saws were modified to be lighter and more "**ice-friendly**," carvers were able to complete finished sculptures using only chain saws.

This use of modern technology increased the productivity of carvers. Standard creations that used to take a competent ice artist 2 to 3 hours to complete can now be duplicated in 45 minutes. And in an industry that values productivity and precision, the use of this technology was quickly embraced.

Ice Sculpting Through the Ages

Some observers point to the glaciers as the most natural and beautiful ice sculptures on the planet. In relative terms, ice sculptures by man are a new phenomenon compared with his rival artist and mentor, nature. Still, man's practice of using ice for shelter, food preservation, and artistic expression is centuries old.

The Inuit of the Arctic Bay area, among many other native peoples of the Arctic Circle, build their well-known homes, igloos, from ice and snow. Crafted from their frozen surroundings, these rounded structures have protected their occupants from the harsh winds and bitter cold of the arctic climate for hundreds of years. Even today, a tourist can opt to stay overnight in a commercially operated igloo facility, such as those built at the Hotel Igloo Village in Kangerlussuaq, Greenland. Other ice hotels, such as those in Sweden and Canada, are also proving to be popular tourist attractions.

Beyond these small shelters of ice and snow, historians note that palaces of ice have been constructed all over the world for more than 250 years. In 1739, the Russians built a grand Palladian palace on the banks of the Neva River in St. Petersburg. The first Winter Carnival in Montreal, Canada, held in 1883, featured a 90-square-foot castle constructed from 500-lb. blocks of ice.

But the largest ice palace ever built on the North American continent was erected in the Rocky Mountains in Leadville, Colorado. In an effort to bolster the mining town's sagging economy, which had collapsed in 1893, the town constructed the Ice Palace to attract tourists to the area. Opened on January 1, 1896, the palace was constructed of 5,000 tons of ice and 307,000 board feet of lumber and covered nearly 5 acres of land. Fully functional, it featured a kitchen, restaurant, dance floor, skating rink, and many enormous ice sculptures highlighting local products. The Ice Palace was officially closed for good on March 28, 1896.

In addition to these oversized works of frozen art, chefs and ice artisans have been providing their guests worldwide with equally stimulating, but smaller and more delicate, sculptures of ice for over 450 years. Miniature vessels of ice were used to chill and serve early versions of ice cream in Italy during the late 1500s. In America, Delmonico's began serving Sorbet à l' Américain in its New York City restaurant in 1867. And while commanding the kitchen staff at London's Savoy Hotel in 1892, Master Chef Auguste Escoffier is credited with presenting his celebrated Pêches Melba in individual swans of sculpted ice.

The carving of ice for the specific purpose of providing attractive centerpieces, and as a novelty, was done infrequently until the late 1800s and early 1900s. As chefs and artists traveled and became worldlier, interest in this frozen art form became more commonplace. The Italian-born chef Luigi Marabini, while working as a pastry chef in London at the turn of the 20th century, had visited the United States and created a 16-foot high sugar sculpture of the Statue of Liberty. Using the same mold, wood chisels, and carpenter's tools, he sculpted a replica from ice. So popular was his work that he began making large ice blocks and sculpting his ice pieces in many countries around the world.

Around 1917, while traveling to France as head chef to the Japanese Imperial Court, Tokuzo Akiyama was impressed by the ice sculptures used to present various savories and sweet dishes. He took this style of service back to Japan, but its popularity did not flourish until the 1930s. The late Shuko Kobayashi, sculptor and educator, is credited with spreading interest in ice sculpting in Japan by chairing the first ice sculpture competition, held in Tokyo in 1955. He also served as the chairman of the first Japan Ice Sculpture Association, and, shortly after the sculpting competition became an annual event, an ice-carving school was established in Tokyo. Annual national competitions in ice sculpture, particularly in sculpting buffet centerpieces, began in 1972.

Gabriel Paillasson undertook the task of reviving the art in his native France. Owner of a pastry shop in St. Fons near Lyon, Chef Paillasson helped found and became president of l'Association des Sculpteurs sur Glace Hydrique (the Association of Sculptors in Ice) in 1989. In 1991, he initiated the first French Ice Sculpture Championship and was a central force behind the Coupe du Monde de la Patisserie (World Pastry Cup) that includes ice sculpting as one of the required competition skills.

Modern Milestones in North American Ice Sculpting

In the United States, Swiss-born August Forster enlisted the help of the Chicago Board of Education and the Cooks and Pastry Cooks Union, Local 88, to found the first culinary school in America, the venerable Washburne Trade School, in 1936. He was among the first to educate others on ice carving when his book, *Fancy Ice Carving in Thirty Lessons*, was published in 1947. Shortly after Washburne opened, Chef Jean Vernet pioneered cooking school programs in Minneapolis and St. Paul, and in 1944 Chef Herman Breithaupt established the Commercial Foods Program at Chadsey High School in Detroit. George Weising further promoted ice sculpting in 1954 with his self-published text, *Ice Carving Professionally*. Weising, proclaimed the leading ice carver in the United States by the National Association of Ice Industries, taught ice sculpting part time at the Culinary Institute of America in New Haven, Connecticut.

However, Joseph Amendola can be credited with being at the forefront of culinary and ice-carving education, working at the Culinary Institute of America since its inception in the 1940s. His special edition of *Ice Carving Made Easy* was printed in 1960, and later editions became a mainstay for ice carving enthusiasts for many years. Chef Amendola also helped to form the National Ice Carving Association (NICA), which now boasts 500 members, and which organizes and sanctions ice-carving competitions across North America.

In the 1980's, Mark Daukas was one of the early pioneers in the use of power tools in ice sculpting. Previously, these tools were more commonly used by the wood construction industry. His well-received use of power tools proved to be an important milestone in the ice industry. Mac Winker's text, *Ice Sculpture: The Art of Ice Carving in 12 Systematic Steps*, self-published in 1989, popularized ice sculpting with the use of templates. Although template use in sculpture pre-dates Michelangelo, Winker's methodical step system changed how most ice sculptors approach their craft.

Then at the end of the 20th century, Ice Sculptures, Ltd. became the first ice sculpting company in the United States to use fully computerized technology in their daily operations when they acquired the Iceculture 5200 CNC router in early 1999. Canadian innovator Julian Bayley adapted advanced computer technology to the sculpting of ice. His CNC router, the CAD-directed Iceculture 5200, and his Iceculture Lathe have provided another level of production efficiency and ice artistry to the sculpting industry.

Ice sculpting has enjoyed an explosion of interest around the globe in recent years. As new technology is developed, more and more craftsmen seek to express their artistic abilities in this most rewarding and exciting art form. Many chefs and ice artists travel hundreds or thousands of miles to sculpt their displays for the benefit of the viewing public.

THE SCULPTURE IS ALREADY THERE

Paul Gaugin said, "Art is either plagiarism or revolution." The artist intends to either imitate something already existing in nature or create a unique and visionary work yet unknown to man. Most of what we do probably falls under the category of Gaugin's plagiarism. We seek to present something already known to man. We try to capture the strength, **proportion**, **balance**, and **movement** of our subject when designing our templates. To represent our subject most favorably with ice, we take time to familiarize ourselves with the theme. Rather than studying another's drawings of the item, we look for existing clay or wood sculptures and photographs that reveal the top, front, sides, and back of our subject. We sometimes even create our own models from clay when we need to better familiarize ourselves with the subject.

Ice sculpting is like many carving forms of sculpture, except it is **sub-zero art**. It is dependent upon the artisan's understanding of, and skill with, the medium and the environment. And it is dependent upon the sculptor's commitment. As Paul Klee once said, "Art does not reproduce the visible; rather, it makes visible." The sculpture is already there. It is up to the artist to remove what doesn't belong. **Visualization** of the finished product is the ability to see the finished sculpture within the ice, a concept first introduced by Michelangelo. Although this gift is natural to a fortunate few, most of us depend on visual aids to assist us in realizing the vision. Once completed, the sculpture should be strong, balanced, and composed of interlocking, flowing, complementary, and contrasting shapes.

STUDYING THE ART

When a person decides he wants to sculpt ice, he may overlook the fact that ice is simply another medium. An ice artist should approach his craft like any other artist and gain a foundation in art. The ice sculptor should first attempt to visualize his subject by making drawings on graph paper and by working with modeling clay or soap. These exercises help familiarize him with the dimension and **scope** of the project. He discovers the **symmetry** and proportion of his subject.

When we began to teach ice sculpting, we could readily see how fast our students progressed in relation to our own, slower progress. We quickly understood and appreciated the advantage of guidance. They were able to benefit from our earlier efforts and mistakes. Although we hope to set a path for learning, it does not come at the expense of exploration. To discourage creativity is to deny Gaugin's revolution, leaving only plagiarism. Our efforts are directed towards the students' conception of ice as a medium for their sculpted art.

Most ice-sculpting courses first teach how to cut ice and then how to make the ice actually resemble the subject. Students learn about ice, tools, and the use of guiding templates. Even though this method is acceptable in learning to be a good carver, we believe it is not sufficient or as beneficial to one who wishes to be a sculptor. We note a difference between carvers and sculptors, and between the approaches each takes to the task.

LEARNING TO SCULPT

There are many organizations, college courses, and schools devoted to the study and appreciation of sculpture. It would be too daunting a task to assume to teach sculpting in its entirety in any one text, particularly when

Figure 1-4. Unfinished work by Michelangelo, from the Galleria dell'Accademia in Florence

Figure 1-5. Pine wood block showing its natural grain

Figure 1-6. Rock showing its natural grain

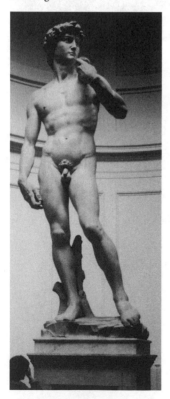

Figure 1-7. Michelangelo's *David*

authored by culinarians. It should also be noted that, although there is very little material available for developing one's skills as an ice sculptor, there is ample information available in the form of books, videos, and designs formatted to the other art media. These can easily be adapted to ice and are worth investigating. We have included several reference texts on sculpting and art in the bibliography of this book that have been useful to our study and understanding.

Furthermore, we suggest that students can learn much about the art of ice sculpting by observing the works created by the world's great sculptors. These works serve as an example of what artists have visualized in the past, and an inspiration for serious ice artists today. The works of great sculptors teach us how to perceive three-dimensional space and how the artist's imagination can activate that space through the use of direction, line, movement, rhythm, and balance.

THE COMPOSITION OF ICE SCULPTURES

Any artist who begins to sculpt first considers the nature of the medium he is using. Be it wood, stone, clay, snow, or ice, each has particular properties that must be recognized. In this text, we explore ice in Chapter 2, "Understanding the Medium: The Science of Ice." Despite the many challenges of sculpting with a **temporary medium** such as ice or snow, the ice sculptor is fortunate because, unlike many other media, man-made ice has no grain. (Natural ice is often formed in layers over time, and therefore has varying textures due to the changes in temperature as it is forming). Wood and stone always possess either grain or fissures that the sculptor must work around. Unless the ice has sustained some damage during handling or formation that has weakened the block, the ice is essentially free of these limitations.

Rules on Composition

In art, composition can be defined, simply speaking, as the make-up of an object. It entails the structure, shape, form, balance, and interlocking nature of the piece. However, it is presumptuous to state any hard and fast rules relative to the composition of sculptures. It is impossible to make all-encompassing statements applicable to all media. Every artist has his own rules and philosophy about sculpting, which partially explains the great variety of works that exist. That being said, there are a few truths to which we adhere as ice artists.

The perceived quality of an artist's work is rarely measured by the subject matter of his work alone. The quality is also found in the composition. The admiration we have for a sculpture of the Buddha in a temple or Abraham Lincoln's statue in his memorial, or even Michelangelo's *David*, is not based on who those individuals were as subjects of art. Our admiration is for the artist and his artistic ability. As a rule, the skill required for making the sculpture is appreciated as much as the actual subject of the sculpture.

Due to the temporary nature of this sub-zero art form and its eventual decay due to exposure to the elements of heat, rain, or wind, *ice sculptures need to be simple in their design features.* Although detail generally enhances the piece, thin lines can appear weak and unbalanced as they melt faster than the rest of the sculpture. The scales and muscle tone of a leaping fish will stand the test of time. A fishing line will not.

Figure 1-8. Michelangelo's Moses, an example of strong line in sculpture

Varied shapes add to the visual impact of a sculpture. A stack of blocks is not anywhere near as interesting as a mélange of forms: cubes, cones, columns, and balls.

Strong lines, **contours,** *and balance sustain a sculpture as it endures a slow, warm demise.* The ice sculpture will be more long lasting if it is composed of strong **primary lines** and shapes. If the sculpture has balance, its visual impact will be sustained while on display.

Rules on Unity

If any "rule of art" exists for sculpting, it would involve the rule of **unity**. For a sculpture to have visual appeal, its various elements must be in physical harmony.

Figure 1-9. Sculpture using contours of shape and form to create interest

Figure 1-10. Sculpture using repetition of form and depth

An artist always tries to create a composition that is unified even though a number of elements are at play within the sculpture. The goal is to achieve **unity with variety**. The trick is to involve enough different and interesting shapes and forms to prevent boredom but ensure that the sculpture remains cohesive.

Unity can best be achieved in one of three ways: **repetition**, **proximity**, or **continuation**. Through the use of *repetition*, using the same form or specific parts of it repeatedly, a sculptor can "tie a sculpture together." The use of *proximity*, where elements of the piece are grouped together, is another effective but relatively simple method of achieving unity in design. The most difficult method to effectively employ is the use of *continuation*, where the sculptor creates a visual path for the observer. Strong lines, edges, and contours become roadmaps the viewer's eyes can follow.

We must also be concerned about confusing **visual unity** with **intellectual unity**. *Visual unity* refers to the unity of the sculpture's elements as they appear to the eye. *Intellectual unity* refers to the unity of a concept not actually seen with the eye, but understood by the mind. However, such an abstract idea may not produce a coherent pattern when brought to the three-dimensional world, and the visual appeal may be lessened.

CONCENTRATING ON THE BASICS

It is an oft-quoted line, but *concentrating on the basics* is fundamental to success in most arenas. Before an athlete can excel in any sport, he must master the rudimentary skills of the game. As the painter must know about color and texture before putting paint to canvas, the sculptor must know about composition and form.

Basic Sculpting Exercises

We recommend concentrating on the basics when students begin to study ice sculpture. The following exercises are useful in learning the craft of sculpting:

- Practice making the four basic forms (see Chapter 5): cube, cone, column, and ball
- Practice sculpting heads, hands, fingers, wings, legs, columns, numbers, letters
- Learn about symmetry and proportion by working with and creating clay models
- Use graph paper to learn about size, proportion, and relationship

Lessons in Design Basics

The following design lessons are useful to note when beginning to design a sculpture. The student will experience less frustration and greater satisfaction by adhering to these lessons:

- Choose a subject matter within realistic expectations. The difficulty of a piece is not so much limited by a student's artistic ability, but by his commitment to practicing and developing his skills.
- Create a drawing or study of the sculpture on graph paper to simulate the dimensions of an ice block. Note the **negative space** and how it may be used efficiently to make attachments or complementary objects for the sculpture.
- When drawing a guiding template (see Chapter 6), concentrate on using strong primary lines to define the basic structure of the sculpture without losing the ability to recognize the subject.
- Examine each component of the larger sculpture. Simplify the approach by reducing the design into smaller, less intricate parts.
- Don't distort the natural shape of an object to fit within the dimensions of an ice block. Learn to fuse ice pieces (see Chapter 7).

Lessons in Sculpting Basics

Often, the beginning ice sculptor lacks confidence and self-assurance as to where to begin cutting into the ice. Not unlike the medical student making his first cut into a human body, the novice sculptor is hesitant about misplacing the cutting edge in the new ice block. His self-doubt usually involves specific location and depth of cut. A few simple tips can help the student through his first attempts:

- Use the template (see Chapter 6) to determine where to etch the design and where to begin cutting.
- As a beginning sculptor, it is best to start working from the top down.
- To prevent breaking off extremities while sculpting, leave ice in areas of negative space to support the location where you are cutting the ice in finer detail. For example, leave the ice intact under an extended arm while detailing the top of the arm. Once the detailing is completed, and you won't be exerting downward pressure, you can remove the ice from below the arm to create negative (open) space.
- Work on the whole project a little at a time; don't concentrate on one part too long.
- Sculpt multiple parts simultaneously to keep dimension and proportion in perspective. Fine-tune all the parts simultaneously to keep the sculpture in balance.

Figure 1-11. Sculpture of a vase, designed with weak detail lines

Figure 1-12. The same sculpture after three hours of melting, with faded detail

- Examine each component of the larger sculpture.
- Occasionally step back from the piece to revisit one's references and notes for guidance. Don't lose perspective and "get lost" in the sculpture. Ask others if they can see the object you are visualizing.

THE SCULPTOR

This book will go into a lot of detail about the medium of ice and the tools with which to sculpt. We will provide information on sculpting and creating templates to aid the beginning artist in achieving his vision. We will show the learner how to develop a subject matter without significant pre-existing skills. However, the student needs to contribute several very important attributes to the learning process to succeed as an ice sculptor.

The Sculptor's Passion

Passion is considered "an intense, emotional excitement or enthusiasm" for an object, person, or activity. The sculptor must possess a passion for the craft to achieve any higher level of artistry. In addition, the student must be sufficiently disciplined to spend the necessary time developing the skills he needs, by studying the text, practicing making shapes and forms, and learning how to artfully interpret guiding templates. This combination of passion and discipline, a strong desire to learn and excel creatively, along with this book and some basic tools, is virtually all that is required to succeed.

The Sculptor's Challenge

Late in his life, Pierre Auguste Renoir, who is considered to be among the greatest French painters, suffered from agonizing arthritis. So severe was his malady that his hands were quite twisted and cramped. It is said that his friend, the legendary artist Henri Matisse, came visiting and observed Renoir struggling to grasp a brush with only his fingertips, experiencing torturous pain with each stroke. When Matisse asked why he continued to paint under such terrible conditions, Renoir replied, "The pain passes, but the beauty remains."

In addition to passion for the art, the ice artisan must have the physical stamina and mental focus to work quickly with this temporary medium, often in uncomfortable environmental conditions. Ice is subject to change by the atmosphere that surrounds it and must be managed accordingly. This, more often than not, requires that the ice artist work rapidly, in cold and wet conditions, on a fragile object that can weigh hundreds of pounds. Herein lie the challenges and the unpredictability that the sculptor must consider when wielding his tools.

This challenge, to create a translucent, luminous, yet transitory sculpture that is of pure origin, lies at the very root of the passion for this most challenging art form.

ARTIST PROFILE

Meet the Artist—Michael Pizzuto

Michael Pizzuto, Certified Culinary Educator, has been sculpting ice since 1970 and maintains an active ice business in Denver, Colorado. His pursuit of learning the techniques of sculpture has taken him worldwide. His advanced training was under Chef Yukichika Iijima, and then he went on to Japan where he trained under the Japanese Master Ice Sculptor Mitsuo Shimizu. Chef Pizzuto is an ACF gold medalist and served as captain for the first USA ice carving team that competed in Asahiakawa, Japan.

Ask the Artist

Q   What do you try to convey with ice as a sculpture medium?

A   *That it is a reflection of life: beautiful, a gift, fragile, unique, and transient as the cherry blossoms in springtime; to be held gently as an art expression without grasping and seeking a permanent thing.*

Q   After carving for over 30 years, starting with chippers and handsaws, what comments do you have about the use of power tools?

A   *Written sources have revealed the use of power tools in Japan and America since the 1800s. The last 10 years of innovative use has definitely changed a predominantly "chisel" mentality to that of a business/production emphasis. Although this is a popular resurgence and evolution in ice carving, I strongly believe there must be a balance of chisels and power tools, for each has distinct advantages.*

2

Understanding the Medium: The Science of Ice

OBJECTIVES

After reading this chapter, you will be able to:

• Explain the transformation of water into ice
• Explain the process of bending ice
• Discuss how and why ice is tempered before sculpting
• Describe how to prevent thermo-shock to a block of ice
• Summarize the use of ice blocks in early America
• Identify three methods of forming ice blocks and sculptures
• Discuss the pros and cons of using colored ice
• Discuss the effect changing weather conditions have on ice

Key Terms and Concepts

ice	sublimation	weight to mass ratio
temper	molded sculpture method	slick ice
refrigeration		thermo-shock
circulating tank method	contaminated	brine tank method
	opaque	plate ice
disturbed	feather	
harvesting	greenhouse effect	

Ice, in the form of glaciers, covers between 25 and 35 million square meters of our world. During the Pleistocene Epoch, some glaciers spread from the Arctic to bury and subsequently erode parts of Asia, Europe, and North America. By 18,000 years ago, this ice sheet had spread as far south as Illinois, Indiana, Ohio, and northern Pennsylvania. The impact on the topography as a result of the movement of great sheets of ice remains visible today, particularly in central New York and throughout the Great Lakes region. In their retreat, the glaciers left behind one of the most important elements on earth: water.

WATER INTO ICE

Water's physical properties are unique. Water is the only natural substance that exists in all three states at temperatures normally found on earth: *liquid* (water), *gas* (steam), and *solid* (ice). The term **ice** can refer to the frozen form of many substances, such as carbon dioxide, which in its frozen form is dry ice. However, when we discuss ice in this text, we are referring to frozen water.

When absolutely still, pure water can be chilled to 15° Fahrenheit (F) before ice forms; however, since water under natural conditions is usually **disturbed** or **contaminated**, ice usually forms at about 32° F. When water freezes, ice crystallizes in a hexagonal system that refracts the light in pleasant, eye appealing ways when cut, similar to a glass prism. The angles between corresponding faces of any two crystals are always identical. In this the ice sculptor has an advantage over the wood carver—ice has a crystal lattice that allows for clean and predictable fracture lines.

Water is also unusual in that the solid form is less dense than the liquid form. When ice forms, it takes up about 9% more space than it did as liquid. This expansion occurs when water molecules move farther away from each other as each crystal forms. Air is captured between the crystals, which gives ice a slightly lower **weight to mass ratio** than water. This is why ice floats in water.

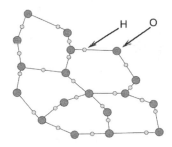

Figure 2-1. Diagram of the molecular structure of ice

The actual molecular structure of ice changes at various temperatures. At 16° F, ice has the same density and volume it has at 32° F. However, from 16° to 24° F, it expands with heat. Upon reaching 24° F, it begins to contract. Then, at 32° F, it begins melting and continues to contract until it almost reaches 40° F, when it again begins to expand.

This knowledge is important to the ice sculptor because the ice block will react differently to cutting when it is at various temperatures. The relative texture of the block will change from soft to hard and back to soft again when the block's temperature fluctuates by only a few degrees.

Bending Ice

Ice bending is a phenomenon that until recently had been considered something of an urban legend among ice sculptors. Those who have lived and worked around ice long enough have observed ice in its many states of development, whether as a frost-coated blade of grass, a branch shrouded in ice, or an icicle hanging from a roof edge. However, bending of ice is a rare occurrence, since many conditions must occur simultaneously to produce a noticeable bend.

Existing ice must first be slowly warmed to a temperature just under 40° F to soften it without its quickly melting. There must also be sufficient weight on one end to create a limited amount of gravity-induced tension, but not so

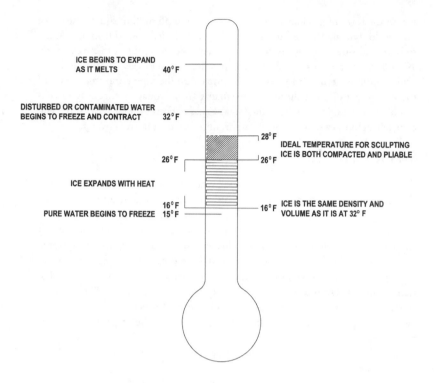

ICE BEGINS TO EXPAND
AS IT MELTS   40° F

DISTURBED OR CONTAMINATED WATER
BEGINS TO FREEZE AND CONTRACT   32° F

                                28° F
                                        IDEAL TEMPERATURE FOR SCULPTING
                                        ICE IS BOTH COMPACTED AND PLIABLE
                   26° F   26° F

ICE EXPANDS WITH HEAT

                                16° F   ICE IS THE SAME DENSITY AND
                   16° F   VOLUME AS IT IS AT 32° F
PURE WATER BEGINS TO FREEZE   15° F

Figure 2-2. Illustration of the effect of temperature on water and ice

Figure 2-3. Elapsed photos of ice bending

much as to snap the ice. To illustrate the process, lay a $\frac{1}{2}$" diameter rod of ice on a table with the short end secured to the tabletop by a weight, and the long end allowed to hang over the table edge.

As the ice warms to nearly 40° F, it will start to expand. This expansion will be directed towards the path of least resistance. The natural gravitational weight of the extended rod will cause the ice to expand and droop downwards. However, the bowing will actually decrease the gravity-induced tension, and the bending process will begin to slow. The average length of time to produce a 90-degree bend in a $\frac{1}{2}$" diameter rod of ice at 40° F is approximately $2\frac{1}{2}$ hours.

TEMPERING

In order for the sculptor to safely remove ice pieces from a full block without the fear of cracking and other temperature-induced problems, whether by saw, chisel, or power tool, the temperature of the ice must be consistent with the temperature of the air around it. For years, sculptors carving in spaces above 32° F have learned to **temper** ice blocks by slowly warming them up to room temperature.

Common Methods Used for Tempering Ice

Ice is generally formed in "ice cans" held in brine solutions that are set at 15° F, or in Clinebell tanks that freeze water at lower temperatures. However, the ideal temperature for sculpting is 26° to 28° F, when the ice is compacted, pliable, and less likely to shatter.

Loading Dock Method

One common method of tempering ice is to cover the frozen block with a large plastic bag, such as one used for leaves or garbage cans, and allow the block to warm to the surrounding temperature. This practice often occurs in an area like the loading dock of a hotel or kitchen, and usually takes 2 to 4 hours, depending on the ambient temperature. The sculptor then proceeds to sculpt in that same area when the ice is ready and safe to cut. However, in some warmer climates, this practice may be impractical due to rapid deterioration of the ice. Wind, blowing debris, and rain can also have a sudden negative impact on the block.

Walk-in Cooler Method

A second method for tempering ice involves warming the block more slowly in a walk-in cooler. The sculptor carefully transfers the frozen block from a walk-in freezer to a large walk-in refrigerator, and allows the block to warm to slightly below the freezer temperature. The block is also covered with a plastic bag with this method. This procedure works best when the sculptor has planned ahead and allowed sufficient time for the process, which can take 8 to 16 hours.

When the ice becomes soft and completely free of all frost, the sculptor should be able to place a wet paper on the ice block and remove it without the paper sticking. If the paper tears when it is pulled off, it is still too cold to carve safely.

Although acceptable, these are not the only methods available for tempering ice. *The key is to keep the internal temperature of the ice consistent with the temperature of the external environment.* This can also be achieved by sculpting inside a walk-in freezer, a walk-in cooler, or outdoors on a cold day. It does not matter if the ice is soft and warm or hard and cold, the air outside the block must be the same as inside the block. Failure to balance internal and external temperatures can cause **thermo-shock** and results in severely cracked and weakened ice. *Contact with metal, such as a chain saw blade or router bit, or water can also crack the ice.* These materials retain heat and can induce thermo-shock problems similar to those caused by warm, moist air.

ICE USAGE IN RECORDED HISTORY

It is not known whether during prehistoric times man used ice as we use it today. Obviously, no records were kept to provide such insight; we can only conjecture about its use. However, mention is made in the Chinese *Book of Songs*, written about 600 B.C., of how ice was harvested and stored in ravines covered with insulating straw—primitive icehouses. Hippocrates wrote of "the pleasures of drinking out of ice" in the 4th century B.C. Alexander the Great had trenches dug and filled with ice and snow to cool hundreds of wine kegs before each of his battles. And historians mention Roman references to ice and snow being used to chill beverages and conserve foods as far back as 52 B.C. when, reportedly, oysters were served on a bed of snow gathered from Apennine Mountain peaks.

In more recent times, from the early 17th century through the beginning of the 20th century, Europeans used ice in holding devices (early iceboxes) for the same purpose. Large blocks of ice were harvested all across Europe, from the polar glaciers of Norway to the frozen Lake Sylans in the Jura Mountains.

Figure 2-4. Raw block being tempered under a plastic bag on a loading dock

Figure 2-5. Raw block being tempered in a walk-in cooler

Figure 2-6. Testing the ice for proper temperature

ICE HARVESTING IN EARLY AMERICA

According to Joseph Jones, Jr., in his book, *America's Icemen*, the earliest reference to the United States ice industry is a patent issued in 1665 to the Governor of Virginia, Sir William Berkeley, to preserve snow and ice. Commercial **harvesting** of ice from ponds and lakes is now a thing of the past. However, its impact before refrigeration was immeasurable. Until the turn of the 19th century, America was content to chill its food and drink in fruit cellars and springhouses. People masked the taste of spoiled foods with spices, and fresh foods could only be safely shipped short distances.

All of that changed in 1805 when Frederick Tudor, known as the "Ice King of Boston," began shipping ice cut from a pond in Lynn, Massachusetts, to the southern cities of Charleston, Mobile, and New Orleans. By 1856, his ice empire stretched as far as Cuba, Jamaica, India, England, and South America. Tudor built a vast and prosperous network of ships, giant icehouses, and local distribution agencies.

The Cape Pond Ice Company was started as the Gloucester Ice Company in 1848 by a blacksmith named Nathaniel Webster. Recognizing the opportunity to supply ice to the fresh fish industry around Gloucester, Massachusetts, Webster dammed a local brook and built his first icehouse. After harvesting his "frozen load" with teams of men and horses, Webster would store the ice in sawdust and salt hay until it was needed in the summer months.

Natural Ice

Axes were first used to chop ice from ponds around 1785. The ice saw soon followed, which allowed the harvester to hand saw evenly shaped blocks. Even so, this proved to be tedious and dangerous work for the harvesters. The introduction of the steam engine in 1870 helped reduce the heavy labor of sawing. This was the preferred method of harvesting until electric saws were introduced around 1912.

From 1800 to 1920 nearly every community in the northeastern United States had its local ice harvesting and storage company. People demanded something better than a steady diet of dried and salted meats. Breweries could work all year instead of only in the winter. The availability of ice was vital to meat packers, dairy farmers, and even the medical community. In 1806, the first shipment of pond-cut ice was sent from the United States to Martinique to help treat victims of yellow fever.

With the invention of the insulated railroad car in 1857, meat shipments became daily occurrences. By 1873, Chicago meat packers were sending fresh beef products to the east coast at the rate of three carloads a day. Ice was becoming even more precious. In 1860, a Chicago produce dealer observed that when salt was placed on ice, the ice melted at a lower temperature causing the formation of chilled air. This led to the invention of refrigeration machinery to make ice. The natural ice industry in the United States reached its zenith in 1886, when its annual harvest reached 25 million tons.

MAKING THE MEDIUM: THE MANUFACTURE OF ICE

When nature could not keep up with demand for high-quality, clean, pure ice, man invented the means for manufacturing ice. Ice manufacturing began in

America around 1910, and the first self-contained household electric refrigerator was built in 1915. By 1925, no significant amount of natural ice was being commercially harvested.

Commercial Ice

The first commercially manufactured ice, known as **plate ice**, was produced in sheets measuring 20' × 10' × 1' and weighing close to 14,000 pounds. The ice was then cut into smaller blocks, known as "cakes," according to the needs of the buyer.

Presently, there are three forms of commercially, or artificially, made ice used for displays: **brine tank method**, **circulating tank method**, and **molded sculpture method**.

Brine Tank ("Can Ice") Method

Until recently, most manufactured ice was made in galvanized cans. In this process, pure, chilled water is placed in galvanized containers designed to produce blocks weighing from 10 to 400 lb. The filled cans are partially submerged in a brine tank filled with sodium chloride or a similar substance. The brine itself is chilled and circulated around the metal cans, slowly freezing the water inside. During the freezing process, small contaminate particles and dust are forced to the center of the block and produce a darker section of slush. The slush is decanted through a hole, and fresh water replaces the slush. After a few days of freezing, a partially **opaque** block is produced.

Although ice produced in this way is generally clean, the **feather** of air running down the block's core leaves an undesirable "snow effect" in the center of the block and therefore in the carvings. Although not perfect, this ice is commonly accepted by many carvers. Using distilled water (free of contaminates) helps to produce clear ice, but it doesn't help to remove all of the air.

Circulating Tank Method

Another more recent method calls for agitating the water as it is being frozen to produce **slick ice**. Small circulating pumps, similar to those used in garden ponds, are placed in block-chilling machines at the surface level of the water. The pumps slowly move the water around as it is freezing from the bottom upwards. This process allows air, minerals, and other impurities to circulate to the top of the ice, thereby producing clear ice blocks. It generally takes 2 to 3 days to form these 300-lb. sculpting blocks, depending on the room temperature surrounding the machine. The pumps are removed just prior to harvesting and before they freeze into the block. The blocks are clear, air-free, and denser than those produced using the brine tank method. Their density causes the ice to be stronger than other ice blocks.

Figure 2-7. Circulating tank

Molded Sculpture Method

There are actually two methods of producing molded sculptures: rubber or plastic molds, and ice mold machines.

First, as an alternative to sculpting raw blocks into finished works of art, operators may choose to purchase rubber or plastic molds that can be filled with water and then frozen. Some types of molds, mostly those made of plastic, are not reusable because they are destroyed when removing the frozen ice figure. The water is not circulated in the mold, and the resultant sculpture can be cloudy.

Figure 2-8. A variety of ice molds

Figure 2-9. An ice mold machine

Other molds, much more costly, may be reused numerous times. These molds are made from two parts: a durable rubber liner that has the finished details of the sculpture, and a fiberglass outer case that provides the needed rigidity to the form as it freezes. Water is poured through an opening in the pattern, and then the water-filled mold is placed in a freezer for several days to harden. These molds have improved in recent years, with larger and more detailed designs available on the market.

A second style of molded ice is made in a machine specifically designed to produce molded ice. Mold forms are filled with water and submerged in a solution of propylene glycol to facilitate even freezing. After 1 or 2 days the mold, complete with a frozen ice sculpture, is removed from the solution.

Obvious advantages to the molded sculpture method are:

- Limited skill and few tools are required
- The appearance of the final product is consistent
- It is possible to produce several sculptures simultaneously, if equipment is available
- It is possible to produce the pieces around the clock

However, in our opinion, the disadvantages are greater:

- There are a limited number of molds on the market, so the customer has fewer options
- All operators can offer the same product
- The molds are limited in size and scope and many only produce small, tabletop-sized pieces
- Finished pieces are often cloudy, since the water is not circulated during the freezing process
- Molds can be very expensive and require storage

- The artist gains little creative satisfaction using molds rather than developing his own sculpting talents

Colored Ice

In the 1950s, carvers used several methods to color their sculptures. After futile attempts to color ice with dyed oils or colored water poured into the core cavity during the formation of the ice, they settled on applying colors after the fact. One common method was to apply aerosol snow spray flakes to the finished sculpture. Individual sections, or the entire sculpture, were coated with the colored spray. Another method involved carefully placing wet, colored crepe paper over the finished sculpture, then spraying it with a thin film of cold water to seal the paper in place. This second method was intended solely for outdoor use.

During the 1980s and 1990s, many ice artists experimented with making sculptures from colored ice blocks. Commercial icehouses added liquid dyes to their machines as the blocks were being made. However, dyes behave as foreign particles in freezing water, so any agitation with air causes them to pool and concentrate in various locations of the block, often at the top. The result is a spottily colored block.

When ice-water blocks are agitated without air, the colors are more evenly distributed, but the finished blocks are cloudy and softer than normal. Although they can be carved, sculptors often find these blocks to be too soft to sculpt.

Another consideration is the faster melting rate of colored ice. Blocks that contain more air cells are softer and melt faster. Additionally, dyed ice often stains the tablecloths and skirting around the sculpture, and can make an unsightly appearance of the buffet table on which it is displayed.

To make a block of colored ice, the sculptor needs 2 oz. of food coloring mixed with 1 pint of whole milk. The colored milk is added to the water in the block chamber, and is then gently and evenly blended into the water to distribute its color. The block is allowed to freeze, without the water pumps running, for 3 to 4 days. Running the pumps will cause the colorants to rise to the surface. Striped blocks can be made by freezing single layers of colored water one upon another.

Gels and colored lighting are highly preferred methods of accentuating and highlighting sculptures with color (see Chapters 10 and 11) and are recommended over the use of colored ice.

THE PERFECT BLOCK

The quality of a finished sculpture is greatly enhanced and affected by the quality of the ice used. Ice that is free of impurities, visible air traces, and large cracks greatly increases the ability of the sculptor to create a memorable work. Sculptors should use only the best ice available, even if it means purchasing it from sources outside their immediate geographical area.

Care must be taken when storing the ice so as to prevent **sublimation** caused by the **refrigeration** process. In sublimation, ice changes directly to water vapor without melting. Refrigeration involves removing warm circulating air, and moisture along with it. Therefore, blocks and sculptures will literally dehydrate if not properly covered and protected from the circulating air.

Figure 2-10. Clear versus cloudy ice

Plastic bags under cardboard boxes work well to cover and insulate new ice blocks and prevent sublimation. It is better to store blocks on plastic, rubber, Ethafoam sheets, or other non-porous material, to make it easier to slide the blocks in and out of storage. Cardboard alone is absorbent and is therefore not the best material on which to rest ice.

Exposure to the elements is often unavoidable. It is important to reduce exposure to wind, rain, humidity, and sunshine as much as possible. Sunlight's ultraviolet rays cause a **greenhouse effect** and melt the ice from the inside. Humidity can cause thermo-shock on a cold, non-tempered block, while rain and wind will erode the ice from the outside. These elements must be considered when designing a sculpture to be displayed under various weather conditions.

ARTIST PROFILE

Meet the Artist—Robert Schultz

Robert Schultz, Banquet Chef-Manager for Grand Rapids Community College (GRCC) in Michigan, has also been serving as an adjunct instructor for the college's Hospitality Education Department teaching courses in Introductory Ice Carving. His enthusiasm for the subject has created a growing demand for the course, filling four sections a year. Chef Schultz has led ice-sculpting seminars in Las Vegas for Michael Roman's annual CaterSource Convention and, over the years, has been very successful in coaching GRCC students in NICA-sanctioned and other ice-carving competitions. Chef Schultz is also a founding partner in Son-in-Law Products, makers of preservative free salsas, BBQ sauces and injectable marinades.

Ask the Artist

Q   What kind of ice do you use in practice and in competition?

A   *We are fortunate that the college has had two Clinebell Ice Block Makers for over 10 years, and a graduate of our program recently donated a third. We only use slick ice for practice and in competition. Most of the time we can make enough of our own, but sometimes we still have to buy ten or twenty blocks...but the quality is well worth it.*

Q   How far in advance can you make the blocks and sculptures before you see any deterioration?

A   *We frequently make blocks of ice up to a month before we need to use them with no trouble, as long as we leave them covered in their plastic bags. We've also purchased cardboard boxes to cover the bagged ice if we know we're going to be storing the ice for any extended length of time. We store sculptures for a few weeks; sometimes the students are working on their first sculptures over a 2- or 3-week period. Even though we have a dedicated walk-in freezer for our ice blocks and sculptures, right where we do our sculpting, we don't like to store sculptures for too long for fear of accidental breakage to their extremities. In any case, we try to keep them covered with plastic to slow their sublimation.*

The Sculptor's Tools and Equipment

OBJECTIVES

After reading this chapter, you will be able to:

- Identify and discuss the tools used by traditional carvers in early ice carving
- Demonstrate and explain proper use of the traditional carving tools
- Identify and discuss tools used in modern ice sculpting
- Demonstrate and explain the use of modern sculpting tools
- Describe various router bits and modern attachments
- Discuss electrical considerations
- Explain the effect of wire diameter and cord length on cord capacity
- Discuss methods for maintaining tools properly
- List the gear and equipment needed for the safe practice of ice sculpting

Key Terms and Concepts

traditionalist	gauge	amperage
modernist	chain saw	voltage drop
handsaw	rotary tool	capacity
rust	bits and blades	Ohm's Law
water bag	resistance	circuit
American Wire Gauge (AWG)	chisel	current
	chipper	conductors
template	condensation	
mise en place	die grinder	

LOOKING BACK WHILE MOVING FORWARD

The ability to use and properly care for the tools available to the ice sculptor are paramount to the sculptor's success. This chapter will discuss the past, future, and present use of ice tools, and will focus on the identification, use, and maintenance of the equipment applied by traditional and modern ice sculptors.

The Past

As alluded to in the preface of this book, ice carvers borrowed their technology from other carving disciplines: chisels from the stone carver and chain saws from the woodcutter. For several decades these tools satisfied the needs of the ice carver. However, it was difficult for carvers to achieve truly life-like representation of flowers, birds, animals, and other living creatures because these tools have a tendency to leave rough edges.

More recently, to eliminate the hard and chiseled appearance created by flat ice chisels, ice sculptors have expanded their tool repertoire to include die grinders, irons, hot water bags, and other devices that allow them to approach the creation of ice pieces as sculpture, not carving.

The authors, like most others of their generation, started working ice with tools typical of the decade. Throughout the 1970s, Japanese handsaws, chippers, and chisels were commonly used, although less expensive wood chisels from the local hardware store were often substituted. Gas and electric chain saws became commonplace in the late 1970s and into the 1980s, but their application was limited. Once improved, lighter electric saws, with reduced vibration and fume-free operation, became the saws of choice.

The 1980s became the decade of the power tool, and **modernist** ice sculpting was born. In addition to purpose-built chain saws, rotary tools, die grinders, drills, and irons were introduced, and sculptures could be created without using ice chisels at all. Surprisingly, power tools actually cost less than a quality set of ice chisels and saws. For example, a rotary tool bit is much easier to purchase or replace than a specialized V-chisel that costs almost 50 times as much—an economic reality that has contributed to the widespread acceptance and use of power tools.

Figure 3-1. Ice lathe

The Future

Now, early in the 21st century, it will be interesting to see what tools and machinery will be adapted and designed for use in ice artistry. As sculptors seek to push the limits of their own abilities and that of their tools, it is likely that new instruments, molds, and power tools will be developed. It is not difficult to imagine that sculptors will be working with finely directed streams of water, air, light, sound, or heat to etch and brand their works of ice in the near future. As sculptors seek to extend their artistic creation further and display works of unthinkable balance, perhaps new methods of strengthening and fusing water molecules will be discovered. Although a distant relative, science has always influenced art.

The Present

Ice sculpting tools have evolved over the last century to include many more devices than the original axe, handsaw, and multi-prong chipper. Today, the professional ice sculptor has a wide choice of tools. To achieve a certain effect, the sculptor chooses the tool specific to the task.

Although **traditionalists** still favor the pure form of carving using only handsaws, chippers, and chisels, few can argue with the efficiency and artistic results achieved with power tools. At present, there are two, sometimes opposing, philosophies surrounding the use of power tools in ice sculpting. A number of carvers, considered traditionalists, have chosen to avoid the use of hand-held power tools. However, of those, a few will still use chain saws. But strictly classical or purist carvers believe that the art of sculpting is compromised when any machines are used. These carvers believe that the use of computer-aided design (CAD) equipment, such as computerized numeric controlled (CNC) routers, corrupts the art by introducing automated production capabilities. They believe that CAD equipment requires less skill to produce ice sculptures. In support of that position, there are even a few ice competitions that prohibit the use of all power tools.

However, a growing number of ice sculptors today favor the safe and proper use of power tools in ice sculpting. They believe that the craft has advanced with their use, and that it is the natural next step for ice sculpting. The analogy to using modern tools in other forms of sculpture is evident, such as with works in metal. It should be observed, however, that tool selection is very personal. The individual sculptor will choose the tools that he is most comfortable using.

The constant evolution of ice sculpting has brought about a challenge within itself. Keeping abreast of new tools and technologies should not be viewed as a dependency on machinery, but as an extension of our knowledge and talent. Customer satisfaction must be the highest priority for the artisan businessman, and developing efficient methods of producing ever-improved sculptures should be the goal for any commercial ice artist.

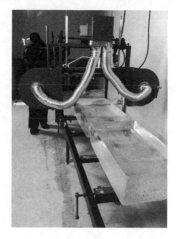

Figure 3-2. Band saw modified for cutting ice

TRADITIONAL VERSUS MODERN TOOLS

This book emphasizes the use of modern power tools, including electric **chain saws**, **die grinders**, power **drills**, **rotary tools**, and **irons** in the making of ice sculptures. They are our preferred tools in our day-to-day production of ice sculptures. Although we were trained in the traditional form of ice carving, using **handsaws**, **chisels**, and **chippers**, we believe power tools are more efficient and capable of producing the best sculptures. No chippers and chisels were used to make the sculptures in this book; *however, all the sculptures illustrated can be created using either traditional or modern tools.*

TOOL IDENTIFICATION AND USE

Although this book is geared towards using power tools, in the interest of introducing all the tools the sculptor has at his disposal we have included a section on traditional sculpting tools, as well as a section on modern sculpting tools, in this chapter.

Traditional Carving Tools

Prior to the practice of using power tools, the sculptor carved his ice pieces with the tools illustrated in Figure 3-3 on the following page. Traditionalists still use them today as a way to preserve the art of ice carving. They can yield beautiful ice figures when used correctly.

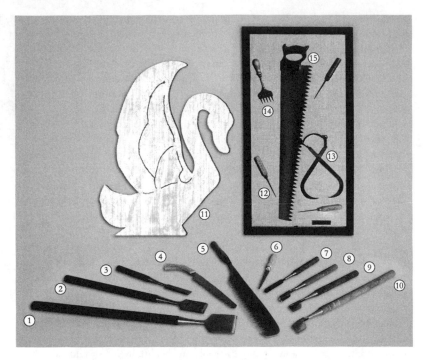

Figure 3-3. Traditional tools of the ice carver

1, 2, 3, 7, 8, 9, 10   Chisels—Originally, ice carvers used carpenter and stonecutter chisels for shaping and shaving. However, wood chisels had at least two faults: they usually had shorter, more impractical handles, and their bevel made them impractical for controlled cuts. Today, an assortment of high-quality ice chisels are available, with various blade shapes, including *narrow flat, wide flat, round (gouge),* and *V (wedge)* shapes.

4, 5, 6, 15   Handsaws—Long before ice carvers used chain saws to cut and split large blocks of ice, they used large-tooth handsaws. Handsaws vary in length and tooth dimension; large-tooth saws are used for rough cuts, and small-tooth saws for finer cuts.

11   Wooden Template—Permanent templates, such as those made of wood, were used before disposable templates became popular. Although their initial cost is higher, re-use of these wooden templates reduces their overall cost and improves design time.

12   Single-Prong Chipper/Pick—A common, old-fashioned household implement, the ice pick is used for chipping smaller sections, cutting and punching small holes, and for scoring the ice, and is useful in tracing and transferring template designs onto a block. The single pick must be kept sharp to be effective.

13   Ice Tongs—Used for safe handling as well as lifting, tongs are practical tools for securely grabbing large, heavy blocks. Tongs come in two styles: the *Cincinnati,* or *compression,* which requires only one hand once the tips are set in the ice, and the *Boston,* which requires both hands.

14   Multi-Prong Chipper—Usually designed with five or six prongs, the chipper is considered the most fundamental of the traditional ice tools. It

Figure 3-4. Using an ice pick

Figure 3-5. Using ice tongs

is primarily used to quickly shave off large sections of ice, scratch texture onto the sculpture's surface, and to transfer patterns. The chipper should always be kept sharp, as a dull chipper will tend to spread out the force of the impact. Spreading the force increases the risk of fracturing the block rather than cutting it.

Using Traditional Tools

Tools are useful only when the artisan knows how to use them. Although we no longer use the following tools for sculpting, our reputation in the ice industry was built using these hand tools. We recommend that students of ice sculpting familiarize themselves with their use and understand their potential. Although these tools can serve a purpose in entry-level sculpting, they may be utilized less when the sculptor moves on to power tools.

Using Handsaws

Handsaws are designed to cut in only one direction. For western-made saws, pressure should only be applied as the saw is pressed forward and facing the ice; applying excessive pressure when drawing the saw blade back is not only inefficient, it also dulls the teeth faster. The sculptor should try to make long, controlled strokes with the blade, letting the blade pass completely through the ice and allowing the ice debris to be released. Handsaws may also be used effectively for rounding and shaping ice. This is accomplished by holding the side of the saw against the ice surface and applying downward pressure while sawing.

Using Chisels

For many years, sculptors have used a variety of chisels to carve their works of ice. Usually made of high-carbon steel, chisels must be kept sharp and free of nicks to be effective. The polished blades shave through ice very easily and can remove large quantities of ice with little effort.

Chisel blades come in various shapes and widths; all are two sided, with an even side and a beveled side. When using a flat-bladed chisel, by holding the beveled side down, the sculptor is able to create sweeping smooth and flat or scooped surfaces. When using the same chisel with the beveled side up, the sculptor can create short but deep cuts.

Figure 3-6. Using a multi-prong chipper

Figure 3-7. Using a handsaw to shave ice

 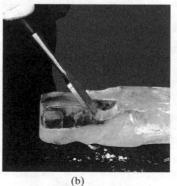 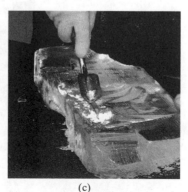

(a) (b) (c)

Figure 3-8. Using a flat chisel (a) with bevel side up, (b) with bevel side down; (c) using a V-shaped chisel

Modern Power and Other Tools Used for Ice Sculpting

Modernist ice sculptors welcome the improvements in the quality of their tools, clothing, and ice made possible through science, and view the changes as progress and the sculpting they facilitate as "state of the art." Not unlike sculptors of other media, contemporary ice artists have successfully used new tools to advance their art. For example, modern metal sculptor Alexander Calder has used power tools to sculpt his oversized works that grace the plazas and lobbies of cities and corporations worldwide.

Most of the tools we use routinely to sculpt are pictured in Figures 3-9 and 3-10.

1   **Ethafoam®**—A brand name for polyethylene sheets. Ethafoam is used to pad work areas while sculpting small and delicate parts, and as a cushion to protect sculpting tools from hard surfaces while they're being used. It can also be used for padding and insulation during transportation of the sculpture.

2   **Chain Saw**—Sculptors favor electric saws over gas because they weigh less and can be used indoors without the danger of exhaust fumes. Electric saws also vibrate less and are therefore easier to hold steady. Originally used only for making larger cuts and to remove big portions of negative space, the chain saw also works for making straight and curved lines, rounding columns, gouging, and sanding. Removing the standard guide bar, around which the chain rotates, and replacing it with a specialty bar (which is manufactured without a guard at the end of the guide bar) is necessary for plunging deep cuts or scoring.

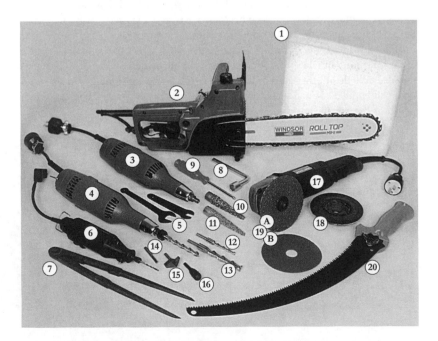

Figure 3-9. Modern tools of the ice sculptor

3 **Die Grinder with Converted Spindle**—A converted spindle has a threaded shaft for screwing on specialized or customized bits (e.g., rubberizers). When converting to a threaded shaft, the sculptor should refer to a licensed electrician or tool repairman to ensure that the integrity of the die grinder is not compromised.

4 **Die Grinder with Normal Shaft**—Die grinders have many attachments to vary the cut. These are primarily used instead of the classic V chisel to make clean cuts, lettering, lines, and other detailing. The collet, which binds the bit to the die grinder, accepts shanks up to $\frac{1}{4}$".

5 **Wrenches for Die Grinders**—Wrenches are needed for installing or removing bits.

6 **Rotary Tool**—Rotary tools, such as those made by Dremmel®, are used with a variety of bit styles for finer detail and delicate finish work, since the collet only accepts bits with $\frac{1}{8}$" shanks.

7 **Compass**—Used to score various-sized circles into the ice.

8 **Chain Saw Socket Wrench**—Used to loosen or tighten the bolt holding the chain cover and guide bar when changing or adjusting the chain.

9 **Chain Saw Phillips Screwdriver**—Used to loosen or tighten the adjusting pin for the chain.

10 **Coarse Rubberizer**—A 16-grit cone rasp used to round, sand, and reach difficult areas of the sculpture. The rubberizer is ideal for shaping areas without removing too much ice by mistake. Using a rubberizer will result in a machined appearance, which may or may not be desirable. The machined marks will quickly smooth when the sculpture is displayed at room temperature.

11 **Fine Rubberizer**—A 36-grit cone rasp used for finer rounding and sanding. This attachment is ideal for more delicate areas and will leave a much smoother surface.

12 $\frac{1}{4}$" **End Mill (Plunge) Bit**—Used for roughing-in, shaping, and gouging in hard to reach areas.

13 $\frac{1}{2}$" **End Mill (Plunge) Bit**—Used for roughing-in, shaping, and gouging. It has a larger diameter than the $\frac{1}{4}$" end mill bit. The shaft of the $\frac{1}{2}$" end mill can be milled down to fit in a $\frac{1}{4}$" collet. The sculptor must use this bit with caution, as it is very aggressive.

14 $\frac{1}{4}$" **Straight Router Bit**—Used for lettering, drawing lines, detailing, and shaping smaller objects.

15 **V-Shaped Router Bit**—Used for making V-lines or grooves. The width of the line or groove is determined by how deep the bit penetrates the ice.

16 **Round-End Rasp Bit**—Used to round and shape small surfaces.

17 **Angle Grinder/Sander**—Used to sand surfaces and shape contours.

18 **Rubber Backing Pad**—Attached to the angle grinder to hold sanding paper in place.

19 **Sanding Paper:**
   a. **16-Grit**—Very aggressive, used for quick and rough removal of ice.
   b. **36-Grit**—Used for smoothing and polishing surfaces.

20 **Handsaw**—Handsaws vary in length and tooth dimension; larger-tooth saws are used for rough cuts and smaller-tooth saws for finer cuts. Ice

Figure 3-10. More modern tools of the ice sculptor

saws are used for splitting blocks and fusing and marking the base. By laying the saw sideways on a piece of wood or cinder block, the sculptor can guide the saw evenly along the base of the sculpture.

21 **Plastic Bag**—A plastic bag can be used to hold hot or warm water for smoothing, rounding, and polishing the sculpture in a controlled and uniform manner. It can also be used to collect dry, clean snow for later use in re-packing snow-filled lines in the sculpture.

22 **Cordless Drill**—Battery-operated drills that require no electrical power cord. Cordless tools tend to lose their charge faster in colder temperatures.

23 **Power Strip with Surge Protector**—When using multiple power cords, a heavy-duty power strip with circuit breaker is useful.

24 **Aluminum Sheets**—Aluminum sheets can aid in evenly melting and smoothing ice, as well as fusing ice surfaces together. Irons are used to heat flat, $\frac{1}{2}$" or thicker aluminum sheets. If the iron is applied directly to the ice, steam holes in the iron result in uneven ice surface.

25 **Freeze Spray or Gum Remover**—Either can be used to join ice pieces together. Caution must be taken to spray the ice slowly and delicately to prevent ice fissures from forming.

26 **Drill with $\frac{5}{8}$" Spade Bit**—Used to drill holes to drain bowls and vodka sockets. May use various-sized bits and hole cutters.

27 **Hole Cutter**—Used to drill larger holes.

28 **Power Brush Wheel**—Used to clean snow or debris off large areas. Attached to a power drill.

29 **Power Brush Cylinder**—Used to clean snow or debris out of hard-to-reach areas, such as sorbet dishes. Attached to a power drill.

30 **Duct Tape**—An all-around tool for the clever sculptor, duct tape is useful for a wide variety of repairs and inventions.

31 **Hand Brush/Whisk Broom**—Used to continually remove unwanted snow and ice chips before they refreeze to the sculpture.

32 **Propane Torch with Auto-Ignite Trigger**—Used instead of a heat gun to clear and clean up the sculpture. No matches or lighter are needed.

33 **Ice Tongs**—Used to lift, hold, or move large blocks. The two main styles are known as *Cincinnati* and *Boston*.

34 **Ice Pick**—Used to quickly break away sections of ice. Also used to score and mark the ice.

35 **CO_2 Tank**—CO_2 gas can be sprayed onto ice to freeze two pieces together. Caution must be observed; otherwise fissures will appear in the ice. May be used in place of gum remover.

36 **Clothes Iron**—A cheap, versatile heating element used to heat aluminum plates for flattening and fusing ice surfaces.

37 **Extension Cord with Rubber Casing**—Should be long enough to give the sculptor room to move around the sculpture without obstruction. Must be rubber coated, brightly colored, insulated, heavy duty, and grounded to an outlet with a GFCI circuit breaker.

38 **Heat Gun**—The heat gun is used in place of the propane torch to round, clean, and gloss the ice.

Using Modern Power Tools

Power tools have proven to be a marvelous means for producing exquisite works of ice art. However, the sculptor must always remain aware that power tools have no sense of what they are cutting into. The artisan must wield the tools properly and safely, and maintain them for safe and effective use.

Using Chain Saws

Chain saws can be used to shape ice in many ways. Most commonly, they are used to slice into sections of ice or to cut straight lines with a high degree of control. Chain saws can also be used to create different widths of gouge cuts, for sanding, for smoothing, and for rounding surfaces. **Note:** You can monitor depth of cuts by marking measurements on the saw's bar with a waterproof permanent marker.

The two main functional components of the saw's chain are the *rakers* and *cutter*. A raker is a guide plate located on the front of each blade, set slightly shallower than the cutting edge of the blade. The raker keeps the blades from digging too deeply as they pass through the ice. Reducing the raker's height will allow the blades to cut more quickly but will damage the ice as it cuts, resulting in a rougher finish. It is best to keep both heights relatively even, since uneven spacing can result in "chain bounce" and compromise the safe operation of the saw.

Warning: Reducing the raker height may produce kickback!

Figure 3-11. Using a chain saw

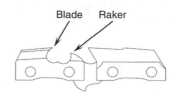

Figure 3-12. Diagram of blade and raker parts of a chain

Figure 3-13. Using a rotary tool for fine detail work

Figure 3-14. Using a die grinder for medium and larger cuts

Figure 3-15. Using a clothes iron to smooth and polish

The cutter, also known as the blade, is the L-shaped, sharpened metal surface of the chain that tapers backwards at approximately a 35-degree angle. When having the chain blades sharpened, it is important to consider the angle at which the blades are sharpened. The greater, or sharper, the angle, the more quickly the chain will cut. However, for this reason, the chain will also dull more quickly because the thinner cutting blade is exposed to the ice.

Some sculptors customize their chains by adding additional cutters and removing rakers. They essentially remove every other raker, resulting in a chain that has a pattern of three cutters followed by one raker. The effect is that the chain cuts more quickly.

The cutting edges of the teeth alternate, and they extend beyond the dimension of the bar. For this reason, all surfaces of the chain can be used for sculpting. The ice artisan views the chain saw more as a "cutting wand" than a slicing saw.

Modern Bits and Accessory Hardware

One of the greatest advantages of using modern power tools is that they can be adapted to the needs of individual sculptors. Rotary tools and die grinders have different bits that can be changed as required, whether for improved usage, or as the bit becomes worn. Some of the newer bits and accessory hardware pieces now available on the market are illustrated in Figure 3-16.

1 **Custom Shaft for GE0600 Makita Die Grinder**—Designed to replace the stock shaft in the Makita die grinder for safe and smooth operations when using large bits. As new tools come to market, more and more large bits will fit these custom shafts.

2 **Large Silver Burr**—The same design as the rubberizer, with the same benefits, but the silver burr is faster in many applications and leaves a smoother finish. It is also more expensive than the rubberizer, and has a tendency to ice up on the tip in certain weather conditions. Use the large Silver Burr when speed is the primary issue. This bit fits the custom shaft.

3 **Dagger Knife**—Designed with a concave cutting edge that allows a wide range of angles when shaping and detailing. The most versatile bit available for shaping and finishing, this bit fits the custom shaft.

4 **Brice Bit**—Designed as a super grinder to perform end mill functions. It removes ice many times faster than the rubberizer. For delicate cutouts it is much smoother than an end mill. This bit fits the custom shaft.

5 **Long Roscoe Bit**—Designed for floating template lines and delicate detail and cutouts, this stainless steel bit is 4.25" long and fits the custom shaft.

6 **Custom Shaft for GD800 Makita Die Grinder**—This shaft has the same threads as the original custom shaft, but fits a larger-model die grinder. The larger die grinder has adjustable speed and more than three times the power of the smaller model, but weighs only one pound more.

7 **Metal Nail Sander**—This tool is the fastest for shaping ice, other than a chisel. It removes chisel marks twice as fast as heavy sandpaper. However, for safety purposes, a grinder handle (handle extension) should be used with the nailsander to protect the fingers, since the edge cuts ice as well.

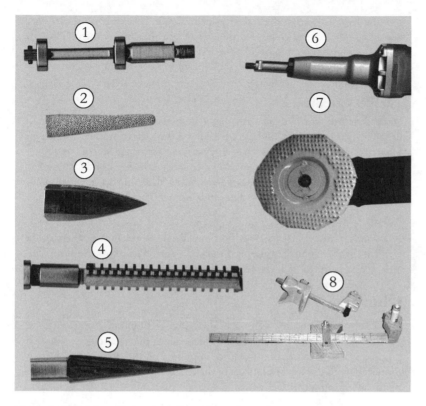

Figure 3-16. Modern bits, tools, and attachments

8   **Layout Jig**—One of the most helpful ice carving tools ever for precision layouts, it makes parallel lines quickly. Similar to a smaller chain saw mill.

CONSIDERATIONS WHEN USING POWER TOOLS

Although modern power tools are relatively simple to operate, the informed sculptor should have a basic knowledge of electricity. It is important to understand the basic terminology used by electricians and to understand electrical circuits and their capacity. The modern sculptor must be able to calculate the amperage needs of his power tools and grasp the effects of cord length, wire gauge, and voltage drop.

Electrical Circuits

Electrical **current** travels a path of **conductors** and conducting devices. There must be a complete path, or, one with no breaks. Current flows in an electric **circuit** according to several laws of electrodynamics. The basic law of current flow is **Ohm's Law**. Ohm's Law applies to all electric circuits for both *direct current* (DC) and *alternating current* (AC). There are two classifications of circuits: *parallel* and *series*. All circuits, including appliances and power tools, use either parallel or series circuits, or some combination of both.

Circuits are designed to handle only a limited amount of electrical **amperage**. Circuits incorporate breakers or fuses to interrupt the flow of current in case the demand exceeds the **capacity** of the circuit. Breakers or fuses are sized according to electrical codes and the electricians that install them. They are rated as 15 amp, 20 amp, or 30 amp and are used to prevent the wires from overheating when the combined total of all connected appliances exceeds those amperages.

Parallel Circuits

Parallel circuits are circuits with many branches. These branches actually become separate circuits, and electricity flows through each one. In this type of circuit, electrical devices, such as a power tool, are arranged to allow all positive poles (for DC) and terminals to be connected to one conductor and all negative poles to another. AC uses a system of black and white wires, while DC uses a system of positive and negative connections.

Series Circuits

In a series circuit, electricity flows from one device to the next in a series. The elements of the circuit are arranged in such a way as to allow the entire current to pass through each element without branching into parallel circuits.

Ohm's Law

Named for its discoverer, George Simon Ohm, Ohm's Law states that the amount of current flowing in a circuit (made up of pure resistance) is directly proportional to the electromotive force impressed on the circuit, and inversely proportional to the total **resistance** of the circuit. The law is usually expressed by the following formulas:

$$I = V/R \text{ or } V = I \times R$$

I is the current, measured in amperes
V is the electromotive force, measured in volts
R is the resistance, measured in Ohms

Extension-Cord Length and Capacity

The size of wire, insulating jacket or shield materials covering the wire, and **voltage drop** are all frequently overlooked considerations that affect power tool operation. Although sculptors (and the general public) often assume that all extension cords function alike, it is important to note their differences and limitations.

An extension cord's wire **gauge** and length affect the power supply available to the power tool. Similar to a gas pipe, the diameter of the conduit determines its capacity to carry the fuel. The greater the wire's diameter, the more electricity it can carry. Smaller wires have smaller capacity and greater resistance. In addition to diameter, wire resistance is also affected by cord length, composition (type of metal), generation source, and demand on the other end. Generally speaking, with extension cords, the wire's diameter and cord length represent the two most important factors to evaluate.

Wire Diameter

The diameter of each wire encased in the jacket of an extension cord is classified by a national standard, the **American Wire Gauge (AWG)**. A typical extension cord uses a three-wire system consisting of hot, neutral, and ground. Most extension cords used on construction sites and in sculpting studios are made from wire ranging in size from 10–18 AWG. The most commonly used sizes are 12-3, 14-3, and 16-3. The first number denotes the gauge of the cord, and the second denotes the number of wires it contains. These cords are readily available from home construction and maintenance retailers, and their sizes are generally stamped on the cord's outer jacket. Each gauge wire has a recommended amperage capacity.

Note: The largest diameter wire has the smallest AWG number.

Cord Length

In addition to the diameter of wire used in making the cord, the length of the extension cord affects its functional efficiency. An extension cord that is too long can create a form of resistance called **voltage drop**. This type of resistance will increase as the cord gets longer, similar to the effect of distance on a runner's energy. The longer and further the runner is from the starting line, the less energy is available to the runner at the finish line. This decline in energy eventually creates a form of resistance and a reduction in speed.

Voltage drop can have severe negative effects on motors. Voltage drop can make a motor run slower, creating carbon deposits on the motor's brushes and decreased efficiency. To avoid voltage drop, it is wise to use the shortest length of cord necessary to complete the sculpture.

Note: Voltage drops should not exceed 10% of the voltage requirement posted on the nameplate. For example, the total voltage drop for a 115-volt chain saw should not fluctuate more than 11.5 volts from the stated requirement. Motors do not perform well on low voltage, although the effect on heating devices like irons is only that they heat more slowly.

Typical Amperage Requirements

In some instances, the sculptor may need to share an extension cord with a fellow sculptor or two. It is not unlikely that an extension cord will be connected to a power source 50' from where the pair of sculptors are working. They may wish to operate their chain saws, die grinders, circular sanders, or irons simultaneously, and with all of these tools tied to that single extension cord. However, the sculptors must first determine how much amperage their tools require and whether the available cord can handle the necessary draw of current.

Consider the hypothetical situation of the two sculptors, both wanting to be able to operate any of their power tools without limitation. Additionally, one artist wishes to keep an iron going continuously to warm an aluminum sheet for fusing. By checking the amperage rating printed on the motor-housing faceplates of the iron and the power tools, the sculptors can calculate their total amperage requirements and compare that sum to the amperage rating of the extension cord. They may discover that the cord is rated too low for the number of tools they wish to operate simultaneously. The typical amperage requirements in Table 3-1 illustrate typical amperage requirements for standard power tools used by ice sculptors. The information on current limits on extension cords in Table 3-2 illustrates the relationship between cord length, cord size (wire gauge), and current limit (measured in amps).

Comparison of Voltage Drop Between # 12 and # 16 Gauge Extension Cords

 # 12 Gauge Wire Voltage Drop

	25 foot	50 foot	100 foot
Heat gun (11.7 amps)	0.97	1.93	3.86
Chain saw (11.5 amps)	0.95	1.90	3.80
Clothes iron (9.2 amps)	0.76	1.52	3.04
Circular sander (7 amps)	0.58	1.16	2.31
3/8" drill (5.5 amps)	0.45	0.91	1.82
Die grinder (2 amps)	0.17	0.33	0.66

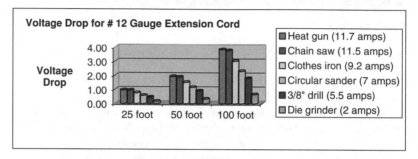

 # 16 Gauge Wire Voltage Drop

	25 foot	50 foot	100 foot
Heat gun (11.7 amps)	2.44	4.88	9.76
Chain saw (11.5 amps)	2.40	4.80	9.60
Clothes iron (9.2 amps)	1.92	3.84	7.68
Circular sander (7 amps)	1.46	2.92	5.84
3/8" drill (5.5 amps)	1.15	2.29	4.59
Die grinder (2 amps)	0.42	0.83	1.67

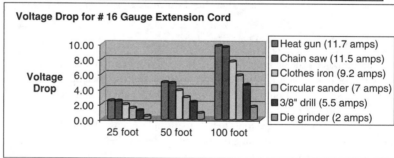

Figure 3-17. Comparison of voltage drop between # 12 and # 16 gauge extension cords

Table 3-1. Typical amperage requirements for sculpting power tools

Heat gun	11.7 amps
Chain saw	11.5 amps
Clothes iron	9.2 amps
Circular sander	7.0 amps
3/8" drill	5.5 amps

Table 3-2. Limits of electrical current on extension cords

Cord size	Cord length		
	25 ft.	**50 ft.**	**100 ft.**
18-gauge	7 amps	5 amps	2 amps
16-gauge	12 amps	7 amps	3.4 amps
14-gauge	16 amps	12 amps	5 amps
12-gauge	20 amps	16 amps	7 amps

Note: The amperes rating may not be listed on the motor-housing faceplate of the power tool. In this case, the watts and volts will be listed instead. The sculptor merely needs to make a quick calculation to discover the amps. The following formula is used to calculate amps when watts and volts are known WATTS/VOLTS = AMPS

For example: 1100 WATTS/120 VOLTS = 9.2 AMPS

Extension Cord Accessories

Occupational Safety and Health Administration (OSHA) regulations require the use of ground fault circuit interrupters (GFCI) on any non-permanent cord used on a construction site. Since ice sculptors use some of the same tools, but often in worse climatic conditions, it only makes sense that ice artisans also comply. Similar to household GFCI, these portable units compare the incoming and outgoing current traveling through the cord and can shut off the power instantly if there is a difference, preventing possible electrocution.

Locking and lighted cords have gained in popularity. The male and female ends maintain a tighter connection, sometimes by being twisted into place. This tighter connection is valued when working around ice and water.

TOOL MAINTENANCE

Proper maintenance of tools is vital to the success of the sculptor. Tools must be sharp, rust-free, and in working order. Maintenance is not only essential to the longevity of these expensive tools, but can also directly affect the quality of the finished sculpture. The Japanese, among many nationalities who sculpt ice, have long believed that one should spend as much time caring for one's tools as in the sculpting itself.

Proper care begins with the sculptor's ***mise en place*** (everything in its proper place). Orderly arrangement of tools, prior to beginning to sculpt, allows for more organized work and prevents unnecessary delays while sculpting. Tools should be placed on foam or towels to keep the blades off the table surface and keep them from rolling around or falling.

Bits and blades of power tools should be inspected for their sharpness prior to their use, and after the sculpture has been completed, in case any need to be repaired or replaced. Most of these are relatively inexpensive and are designed to be disposable.

The following procedure for cleaning bits, blades, and chisels should be carried out immediately after each sculpting session:

1. If rust is present, rub rust remover on the surface, then warm the bit, blade, or chisel with boiling water—cold metal will collect condensation quickly.

2. Wipe the item completely dry with a soft cloth.

3. Coat the metal item with a light film of oil.

4. Wrap each piece individually, or place in separate slots in a storage tray so they will not damage each other.

Saws and other power tools need to be oiled regularly, and their power cords need to be inspected frequently for cuts, cracks, and exposed wires. A damaged power cord can cause shocks and arcing of electricity.

Attention to the condition of the chain on the chain saw is also vital. A normal chain can be used about 10 times before the cutters need to be sharpened. This can be done by the sculptor or by a hardware store employee; however it is highly recommended that a skilled professional sharpen chains and other cutting tools. An improperly sharpened chain can be a safety hazard and can also negatively affect the quality of the sculpture. Uneven rakes and uneven angles on the blades can cause the chain to grab the ice, creating a dangerous kickback instead of smoothly cutting through the ice. Carbide tip chains can last 10 times longer than standard chains, but are much more expensive. Either way, the chain must be sharp to produce a good sculpture.

It is advisable to keep additional sharpened chains on hand, since chains can dull or break. The guide bar of the chain saw should be flipped over occasionally because sculptors tend to favor the bottom of the blade, and guide bar rotation prevents uneven wearing.

Safety Clothing and Gear

In addition to using the proper tools while sculpting, the ice artist protects himself from the elements and possible accidents by dressing appropriately and defensively. Proper selection and care of clothing and safety gear is a vital part of successful sculpting. The most important items are shown in Figure 3-18.

Sculptors must be able to move unrestricted by their clothing, which should also have no dangling or loosely tied straps. They must also protect their extremities from the elements without impairing vision, movement, or dexterity.

And, of course, keeping the body warm and dry is extremely important. The sculptor has to be able to work comfortably for several hours in chilly and wet conditions. Periodically changing gloves, socks, or any other article of clothing that may become wet during the course of sculpting is a proactive means of remaining warm and comfortable.

1   **Weight Belt**—Gives added support to the lower back when lifting or bending.

2   **Rubber Rain Suit**—Worn as insulation against wet elements, such as chipped ice, slush, and water.

3   **Rubber Boots**—Known as "Wellingtons" or "Wellies" in the United Kingdom, any version of these oversized rubber boots keep feet warm, dry, and protected from electrical shock. An Army–Navy surplus store is a good place to find very high quality rubber boots at a fair price.

4   **Gloves**—An absolute requirement when using power tools, leather gloves help protect the sculptor's hands from abrasions. However, dry cotton

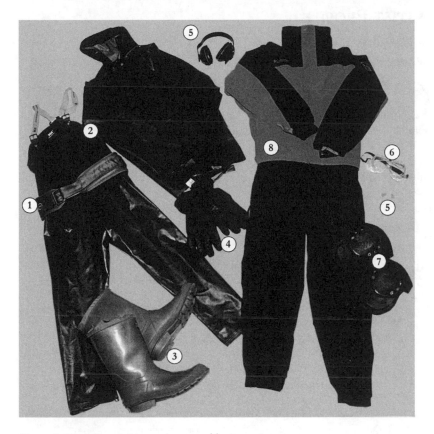

Figure 3-18. Safety clothing and gear used by ice sculptors

gloves are best for holding and carrying finished ice pieces. Rubber gloves that extend well beyond the wrist can be used when handling wet slush or holding an area where water is being applied.

5   **Ear Protection**—Either actual rubber-like plugs or coverings similar to headphones, they protect the sculptors' eardrums from the extremely high decibels produced by power tools. Most sculptors prefer the headphone style since they also protect their ears from flying ice chips, and can be easily slipped off and on.

6   **Eye Protection**—Protective eyewear should always be worn when using any power tool. Flying ice can be a dangerous projectile. Plastic goggles for wearing over standard eyeglasses, or safety glasses with wraparound sides are commonly available. *Standard eyeglasses are not impact resistant and are not sufficient to protect the eyes.*

7   **Knee Pads**—Sculptors often wear knee protection when sculpting close to the ground. While the preferred position for sculpting is standing with the ice at eye level, it is not uncommon to kneel when applying finishing details.

ARTIST PROFILE

Meet the Artist—Julian Bayley

Canadian Julian Bayley came to the ice hospitality business by way of a 25-year career in advertising and marketing, in addition to off-premise catering. His skills in business have enabled him, with the help of his family, to build a company of 28 employees that specializes in ice block formation, commercial ice sculpting, and the development and sale of specialized ice sculpting equipment. His CNC router and ice lathe have been distributed across North America and Europe. Much of the commercial awareness that ice sculpting has received in recent years can be attributed to Julian's innovative approach to ice production and marketing.

Ask the Artist

Q   Where do you see new developments in the industry?

A   *Transportation will be a key area. Other developments will take place in the business sector, addressing liability and food safety.*

Q   What other developments do you see occurring with ice-sculpting tools?

A   *We have modified a drill press to work in conjunction with a lathe. That machine, for instance, can hollow out vases that can be turned on the lathe. These sculptures will work nicely as centerpieces to hold flower arrangements. Other developments include a number of specialized accessories for power tools used every day in freezer studios.*

CHAPTER

4

Safe Practices and Procedures

OBJECTIVES

After reading this chapter, you will be able to:

- Identify and discuss the five elements of safe sculpting
- Take preventative steps to ensure the safety of yourself, your guests, and your sculpture
- Discuss the proper methods for moving ice, including lifting and lowering
- Set up a safety zone for sculpting
- Identify and discuss how to prepare for an emergency situation
- Create a waiver of liability
- Safely display a sculpture
- Safely dispose of a sculpture

Key Terms and Concepts

protection
ground
greenhouse effect
ground fault circuit interrupter (GFCI)
insulate
safety zone
sculpting buddy
jig

OUTLINE

Elements of Safety
- The Individual Sculptor
- Clothing
- Tools
- Electricity
- The Display Environment

Moving Ice Safely
- Rolling Sculptures
- Lifting and Carrying Ice
- Stacking Ice Blocks
- Leveling a Pillar

Setting up the Sculptor's Work Area

Preparation for an Emergency
- Sculpting Buddy
- Emergency Supplies, Equipment, and Information
- Emergency Information

Displaying Sculptures Safely

Disposing of Sculptures Safely

Artist Profile

Although safety is always a consideration for professional sculptors, most textbooks, training sessions, and competitions seem to overlook its importance.

Adherence to safe practices and procedures supercedes any need associated with ice sculpting. Said another way, *the sculptor is more important than the sculpture.* It is the sculptor's responsibility to ensure that he is working under the proper conditions. The sculptor has it within his ability to protect himself and those around him from serious injury when sculpting. The authors believe that this subject is of ultimate importance when teaching students to sculpt—greater than any other lessons taught about ice sculpting. Furthermore, since sculpting is their livelihood, the authors know they must practice what they preach if they are to enjoy a long and healthy career.

ELEMENTS OF SAFETY

This book will approach the topic of safety by considering the essential elements of ice sculpting. There are many variables that can affect the safe completion of a sculpture, and the professional ice artist must consider each of these elements before, and during, sculpting.

The Individual Sculptor

The person doing the sculpting has the most to do with creating a safe environment. The sculptor must learn about safety and then be disciplined enough to follow the proper procedures. He must take personal responsibility for his actions, be organized in his work, and always adhere to safe practices. All sculpting tools can be deadly weapons in the hands of an immature or careless individual.

Personal Responsibility

The individual sculptor must recognize when he is fatigued or unable to safely operate chain saws and other power tools, and be willing to rest as needed. Food fuels the body, and a person burns many calories when sculpting. Dehydration also occurs when the body has not received sufficient water. Time must be taken to rest and eat, as accidents happen more frequently when one is tired.

The sculptor must also know his personal limits when attempting to sculpt a difficult piece in a limited period, such as during a competition. Loss of focus can quickly lead to an accident, just as much as poor judgment can. One should always work within the safe limits of the situation.

The ice artist must be vigilant, always aware of himself and others, his surroundings, equipment, and the ice display he is working on. A proactive attitude towards safety will greatly reduce the chance of accidents.

Organization

How the sculptor organizes his work site and tools affects the outcome of a sculpture. A cluttered tool table or work area is an accident waiting to happen. Proper organization also saves time and effort. Tools that will no longer be needed should be properly stored, allowing the optimum table space for remaining work. Time-saving devices, such as drill bit cases or wooden stands for rotary tool bits, reduce unwanted clutter on the tool table and increase productivity.

Electrical cords must not become tangled or allowed too close to the cutting blades. Accidents happen when sculptors fail to safely arrange their electrical cords; whenever possible, cords should hang from above to avoid tripping people or being cut inadvertently.

Templates should be grouped and organized for easy access. Paper can be a nuisance on a windy, wet day, and the professional sculptor knows to organize and protect his templates from the elements.

Practices

Safe practices by the sculptor also improve the probability of success. If he makes a conscious effort to develop and use safe practices, taking precautions will become second nature. This attention to personal safety instills a subconscious pattern for future behavior.

Use two hands. The sculptor should make a conscious effort to always operate the power tools with both hands. The two primary reasons are to gain better control of the tool and to keep an idle hand out of harm's way.

Take care when lifting. Proper lifting and handling of the ice will also reduce or prevent unnecessary back strain. When possible and appropriate, use two-wheel handcarts and mechanical lifts to assist in transporting and raising the ice. A byproduct of proper lifting is less fatigue, thereby reducing the probability of an accident.

Work at eye level. When possible, raise the sculpture onto a sturdy table protected with material such as Ethafoam to improve vision and reduce back strain caused by excessive bending.

Keep the work area clear. Avoid buildup of water, slush, and ice chunks by setting the area up properly from the beginning. Provide for proper drainage, and keep a push broom and/or long-handled squeegee nearby to periodically sweep away any potentially dangerous debris.

Turn off all power tools before unplugging them. Conversely, always check to be sure the tool is turned off before plugging it into a live electrical circuit or power cord. All too often, the sculptor or another artist will forget to check, and an injury may happen when the tool is again connected to a live power source. Errant cuts to the sculptor, particularly severe abrasions to the hands, are often the result. This is a very common accident that can easily be avoided through proper practice.

Have a plan in case of an emergency. Prior knowledge of modes of transportation, telephones, and hospital locations in case of an accident is good practice, as is never using chain saws or power tools without another person present. Always have a complete first aid kit on hand when sculpting.

Clothing

Proper clothing aids the sculptor in achieving his best work. Clothing that is loose fitting and flexible allows the sculptor to move without restriction. However, avoid wearing long scarves, hats, or any other clothing or jewelry that may tangle.

Protective clothing, including insulated steel-toed rubber boots, safety glasses, leather or neoprene gloves, rubber aprons, and earplugs or headphones provide all-important armor against injury. Additionally, wearing a weight belt or back-support vest may protect the lower back when lifting heavy objects.

The professional sculptor knows to be proactive against both the weather and body strain. An investment in quality clothing and protective gear is an investment in safety and should not be discounted. Army surplus stores, camping and outdoor recreation stores, and safety equipment distributors or retailers are all good sources for clothing and gear. When considering clothing, the key word to remember is *protection*.

Hand Protection

Selecting proper hand protection requires some forethought. Different glove materials serve different purposes, and the sculptor may want to have different gloves available for different purposes. It is a good idea to have several pairs of the same type glove for rotating while working, to keep hands dry. The following list reflects the authors suggested glove types, given the varying activities involved in sculpting:

- **Leather**—Best to wear when carving with power tools, chisels, chippers, or handsaws because it protects against abrasions. However, leather becomes slippery when wet and hardens as it dries, thereby losing its effectiveness for gripping tools.
- **Neoprene or Rubber**—Best material for keeping the hands dry when handling slush and snow and working with water.
- **Cotton Knit**—Best material for gripping ice blocks or finished sculptures. However, several pairs may be needed for prolonged wear, as these gloves become wet and cold relatively quickly.

Loose straps on gloves can cause serious accidents. Wrapping duct tape around the straps can ensure a secure fit.

Ear Protection

Ear protection is needed primarily to insulate the eardrum from the high decibels and high-pitched noise from the motors. There are two kinds available:

- **Rubber or Foam Plugs**—Less intrusive and obvious to an onlooker.
- **Plastic Head Muffs**—Easiest for the sculptor to slide off and on as needed. They also protect the whole ear from flying ice chips.

Eye Protection

Eye protection, whether a person normally wears eyeglasses or not, is a very important but often overlooked necessity. Ice chips, slush, and water fly off power tools, such as grinder pads and chain saw blades, at tremendous speed. Although less likely, other materials, like rubber matting, Ethafoam, and cardboard, could become dangerous projectiles.

Three common forms of eye protection are:

- **Rubber or Plastic Goggles**—As these can fit over the sculptor's prescription eyewear, sculptors who wear glasses often wear goggles. They are also suitable for those people who don't wear glasses.
- **Shatter-Resistant Safety Glasses**—These glasses are made of durable material and have side panels on their stems for additional protection. Safety glasses can be ordered with prescription lenses.

- **Safety Helmets with Face Shields**—Safety helmets have long been used around construction sites and other locations where falling debris is commonplace. Clear, impact-resistant plastic face shields can be attached to some of these helmets to protect against flying debris; however their use in ice sculpting is rare at present. A mesh shield, like those used by brush cutters, is also effective.

Foot Protection

Foot protection usually receives the attention that it deserves. Most sculptors have rugged, insulated footwear that can hold up against the elements. However, it is our opinion that there is only one material that is best for ice sculpting, especially outdoors: rubber.

The authors have worn many types of rubber, plastic, cloth, and leather shoes and boots during their years of sculpting outdoors. After considering the merits of each, no other boot can compare to an insulated, calf-height rubber boot of single piece construction, with anti-skid soles. These boots are warm, waterproof (and watertight), grounded against potential electrical shock, and skid resistant. Our source for these boots has been our local Army–Navy surplus store. The boot should also have steel toes to protect the foot from sharp and heavy objects. Protecting the feet from the harsh elements of weather, fractures caused by the weight of falling ice, and cuts from the sharpened edges of sculpting tools are all good reasons for investing in quality footwear. **Note:** The use of steel-toed boots is becoming a legal requirement in some states.

Back Protection

Back-support vests and weight belts are useful to sculptors of all ages and levels of physical fitness. The back can be easily injured when lifting improperly. Even low weights can cause back distress when muscles are aggravated. Two common styles of back support are:

- **Weight Lifter Belts**—These leather belts are buckled around the upper waist of the wearer, and are designed to support the lower lumbar region.
- **Stockroom Back Braces**—These braces resemble vests and are generally made of reinforced nylon and cloth. They and are wrapped around the wearer, then tightened with Velcro straps.

Sculptors should be aware, however, that neither a support vest nor a belt can protect from excessive or improper lifting. Two-wheel handcarts and mechanical lifts should be used whenever possible to move and raise blocks and sculptures.

Tools

For maximum safety, tools must be properly selected, adequately maintained, and used as the manufacturer intended. Tools used for the wrong purpose or handled improperly can cause injury.

Proper Choice and Use

You get what you pay for when it comes to tools. The ice artist must first decide what tool is needed and then how much he is willing to pay for it. Then, a review of which tools are available and their cost will dictate the buying decision. We consider some tools as *disposable,* when we know their use expectancy is shorter than other tools. A clothes iron is a good example of this kind of tool. We spend minimal money on our disposable tools, and the necessary money to buy superior permanent tools.

Many power tools, such as chain saws and die grinders, have a longer use expectancy, particularly if they are of good initial quality, but they have disposable parts that wear out from grinding, cutting, and drilling.

Proper Care

To function properly, a tool and its parts must be cared for adequately. It costs only a few dollars to have an electric saw's chain sharpened at a hardware store, and the difference between sculpting with a sharp chain and a dull one is immeasurable. Also, a good hardware store will inspect the chains for their safe and useable condition. We maintain a large supply of chains that we rotate out to have serviced. Our chains are stored in an oil bath or coated with an oil film to prevent rust.

Several years ago, a machinist recommended that we use a particular brand of lithium grease on our chain saws and Iceculture 5200. The USDA had approved the brand name that he recommended for use in federally inspected meat and poultry plants. Because we often use our sculptures around food, we thought it was best to take this precaution. We lubricate our chain saws' bar sprockets and oil reservoirs frequently, according to the manufacturer's recommendation. However, we have noted that we must lubricate even more frequently when using lithium grease compared to a petroleum-based lubricant.

Electrical

In addition to ensuring that electrical cords do not become tangled or cut by the saw, the sculptor must be constantly aware that he is using electrical tools around water. The possibility of shock, or even electrocution, does exist. To ensure a safe electrical environment, lines should be properly grounded, circuit breakers and **ground fault circuit interrupter (GFCI)** circuits and plugs used, and all electrical cords routinely inspected. To further protect against electrical shock, rubber boots should be worn.

Insulation and Connections

Before plugging in any power tool, the sculptor should inspect the cord for accidental nicks and cuts. These nicks and cuts can result in arcing, and cause a shock or burn. A simple examination of the cord will prevent this sort of mishap.

We recommend using only three-pronged, brightly colored, heavy-duty and insulated rubber-coated extension cords for ice sculpting with power tools. Each of these features adds a unique element of protection when using power tools near water and ice. We also recommend tightly fitting rubber connections between power cords, and securing connections with rubber or duct tape to prevent water seepage.

Grounding Power Tools

If you decide to modify the length of a power cord, be sure to have a qualified electrician perform the work. Saving a few dollars on the cost by doing the work yourself is false economy. Professional electricians guarantee quality workmanship and safe use of the materials. Using GFCI plugs and circuits is paramount to working safely around water.

The Display Environment

Weather, temperature, lighting, room dimension, traffic patterns, dining and buffet setups, and many other factors make up the display environment. The professional sculptor must study the environment in which the ice is to be displayed and consider its impact on the sculpture. This attention to detail is necessary to ensure the stability of the finished sculpture, as well as for the protection of guests and food displays.

Working Outdoors

Wind and sunshine greatly affect a sculpture's stability, and care needs to be taken to consider the effects of nature on the ice. Ice can suffer from the **greenhouse effect** by prolonged exposure to sunlight, which weakens the sculpture from within. A strong gust of wind may slowly erode or topple an otherwise secure ice display. Sometimes canvas tarps and tents are necessary to protect the ice and sculptor from the elements.

Working Indoors

The room where a sculpture will be carved or displayed must have a proper infrastructure, with certain elements that can either be controlled or provided. When a sculptor views a room where he is to work or display, he must take into consideration and secure the following:

- Proper lighting
- Proper drainage, considering the size and form of the sculpture, expected length of display, lighting, and other temperature considerations
- Proper ventilation
- Proper distance from air ventilation ducts
- Proper distance from potential heat sources, such as chafing dishes with Sterno, fireplaces, or electric heat lamps
- Proper distance from electrical outlets (to prevent the spray of water and slush from causing electrical shortages)

MOVING ICE SAFELY

Because ice is hard, cold, heavy, and slippery by nature, caution must always be observed when moving full blocks and sculpted pieces. There are many potential problems inherent in moving ice, so the sculptor must be vigilant throughout the process. Chapter 9, "Methods of Transportation," discusses the "Five P's of Ice Sculpture Transportation" in detail; however, in relation to safety, we offer the following information.

Before actually moving the ice, the sculptor should inspect the route the ice will be traveling to look for obstacles and rough or uneven terrain. Sometimes the sculpture must be moved through high-traffic areas. This congestion will slow the safe movement of the sculpture and could result in an accident. Getting help moving the ice is always advisable. The following procedures can be beneficial in moving ice in a safe and secure manner.

Rolling Sculptures

The first task is to note the possible temperature extremes between where the ice is and where it is going. For example, if it is going from an area that is above freezing directly to a banquet room for display, then the ice has tempered and it will be less brittle. However, if the ice is going to the display area directly from a walk-in freezer, it will be at its most fragile. The slightest vibration could cause a crack. Care should be taken to let it warm to the room before moving it any distance.

Moving an ice block or sculpture any appreciable distance is best done with a sturdy cart or two-wheel dolly on which the ice can be rolled to its ultimate destination. Before the ice is placed on the dolly or cart, the vehicle needs to be prepared for the process. First, it should be padded to eliminate fractures to the ice. Carpeting, Ethafoam, or rubber will buffer the ice from the metal surfaces and help keep the ice intact. Wrapping the padding in duct tape will keep the ice from sticking to it and prolong the life of the padding.

Second, if using a two-wheel dolly, the tires (which should be air filled, not solid rubber) must be inflated equally to ensure level transportation.

Once the ice is on the cart or dolly, it should be secured by lashing it with straps or ropes. When rolling the ice cart, the sculptor can maintain better control by pulling it rather than pushing it. Slow steady movements are best, as the weight of the ice on the cart can cause too much momentum to safely control. *Beware! Haste can make waste!*

When taking the ice off-premise, the sculpture must be stabilized, but transportable, when moved from one location to another. The sculpture should first be wrapped in insulating blankets or bubblewrap before being secured to a two-wheel dolly or hand truck. The sculpture, strapped to the hand truck, is then secured to the wall panel of the truck for transportation.

Lifting and Carrying Ice

We subscribe to the philosophy, *The best muscle for lifting is the one in your head.* More good advice is to get the assistance of others when lifting the ice. As the adage says, *many hands make light work.* When available, the sculptor should use mechanical lifts for raising and lowering ice sculptures.

Cotton gloves are best for lifting ice. When dry, they grip securely, allowing for a tighter hold on the ice. Handle the ice from its thickest elements, as they are the least likely to break. Lifting properly is best accomplished by placing the stress on the most powerful muscles in the legs. Protect your back from strain by keeping it straight while bending at the knees. Always use proper technique when lifting.

Always make sure that the tongs are firmly in the ice. If tongs are placed on a crack the ice may break off at that point. If a raw block begins to fall, never try to catch it. The weight of the block, coupled with its gravitational force, is too much to handle.

The sculptor should always try to carry the ice as little as possible and use a cart or dolly for the major length of the journey. Protection with proper clothing is important because direct skin contact with the ice may cause discomfort and will begin to soften the ice, making it more slippery to grasp.

Figure 4-1. Proper body position and form for lifting ice

Steps in Lifting a Raw Block

Recognizing the shear bulk and weight of a standard block of ice, it is important to follow these steps in lifting a raw block:

1. Inspect the raw block for damage or flaws that may hinder the process of lifting the block now or the finished sculpture later.

2. Make sure the bottom of the raw block is level and free of debris. If the block is not level you may wish to lay it on its side and square off the base with a chain saw.

3. Inspect the surface area where the block is to sit, to ensure it is also free of debris.

4. Using both hands to grip the tongs, place the pincers into the sides of the ice, approximately 4" from the bottom corner.

5. With feet spread shoulder-width apart, legs bent at the knees, and back straight, pull the block up using your legs and arms, *but not using your back*.

6. As you lift, carefully place your foot at the bottom corner of the block closest to you. This action will prevent the block from slipping forward while lifting.

7. Be sure to control the block as it comes to rest. Do not allow the ice to slam onto the ground.

Steps in Lowering a Raw Block onto Its Side

Just as it is important to know how to lift a raw block, there are important steps to be followed in safely lowering a block of ice.

1. Inspect the raw block for damage or flaws that may hinder the process of lowering the block now or the finished sculpture later.

2. Place a sheet of Ethafoam that is at least the same length and width of the block on a level surface.

3. Using a handcart, position the upright block of ice towards one end of the Ethafoam. Set the block down with the narrow side of the ice parallel to the Ethafoam.

4. Stand on the Ethafoam in front of the ice with the narrow width (10") facing you.

5. Using both hands to grip the tongs, place the tong's pincers in the center of the ice, approximately 4" from the top of the block.

6. Tug on the tongs to ensure that the grip is firm.

7. Using the tongs, slowly pull the top of the ice forward, towards you.

8. Control the lowering with the tongs, and gradually bend at the knees while maintaining a straight back as the block descends as slowly as possible. Allow gravity to do the work of lowering, while you control the rate and direction.

9. If the block slips from the tongs, the Ethafoam should absorb the fall and prevent damage to the ice.

Stacking Ice Blocks

Designing an ice sculpture properly for display is an important part of the entire process. This is especially true when doing multi-block displays. There are basically two approaches to these large, expensive, time-consuming, physically exhausting, tremendously rewarding efforts. One consideration is to build a wall of ice by stacking full blocks in a staggered pattern like a brick wall. The artisan then sculpts the intended design by removing the unwanted ice.

The other method, which we prefer, is to design multi-block ice displays in modular sections. When components are designed and sculpted before building the display, there are often fewer full blocks to lift when assembling the final, massive sculpture. However, this method requires planning and precision cutting by the artisan. Mistakes can be fixed, and some finish work can be done after assembly, but the up-front planning is of the essence.

A multi-block display was created by Chefs Finch and Maxfield for the 2000 Plymouth Ice Spectacular. The ice wall measured six blocks high (resting on a seventh row of ice blocks, laid on their largest sides, to serve as a base) by five blocks long. The sculptors intentionally did not stagger the rows of blocks; rather they used the fuse lines to simulate the longitude and latitude lines of a map to enhance their "Map of the World." Each block was sculpted prior to being set in place and fused to the entire display. The rows of blocks became narrower as they were placed upon the preceding row. The top row of ice blocks measured 3" thick, compared to the full thickness of 10" blocks setting on the 20" base.

When stacking blocks, much consideration must be given to the surface on which the ice will be placed and the environment around it. Some ground is soft and will give way, causing the sculpture to sink. Blacktop surfaces absorb the sun's rays and warm over time, causing the base to soften. Open and flat areas, although roomy for building displays, may also be windswept. Care must be taken to allow plenty of room around the display for a safe work area and a protected area for the spectators, in case the sculpture falls. The sculptor also needs to be aware of what is overhead. Tree limbs and power lines don't mix well with ice sculptures.

Steps in Stacking Ice Blocks

The process of stacking ice blocks is as follows:

1. Select a solid surface on which to build that is as level as possible.
2. Create a level first course of blocks:
   a) Lay blocks closely together, end to end.
   b) Using a carpenter's level and ice pick, score a level line into the ice.
   c) Using a chain saw, remove large sheets of ice to create a new and level surface.
3. Plane off the surface of each course of blocks using a heated aluminum sheet (a minimum of a $\frac{1}{2}$" thickness).
4. Constantly check the ice with a bubble level to ensure the wall is level on all sides.
5. Alternate joints of the ice blocks, like a brick wall, for added strength and to prevent seams from widening as the ice melts.

Leveling a Pillar

In addition to block walls, pillars are a common part of multi-block displays. However, they can become a safety problem for both the display and people around the display. When not properly formed and leveled, pillars can

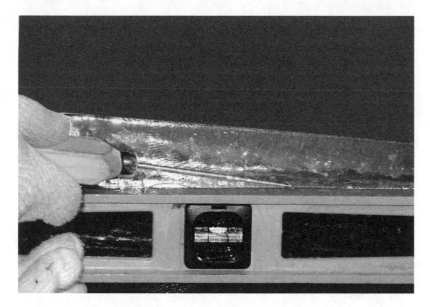

Figure 4-2. Using a bubble level and ice pick to create a level first row

become unbalanced and weaken the overall display. Care must be taken to level a pillar properly before it is added to the display.

Steps in Leveling a Pillar

To level a pillar, the sculptor must make a **jig**. The materials required include:

Figure 4-3. Pillar jig

- Two 12" × 40" × $\frac{1}{2}$" pieces of plywood
- Four heavy-duty corner brackets
- Eight $\frac{1}{2}$" wood screws

Screw together the two pieces of plywood with the corner brackets evenly spaced out on the outside surface of the now L-shaped jig.

1. Lay an ice pillar on a piece of Ethafoam. Anchor one ice pick in the Ethafoam (as close to the ice as possible) on each side of the pillar, towards its center. This will prevent the pillar from rolling around.
2. Using a chain saw, slice $\frac{1}{2}$" off each end, making the surface as flat as possible. Clean off any snow or debris.
3. Lay the pillar flat in the wood jig, $\frac{1}{2}$" from the bottom edge of the jig.
4. Place a 20" × 40" piece of warmed aluminum against both bottom edges of the jig.

Figure 4-4. Using the pillar jig to level the ice

5. Make sure the sides of the pillar are completely flat and tight against the inside surfaces of the jig. Firmly holding the warmed aluminum to the bottom edges of the jig, slowly push the pillar back and forth across the warmed aluminum until there is no longer any gap between the two.
6. Repeat this same process on the other end of the pillar.

SETTING UP THE SCULPTOR'S WORK AREA

When sculpting a large multi-block display, a staging area is often set up near the main display for storing additional dry clothing, tools, equipment, and raw ice blocks. These items can get in the way during sculpting and potentially cause accidents. The staging area can also be used for producing smaller components that will be joined to the larger display. Generally, this staging area is also near sources of electricity and water.

Whether the sculptor needs a separate staging area for a multi-piece display, or just one location for sculpting, there are basic elements required to organize a proper work area:

- The location needs to be ample for the tasks at hand and established as a **safety zone** (see Chapter 8) work area, with established boundaries. Boundaries should be identified by something bold and obvious like yellow police barrier-type tape. This type of safety tape is readily available.
- The sculptor needs to work within the designated safety zone boundaries, and the viewing public needs to remain outside the barrier tape.
- The area needs to be organized and free of clutter.
- A padded table for tools and finish sculpting must be available.
- A second table with padding, rubber mat, or even a wooden skid (although the last is the least desirable to use in our opinion) on which to sculpt the ice.
- A snow shovel, long-handled squeegee, or broom for removing slush and water.
- A grounded electrical source, ideally hanging from overhead.

We will discuss the safety zone and work-area setup in more detail in Chapter 8, "The Studio."

PREPARATION FOR AN EMERGENCY

Part of the process of working safely is to plan for emergencies. A professional sculptor realizes that safety and health are vital to their ability to sculpt and work. Planning ahead reduces risk and increases the likelihood of continued safety.

Sculpting Buddy

First and foremost, having someone responsible and aware of the sculptor's activities while he is sculpting is an excellent way to protect the sculptor and prepare for an emergency. A **sculpting buddy** can provide a second pair of eyes to note areas where safety is being compromised, and can intervene before accidents occur. He can be helpful in keeping people at a safe distance from the sculptor's tools and sculpture. Additionally, a sculptor is likely to develop a more organized approach when sculpting with someone who is familiar with the design and procedure. Organization leads to reduced risk of accidents. The sculpting buddy can also share the weight when lifting ice, making for a safer and lighter load. And, in the worst case scenario, having an assistant present can save your life if first aid or transport to a hospital becomes necessary.

Emergency Supplies and Equipment

Planning ahead also involves identifying necessary information in case of an emergency, and having the needed equipment and supplies at hand. The following items represent the basics in emergency contingency planning.

Medical Kit

Although most sculptors are not trained as emergency medical technicians, they should know something about basic first aid for abrasions, cuts, and fractures. The sculptor should know how to clean and dress a small wound, how to apply compression to larger wounds, and how to splint a minor fracture to fingers. When in doubt, always have trained medical personnel administer to wounds or fractures.

Communication

In this day of cell phones, it is best to have a dependable telephone handy while sculpting. This is vital if a serious accident should occur. Necessary telephone numbers should be readily available.

When sculpting in a foreign country where the primary language is different from the sculptors', forethought and planning need to be given to communicating effectively. Plan to have an interpreter available to explain the rules, help with organizing the safety zone, and assist in emergencies.

Transportation

Although it is unlikely that a sculptor would have to be moved to a hospital as a result of an accident from sculpting, it is a possibility. If this were the case, then time would be of critical importance.

The cautious sculptor should have reliable transportation readily available and nearby, as well as a driver (such as the sculpting buddy) identified who knows the route to the hospital or medical facility that has been previously identified.

Emergency Information

Emergency information is one of those things in life one hopes never to need, but is necessary to have at a moment's notice. Often the sculptor is working away from his own facility. If a serious accident were to occur, it might be difficult for others to assist without some basic information. The cautious sculptor should carry emergency information, particularly when performing off-site work. This information should include:

- Full legal name
- Home address and telephone number
- Name and telephone number of several people to contact in case of emergency
- Blood type
- Related medical information, including prescriptions and allergies to any medications
- Name and telephone number of primary physician
- Preferred treatment center or hospital, if any
- Personal health insurance card or information

Those involved in teaching others to sculpt ice should make a practice of requiring this information on the first night of class and keeping it organized and available in case it is needed in the future.

Waiver of Liability

Participant Waiver of Liability and Release Forms should be considered when teaching others to sculpt or work with sharp tools. The instructor or mentor needs to make it perfectly clear to the student or apprentice that accidents can occur. The learner must accept full responsibility for his or her actions, and hold the instructor and the organization blameless should there be an accident. *For this reason, we do not instruct any student who is not of majority age, or one who will not agree to take responsibility for his or her own actions.*

The institution that is sponsoring the instruction should select the waiver form that is best suited for their circumstances. Each state's legal system is different, and for that reason it is imperative to contact the Risk Management Office or Office of General Counsel of the sponsoring institution. It would be unwise to merely copy another state's waiver forms without also ensuring the legally acceptable use of language contained in the form relative to the sponsor's own state laws.

The following components should be included, since they have a better chance of being upheld in a Court of Law:

- The form should boldly and clearly state that it is a Waiver and Release of Liability
- The wording on the release should immediately follow the heading, such as shown in Figure 4-5.
- Since the waiver and release is a contract, there must be consideration such as "in consideration for receiving permission to participate in ice sculpting classes …"
- The signatures should immediately follow the wording on the release

All of the above should be on one side of a page.

That said, there is no better legal or ethical preparation than providing sufficient and effective training for students and apprentices. Proper guidance and adherence to safety practices will, in the long run, serve everyone's best interests. Should an unfortunate incident arise, the legal system, among others, will primarily evaluate the *actions* of the instructor and the student. Measures of safety that were practiced by the instructor and class mean far more than any warning poster or signed waiver and release of liability form.

DISPLAYING SCULPTURES SAFELY

Safe and proper display of ice is the responsibility of the professional ice artisan. Ice can be either a stunning addition to a buffet arrangement or a disaster about to happen. It all depends on the knowledge and expertise of the staff displaying the piece. Chapter 10, "Displaying and Lighting for Effect," will go into detail about the proper procedures to follow when displaying ice.

PARTICIPANT WAIVER AND HOLD HARMLESS
FORM THE TEXAS A&M UNIVERSITY SYSTEM

1. In consideration for receiving permission to participate in
_____ (herein referred to as ACTIVITY), which is
sponsored by _____ (herein referred to as
SPONSOR), a component member of The Texas A&M University System, I hereby
**RELEASE, WAIVE, DISCHARGE, AND COVENANT NOT TO SUE, AND AGREE
TO HOLD HARMLESS** for any and all purposes SPONSOR, The Texas A&M University
System, the Board of Regents for The Texas A&M University System, and their officers, ser-
vants, agents, volunteers, or employees (herein referred to as RELEASEES) **FROM ANY
AND ALL LIABILITIES, CLAIMS, DEMANDS, OR INJURY, INCLUDING DEATH**
, that may be sustained by me while participating in such activity, or while on the premises
owned or leased by RELEASEES. I acknowledge there may be physically strenuous activities.
I know of no medical reason why I should not participate.

2. I am fully aware that there are inherent risks involved with ACTIVITY, including but not limited to_____,
and I choose to voluntarily participate in said activity with full knowledge that said activity
may be hazardous to me and my property. **I VOLUNTARILY ASSUME FULL RESPONSI-
BILITY FOR ANY RISKS OF LOSS, PROPERTY DAMAGE OR PERSONAL INJURY,
INCLUDING DEATH** , that may be sustained by me as a result of participating in said activity. I further agree to indemnify and hold harmless the RELEASEES for any loss, liability, damage or costs, including court costs and attorney's fees that may occur as a result of my participation in said activity.

3. I understand that RELEASEES do not maintain any insurance policy cover-
ing any circumstance arising from my participation in this activity or any event related to that
participation. As such, I am aware that I should review my personal insurance coverage.

4. It is my express intent that this Covenant Not to Sue and Agreement to Hold
Harmless shall bind the members of my family and spouse, if I am alive, and my heirs, assigns
and personal representatives, if I am deceased, and shall be governed by the laws of the State
of Texas.

5. In signing this Covenant Not to Sue and Agreement to Hold Harmless, I
acknowledge and represent that I have read the foregoing Covenant Not to Sue and
Agreement to Hold Harmless, understand it and sign it voluntarily as my own free act and
deed; no oral representations, statements, or inducements apart from the foregoing agreement that has been reduced to writing have been made. I execute this document for full,
adequate and complete consideration fully intending to be bound by the same, now and in
the future.

SIGNED this _____ day of _____, _____.

Participant: _____

Printed Name: _____

Parent or Legal Guardian: _____

(If Participant is under 18 years old)

WITNESS: _____

Printed Name: _____

INSTRUCTIONS TO SPONSORS

1. *Complete all blanks in form prior to execution.*

2. *Provide copy of executed form to Participant.*

3. *If a special event or other policy of insurance is in effect for the Activity, delete paragaraph 3 and initial.*

4. *Attach additional pages as necessary to describe Activity or Inherent Risks, and have Participant initial all such pages at the time of execution of this document.*

5. *Keep this release on file in appropriate office of Sponsor.*

<u>**OGC Approved 08/03/01**</u>

THE TEXAS A&M UNIVERSITY SYSTEM

Figure 4-5. Example of a Waiver of Liability (Note: This example does not constitute legal counsel.)

DISPOSING OF SCULPTURES SAFELY

Even after ice has been safely sculpted, transported, and set in place, the responsibility for staff and guest safety continues. For a truly grand experience, from beginning to end, drainage must be dealt with and the sculpture must be disposed of properly, which includes safely. The following steps and procedures are common to the process:

- Identify and inspect the path on which the disposed items are to travel. Remove any obstacles that may hinder the process.

- Gain assistance from as many people as are needed to perform the work safely.

- Remove the drain bucket from under the sculpture before moving the sculpture. If the pail is too full, transfer some of the water to a second vessel for disposal. Care should be taken to prevent spills, which could damage the floor covering or cause the floor to become slippery.

- If necessary (and possible), reduce the size of the sculpture by breaking it into smaller, lighter parts with an ice pick.

- Wear dry cotton gloves for improved grip on the ice.

- Wrap the sculpture in a moving blanket to prevent water from dripping onto the floor when leaving.

- After gaining permission from the facility, dispose of the sculpture in an area of low foot traffic. Often a spot near the loading dock or large drain is suitable for this purpose.

ARTIST PROFILE

Meet the Artist—Lyde Buchtenkirch-Biscardi

Lyde Buchtenkirch-Biscardi, CMC is the only female Certified Master Chef in the United States. Lyde was a member of the 1980 United States Culinary Team that represented America at the Internationale Kochkunst-Ausstellung in Germany, where she earned a gold and a silver medal. Lyde also earned gold medals for her centerpiece work in marzipan and pastillage, when she represented the U.S.A. as a member of the American Team at Japan's World Culinary Contest, and at the Austrian International Cooking Competition, both held in 1983. A very talented culinarian, Chef Buchtenkirch-Biscardi is also an amazing ice sculptor, wood worker, and iron sculptor. After 25 years of teaching, Chef Buchtenkirch-Biscardi recently retired from the Culinary Institute of America, although she remains a popular ice-sculpting instructor through the Institute's Continuing Education department.

Ask the Artist

Q   What do you think is important when you teach ice sculpting?

A   *There are many important areas that I cover, but two come quickly to mind. First, I always start by stressing the necessity for safety. Nothing can be of more importance to me. Secondly, I like to have my students touch the ice within hours of the first day I teach them. They get very excited at the chance to work with the ice.*

Q   How do you approach teaching safety to your students?

A   *It's very simple; safety is about personal responsibility. I stress to my students that each person must be committed to the safety of those around him or her, in addition to themselves. It's like operating an automobile; the driver must practice defensive driving by being aware of their surroundings. Ice sculptors must also be vigilant to what is happening around them.*

II

Working With Ice

Mastering Shapes and Forms

OBJECTIVES

After reading this chapter, you will be able to:

- Discuss the concepts of shape and form and their relationship
- Discuss the concept of the internal sculpture
- Discuss the concept of how sculptors view their work, including strength of lines and focal points
- Describe how sculptors can create the illusion of space
- Describe how sculptors can shade their work
- Explain how sculptors can create the illusion of movement
- Define additive versus subtractive sculpture
- Explain how the four principle forms are the foundation of sculpting

Key Terms and Concepts

shape (noun)	static	additive sculpture
shape (verb)	kinetic	illusion of space
negative space	horizon level	illusion of movement
strong lines	mass	picture plane
primary shapes	volume	
form (verb)	subtractive sculpture	
form (noun)	armature	
focal point		

THE MANY USES OF *SHAPE*

Shape is both a noun and a verb when discussing the figure and fashion of ice. It is important to understand both uses in sculpting. It is also important to note the relationship between shape and form, and how the one becomes the foundation for the other.

Shape as a Noun

The common definition for the noun *shape* is the characteristic surface or contour of a particular item or group of items. It is the standard, or, universally recognized, two-dimensional spatial form that appears in the outer crust or skin of an object. Finished sculptures and works-in-progress are described by their primary shape. Terms such as circular, oval, square, rectangular, and triangular are common descriptors.

Shape as a Verb

Shape as a verb means to give an item a specific configuration. We modify ice blocks by shaping them. Using our tools and guided by our artistic vision, we set about sculpting the finished piece by shaping sections of the ice, portions at a time. We remove ice that is unwanted and that occupies an area of the original ice block deemed **negative space** to reveal the desired finished piece.

BETWEEN *SHAPE* AND *FORM*

A shape, when made three-dimensional, is called a **form**. Form is also often used to describe the total visual organization of a sculpture. The word *shape* describes a work's outer boundaries. However, *forms* have **mass** and **volume**. Templates have shape, ice sculptures have form; forms are derived from shapes.

Form as a Noun

The noun *form* means a general structure or figure of an animal, person, or object; it is also used to describe a particular ice mold. Adjectives, such as rounded, cubic, columnar, and conical describe an object's form.

Form as a Verb

The act of *forming* is to create a particular sculpture. We make the simple foundation of our sculpture by blocking-in or roughing-in our block of ice, refining it into a finished work. Forming is the removal or addition of ice as we sculpt.

VIEWING THE WORK

Sculptors commonly discuss works as having good shape or bad shape, also **primary shape** and empty shape. Good shapes can be described as symmetrical, even, and well balanced, while bad, shapes appear asymmetrical, disparate, and ill-conceived. Primary shapes have **strong lines**, and they are essential for well-proportioned and well-defined sculptures. They become the foundation on which good shapes may be built. Empty shapes convey unnecessary and frivolous use of ice and detract from the finished sculpture. As the eye focuses on various points on the lines of the object from a fixed position, the shape changes but remains connected. As the observer moves around the perimeter of the object, the object appears to reach out towards the observer.

A successful ice sculpture is one that has outward growth. It must appear as if it radiates its shape from a central core, like an **armature**. Due to their nature and how they are displayed, ice sculptures are rarely viewed from a single, fixed position. The entire form is seen as the observer passes by the sculpture. Artists refer to this display concept as "sculpture in the round," as the form engages the viewer from every direction. In all of nature's creation, there are examples of good shapes and forms. A twisted tree trunk, curved bunches of bananas, perched eagles, and bent sheaves of wheat all have strong lines coupled with good shape.

Seeing the Internal Sculpture

We also consider works from their *internal orientation* as well as their external appearance. That is to say, when a person observes an ice sculpture, they are imagining the unseen but implied inner sculpture plus the tangible outer structure. As an example, a properly sculpted bouquet of balloons held by a clown suggest lightness and air, even though the balloons possess the same mass as the rest of the sculpture. The effective use of shape and form provides the illusion.

The Strength of Lines

A sculpture that consists of strong lines and good form can stand against erosive forces. We have all witnessed, either in person or through photographs, timeless works of art that have weathered or chipped but remain attractive to the beholder. Even though the giant Sphinx of Giza has lost most of its nose and its body has been scoured by sand and wind, it remains an example of exquisite stonework. This work, and many more like it, continues to be appreciated for the artistic merit of what survives the damage.

Figure 5-1. The Great Sphinx of Giza

Figure 5-2. *Winged Nike*, an example of high relief

Focal Points

Generally speaking, a **focal point** is a design element that differs from the others in the sculpture. When a pattern is disrupted by a differing shape or form, the observer's eyes are immediately attracted to the contrasting design. Sculptors use this technique when they wish to emphasize a certain element in their sculpture. The following are some common methods for creating focal points:

- Using a geometric form (such as a ball or cube) when most components of the sculpture are irregular and incongruous
- Superimposing elements sculpted in high relief on a flat background
- Breaking a horizontal pattern with occasional vertical forms
- Using contrasts in size
- Isolating an element
- Using strong primary lines to lead the observer's eyes to the object

The *absence of a focal point* can also be the intent of a designer. Consider the appearance of a woven piece of upholstery, where a pattern or focal point might be too distracting. We have all seen posters or wallpaper with row upon row of the same pattern, repeated continuously. The intent here is to *not* attract our eyes to a particular location. In ice sculpture, we accomplish this by creating long, flowing sections of the sculpture with a consistent texture, either smooth or rough. However, generally speaking, an ice sculpture needs to have focal points. Otherwise, it will appear to be some monolithic mass of frozen water serving little purpose.

The Illusion of Space

Several art forms are two-dimensional and rely on the artist's skill in creating an **illusion of space**. Because canvas and paper are flat, and paintings and drawings on them are also flat and remain on the **picture plane** (the frontal plane of the canvas or paper), the artist must use visual illusions to create depth or distance. Some artists view the picture plane as a window that they look through to see their work of art.

The ice sculptor must also "look through" the surface of the ice, the picture plane, to see the sculpture within the block. The ice artisan can create the illusion of space, as well as *real space*, in his own three-dimensional ice art. Sculptors use *size*, *scale*, *transparency*, *overlapping*, and *vertical location* to create illusions of space in their sculptures.

Size

For centuries, artists have noted how *size* differences within a sculpture or painting easily give the illusion of space and distance. It requires relatively little skill to create this comparison of figures, yet the results are effective. Abstract forms, as well as geometric shapes, can be effectively displayed in various sizes to create a spatial illusion.

Scale

Often in early works, some figures were portrayed larger than another figure in the same painting or sculpture to communicate their importance. This practice was common in Egyptian sculpture, when Pharaohs were depicted much larger than other, lesser mortals standing nearby. In this case, *scale* was not used to create an illusion, it was used to communicate a message. Superiority, distance, or space between the objects is represented by the use of scale.

Transparency

When two forms overlap and both can be fully seen, they are considered to be *transparent*. A popular sculpture for Valentine's Day is a silk rose encased in a sculpted heart with the snow-filled message of "Happy Valentine's Day" engraved on the front surface of the sculpture. The rose is fully visible deep within the sculpture.

Overlapping

Overlapping, commonly used to suggest depth, occurs when portions of succeeding figures within the sculpture are blocked from view. It also works well when the succeeding figures are gradually reduced in size. A good example of this illusion is when an oversized hand of playing cards is fanned out in a sculpture. Each card partially blocks the one following. It's even more convincing when portions of each card become progressively smaller.

Vertical Location

The illusion of *vertical location* is based on ocular reality. Standing upright and viewing a sculpture or scene before us, the closest place is the ground at our feet. As we slowly raise our head and focus our eyes upward, we perceive

Figure 5-3. A transparent ice sculpture

objects as farther away, until we are staring straight ahead at eye level. This view with our eyes is called the **horizon level**. Those elements viewed near the top of a sculpture that is set on a table for display will appear to be the most distant, and those at the base will appear to be the closest.

Negative Space

Negative space is the area within a sculpture that was once occupied by ice, but is now open space because the unwanted ice has been removed. The artistic use of negative space lends excitement to the composition by allowing space to "run through" the sculpture, rather than only around it. A sculpture that weaves negative space into its design is much more interesting and is considered more difficult to sculpt by competition judges.

Shading and Reverse Shading

Shading is the process of roughing up the ice to provide contrasting texture. *Reverse shading* is leaving an area smooth and roughing up the areas around it. The rubberizer bit works very well for this task. This technique is often used when the artist is depicting fur on an animal.

■ = negative space

Figure 5-4. Illustration of negative space

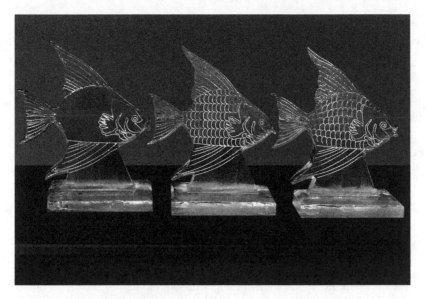

Figure 5-5. Illustration of repetition and rhythm in the fishes' scales

Repetition and Rhythm

Rhythm is based on the measured repetition of a design feature in a piece of art. Sculptors often repeat similar elements to create a pattern in their work. They may vary the frequency and size to affect the rhythm of the piece. In Figure 5-5, note the visual difference between the fish sculpture with even rows of the same-sized scales compared with the fish sculpture with rows of variously sized and spaced scales. The variance in the rhythm within the same sculpture is visually more stimulating.

The Illusion of Movement

Most sculptures are **static** in nature and design. They are displayed in a set position and the observer moves around them. A few sculptures, like mobiles, are designed to move on their own. These sculptures are said to be **kinetic**. However, very few ice sculptures have been designed to really move on their own. Those that have been designed to move are most often displayed on revolving ice stands that feature gel- (or colored-plastic sheets) covered lights.

Truly kinetic ice sculptures are much more difficult to create. The working double Ferris wheel (see Figure 5-6), which incorporated a motor into the sculpture to move the cars, and the full-size, fully-functional pool table, with cues and billiard balls also made from ice, that are featured in this book, are two such examples.

Sculptors often seek to create the **illusion of movement** in their sculptures. That is to say that the sculptures are actually static, but the sculptor wishes to imply movement. This is best accomplished by sculpting something familiar to the observer. For example, we all know what a bird looks like perched on a branch. If the sculptor creates a work similar to that memory, we

Figure 5-6. A motorized Ferris wheel

understand it as static. However, if he creates an ice sculpture of an eagle with its wing feathers outstretched and swept back, and its talons reaching forward grasping a curved salmon, then our memory is of a bird flying and in our mind's eye we *see* motion. And if its beak is open, as if screeching in triumph, we might even hear the sound.

The angles of the primary lines in the sculptor's design can also imply motion instead of stasis. Horizontal and vertical lines are static, while diagonal lines imply action.

ADDITIVE VERSUS SUBTRACTIVE SCULPTURE

All sculptures are of two basic forms: *additive* or *subtractive*. In **additive sculpture**, the artist usually starts with a central core or armature on which to build the sculpture. A sculptor who models in clay has the ability to grow a sculpture by adding layers of clay upon previous layers. Ice artisans who fuse their displays beyond the block's original dimensions are also practicing additive sculpture.

Conversely, stone carvers remove unwanted medium to reveal a sculpture that appears to have come from within. This removal of medium is known as **subtractive sculpture**. An ice sculptor can practice both forms of sculpting on the same block of ice by removing unwanted ice to create form and negative space, and fusing ice back on to the main body of ice to extend the sculpture's size.

SHAPING

To create a truly exquisite ice sculpture, one that can be appreciated even after it has partially melted away, requires the use of strong primary lines and well-proportioned shapes and forms.

Addressing the Sculpture

When approaching a block, the sculptor needs to understand that the finished sculpture will have a three-dimensional appearance. It will consist of a front, sides, and back. Each of these "faces" must have depth and detail. Unlike an artist working with clay, who builds outward from the center, the ice artist begins at the outermost surface, removing layers to reveal the sculpture's finished dimension. The accomplished sculptor can mentally view these depths of dimension while working with a two-dimensional template (see Chapter 6, "Sculpting with Templates"). The template provides the outer framework the sculptor is to work within, but the artist must bring proper depth to the creation so that it has form.

Build Shape on Shape, Form on Form

When the artist studies the model to be replicated in ice, he should note the primary geometric shapes that comprise the model. The sculptor starts by identifying the squares, circles, rectangles, and triangles, that make up the shapes of the figure. The artist then converts each shape to a form by adding depth and dimension.

When learning to sculpt or draw freehand, many artists reduce the sculpture to sections of basic forms. Each section is considered its own sub-sculpture. Even as a sub-sculpture, these sections comprise the four principal forms:

Figure 5-7. The four principal forms

cube, ball, column, and *cone*. Almost all the designs you conceive of can be created from these four forms.

When fashioning a sculpture, the artist actually builds forms, albeit smaller ones, on larger forms. As an example, consider the basic dimensions of a dog. In the simplest design terms, the main body could be sculpted as a horizontal column, or even oval shape. The legs are basically cones. The head could be a ball on a cube-formed neck. Detailing transforms the collection of basic forms into a finished sculpture.

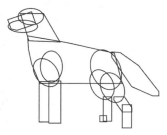

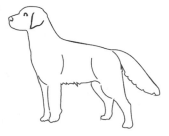

THE FOUR PRINCIPAL FORMS

The ice artisan needs to practice each of the four principal forms; mastery of the basics is paramount to success down the road. As mentioned, the four principal forms to be mastered are *the cube, the ball, the column,* and *the cone*.

Rounded and curved shapes are a bit more difficult to carve than simple straight or flat cuts. Unfortunately for the novice sculptor, it is hard to find many subjects in nature that consist of anything other than a collage of rounded or curved shapes. To sculpt these more difficult shapes with the ease of the straight flat cuts, the student should reduce the curves to a series of flat cuts, called planes.

Figure 5-8. Using forms to create a design

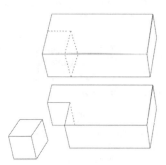

Figure 5-9. Sculpting a cube

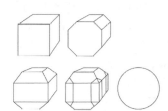

Figure 5-10. Sculpting a ball

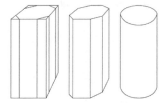

Figure 5-11. Sculpting a column

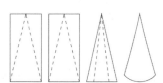

Figure 5-12. Sculpting a cone

ARTIST PROFILE

Meet the Artist—Dan Hugelier

Chef Dan Hugelier, CMC, hails from Michigan, where he now serves as a full-time Chef-Instructor at Schoolcraft College and is owner of Culinary Concepts International, a consulting firm to the foodservice industry. He is a certified judge for NICA and the ACF. With over 30 gold medals, Dan is a highly skilled competitor in hot food, cold food, and ice sculpting competitions. Chef Hugelier was a member of the 1980 U.S. Regional and 1984 and 1988 U.S. National ACF Teams that represented the United States at the "Culinary Olympics" in Frankfurt, Germany. Chef Hugelier's huge sunburst ice sculpture, which anchored the U.S. Team's Cold Food Display table in 1988, is legendary among culinary competitors for its functional use and spectacular, eye-catching appearance.

Ask the Artist

Q Ice sculptures were rarely seen at the Internationale Kochkunst-Ausstellung as part of a team's display prior to 1988. What was the purpose of the huge sunburst of ice on the American team's table?

A *We were going for a whole new look at displaying our cold food. Prior to that competition, teams hardly used risers or linens to dress their show platters. We sought to have an eye-catching, elegant display that would equal the quality of the food. Additionally, all teams had problems with their aspic work melting on their showpieces as they set them under the warm lights of the show hall. The ice fan I created actually radiated cool air down over our pieces, and the aspic remained intact. The ice sculpture was an important part of our team's success that year.*

Q When you were Executive Chef at the Amway Grand Plaza Hotel, you and your staff used to create exquisite ice displays outside the entrance to the hotel. What was their purpose?

A *For the holiday season in December, every year we would make a life-sized Santa Claus in a sled being pulled by his reindeer. We found that it was an attraction for the community and for the hotel's guests. The hotel always gained news coverage from the displays, which was important for our image in the community—plus it was good business. Besides, it was an opportunity for my staff and me to sculpt a lot of ice. We all enjoyed it!*

Sculpting with Templates

OBJECTIVES

After reading this chapter, you will be able to:

- Describe how early sculptors and painters used templates
- Discuss the application of templates in ice sculpting
- Discuss the uses for wood, plastic, and paper templates
- Describe how to make a paper template using several methods
- Explain how to make a multi-view template
- Explain the concept of master templates and production templates
- Explain the use of a sub template

Key Terms and Concepts

design template	cartoon	plotter
opaque projector	master template	production template
overhead transparency	sub template	scoring lines
	plunge router	

Design templates are used for assisting the sculptor in defining the proportion and shape of a sculpture within a limited space. Templates are regularly used with all media that are sculpted, including those media that are carved rather than modeled, like stone, wood, soap, and ice.

A TIME-TESTED METHOD OF DESIGN

After finishing his beloved statue of Moses, the renowned Renaissance sculptor Michelangelo examined his work, then, in a fit of anger, struck at the stone knee of his masterpiece. Crying aloud, he passionately pleaded, "Why dost thou not speak?" It was Michelangelo's compulsive search for divine perfection that fueled his artistic drive to become one of the greatest artists, architects, and sculptors of all time.

The use of patterns or templates in art has been in practiced for centuries. The greatest artists in history, including Michelangelo, Leonardo da Vinci, and Raphael, all used methods for tracing their designs onto their medium. *Design Templates* are a very accurate way to transfer a design onto a block. They are almost always used in ice competitions and whenever accuracy and uniformity are crucial.

In fine art, a **cartoon** is a full-scale preparatory drawing done on heavy paper. The term derives from the Italian word *cartone,* meaning cardboard. In the Renaissance period, the cartoon was placed over damp plaster and then holes were pricked along the outlines using a pinned roller device, similar to a pizza wheel, to transfer the design. A bag containing powdered charcoal was "pounced" across the template pinholes to create a dotted pattern on the plaster. After removing the cardboard, the artists used the charcoal dots as a guide to create their works.

Today, ice artisans create patterns, called templates, to transfer their designs onto the ice before cutting. The sensible idea is to make mistakes on paper, not ice.

DESIGN TEMPLATE STYLES

Templates can be made of wood, plastic, cardboard, or paper, depending on what they will be used for and whether they will be reused. The following are the most widely used styles of templates. However, most sculptors use paper templates, although wooden or reusable templates are used for routinely made designs.

Wooden Templates

Wooden templates can be used many times, which is their greatest attribute. They can be put directly on the ice, and traced with an ice pick to delineate the silhouette. A limited number of holes and larger slits can be cut through the template to allow scoring of the strong lines that will help keep the sculpture components proportional. Wooden templates must be simple and without a lot of complicated detail. While their use is commonplace, paper templates are used more frequently.

Using Wooden Templates as a Jig

The sculptor may wish not only to trace a design around the wooden template, but also to actually cut out the pattern. To do so, the wooden template must have several metal screws drilled through it at regular intervals, with their pointed ends extending out the other side.

With the ice laid down horizontally, the template is positioned proportionately onto the block with the pointed tips of the screws resting on the ice. After a few minutes, the ice will temper, and the screw tips will sink into the ice thus securing the template enough to prevent its slipping.

Using a **plunge router**, the artist should adjust the end mill bit so that when it is resting on the template, the upper flat portion of the bit extends beneath to the exact thickness of the template. This will prevent the cutting blade of the bit from hitting the wood and damaging the template's edge. If blade depth is adjusted properly, the sculptor should be able to rest the router on the template so that the non-fluted edge of the bit can use the template as a guide to follow in cutting the template's shape.

Coating the wooden template with paint, varnish, or some other form of sealant will protect the wood from water damage and reduce the risk of warping, and therefore will extend the potential life of the template.

Plastic and Cardboard Templates

When using a hard template, such as plastic or cardboard, the design is cut directly out of the material using heavy shears. Although these templates are more expensive to produce and are somewhat difficult to create, they do have a reasonable life span. However, these templates are often difficult to trace, as they have a tendency to slide around on the ice.

Reusable Templates

Mac Winker, co-author of *Ice Sculpture: The Art of Ice Carving in 12 Systematic Steps*, uses a method of transferring template designs to blocks without destroying the template. He uses a chipper to poke holes through the template, following the design lines. He then removes the plastic-coated paper template and scores the ice along the line formed by the holes. This process allows him to reuse these flexible and durable templates.

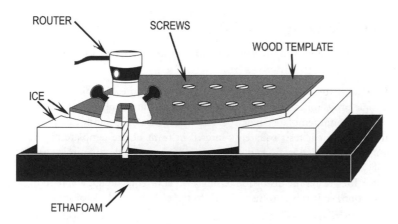

Figure 6-1. Wooden template used as a jig, using a router bit

Paper Templates

By creating a template with paper, a sculptor can perfect the design before applying it to the ice. Paper templates can then be frozen onto the ice, and the sculptor can use either a die grinder or a chain saw to cut through the lines on the paper, and thus transfer the lines directly onto the surface of the ice.

Paper templates have several advantages over other types. They are cost efficient, lightweight, and much easier to transport than other kinds of templates. Due to the fact that they are frozen to the ice, they can be applied faster and be traced with the actual cutting tools, which reduces on-site prep time. Another great advantage is their ability to be modified, refined, and reproduced quickly and inexpensively. The use of paper templates allows for more detail to be traced onto the ice, which makes it easier to see the **scoring lines**. These scoring lines can be color coded, and written notes can be applied to the paper template regarding cutting depths and tool usage. Their size and flexible material also allows them to be stored folded or in a small artist's valise.

The paper template's one slight drawback is that it is destroyed by tracing and so has to be picked up, piece by wet piece, and discarded. While paper templates must be used when the raw block is still very cold, their advantages far outweigh their disadvantages, making them the template of choice for many modern ice sculptors.

TEMPLATE DESIGN AND CONSTRUCTION

When making a template, the sculptor needs to know the dimensions of the ice block. Additionally, the sculptor must have a sketch or picture of the design.

Drawing the template can be done freehand or using a grid pattern like graph paper; however, the most efficient way is to use a projector to capture a design on template paper. The projector displays the design onto paper that has been taped to a wall. The paper is the same size as the block of ice being sculpted. The sculptor then traces the design onto the paper, creating the template.

Tools for Making Templates

Sculptors use the following instruments to prepare templates, as shown in Figure 6-2:

1   **Opaque Projector**—More versatile than an overhead projector, the opaque projector can project any images, from photograph, magazine, or drawing, onto template paper. It is imperative that the projector be positioned so that it rests squarely centered in front of the template paper onto which it will project. If the projector is at an angle, the projection will be distorted. The further the distance from the projector to the paper, the greater the distortion. Using a larger original design will reduce distortion, so it is best to use designs to the capacity of the projector.

2   **Template Paper**—This is the paper on which projected images are traced, and which is later placed on the ice. Template paper comes in basically two forms: newsprint, and on large, white rolls. Newspapers are

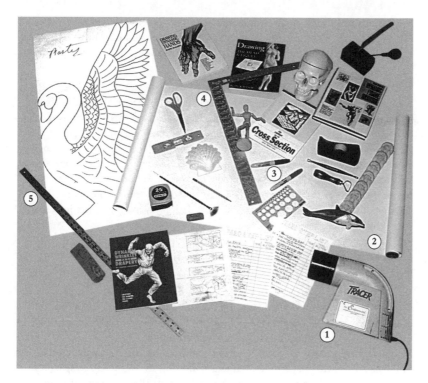

Figure 6-2. Tools for making paper templates

printed on newsprint, and partial rolls are often left over which are too small for the newspaper printer to use for a "run." The local newspaper often makes these end rolls available at a reasonable price. White rolled paper is used by butchers as table coverings and for crafts. It is readily available from craft stores and butcher supply stores. We prefer the white paper, as it is more convenient and substantial and less likely to tear during use. The paper comes in 24" rolls, and it is recommended to cut the roll to a width of 20". The sculptor will then only have to roll the paper out and cut it to a length of 40" to have the standard frontal dimensions of a raw ice block on which to trace projected images for use as templates.

3 **Waterproof Marker**—These pens are used to mark the design of a sculpture onto the template paper. Brands such as Majic Ink® are oil based and are preferred because they do not bleed into the ice.

4 **Square**—This is an L-shaped carpenter's tool used for making right angles. The larger all-metal squares are the most useful.

5 **Metal Yardstick**—This provides a means to draw a straight edge or to measure distances and dimensions.

Making Paper Templates

The sculptor may choose from a variety of methods for enlarging, sizing, and transferring his designs onto paper. Depending on what equipment may be readily available, the sculptor has several options. The following list represents the most common and acceptable methods of transferring patterns onto paper for template construction. We have used all of these methods, but prefer to use the **Opaque Projector Method** and **CAD Method**.

Opaque Projector Method

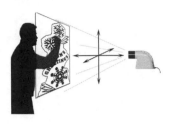

Figure 6-3. Using an opaque projector

This method of making templates is a very simple, one-step method of projecting the desired image onto the paper. The sculptor either draws his own design on a small 5" square piece of paper, or uses an existing design, logo, clip art, or photograph. It is then projected onto the 20" × 40" paper mounted to a wall. The projector must be square to the wall or the image will be distorted. Using a waterproof marker, the artist then carefully traces the pattern, which must fit within the paper's (and ice block's) dimensions. The obvious advantage is the flexible use of any design, as long as it fits into the viewfinder of the projector.

Overhead Transparency Method

This widely used method involves two steps for projecting the image onto the template paper. The artist must first make an **overhead transparency** of the selected design. This is done by placing transparency film in the paper tray of a copy machine, then making a photocopy of the picture, logo, sketch, or other design source onto the transparency film.

The sculptor then projects the image, captured on the transparency film, onto the 20" × 40" paper mounted to a wall using an overhead transparency projector. As with the first method, the artist traces the pattern with waterproof markers.

The advantage of this method over the opaque projector method is the availability of overhead transparency projectors and copy machines. Nearly all hotels, banquet halls, and colleges have them; opaque projectors are not as readily available.

Tracing Method

This "low-tech" method requires only a large window or a light box. However, the artist must first create a full-size original or *master template,* with darkened lines, from which to trace. The master template is taped to one side of a large clear window, with its design showing through the window. A piece of transparent template paper is mounted to the other side of the window, squarely facing the original. Looking through the new piece of paper to the design behind it, the artist traces the original design onto the new paper with a waterproof marker.

This method is practical for making *production templates* from master templates once the full-scale size of a template has been made. However, someone has to create the full-size master template first.

Copy and Poster Machine Method

Although not the most common method for making a template, this is the most accurate method for enlarging and reproducing a design. The artist merely takes the logo, sketch, photograph, magazine page, or clip art to a copy center where they make enlarged copies and posters. For a fee, they will make a precise enlargement on their paper stock. Most copy stores and many colleges and schools have these machines, but the cost for this service makes this method impractical when making many templates. And the final product may not be on paper that is exactly 20" × 40".

CAD Method

The computer-aided design (CAD) method requires someone skilled in CAD software to design the template on a computer. It is then either printed in full scale on a **plotter** or printed in reduced scale on a traditional printer for use with a projector method.

This method provides very accurate sizes and shapes, and is a preferred way of making multi-view templates that correspond well with each other. These templates are very useful in competition for their accuracy, and for allowing the artist to create often very original designs. They are also useful when planning large, multi-block sculptures. CAD allows for the *master template* of original works to be stored on a computer for later access or modification.

Although not often accessible to sculptors on their own, most colleges have computer and technology departments where CAD is taught. The serious ice artisan can take classes to learn this skill, as we have, or they can befriend someone already trained in CAD (also, as we have).

VIEWING THE SCULPTURE'S OTHER SIDES

Making appropriate templates for each side of the sculpture will enable the sculptor to preview the finished design. This helps the sculptor to develop a mental image, as well as provide cutting guidelines for each side of the ice block.

The side templates will show the sculptor where to cut into the ice. He must score the inside of the ice so that, once the front silhouette view is cut, these cuts made on the left and right sides of the block can act as guidelines for the side-view rough cuts.

Creating Four-Side-View Templates

To accurately represent a subject to proper scale, and to aid the sculptor in fitting the sculpture into the available ice, several corresponding templates are designed to address the multi-dimensional nature of their work.

Step 1: About 4" in from the left side of a piece of tracing graph paper, which is placed in the landscape direction, draw a rectangle exactly 2" wide × 4" tall (Figure 6-4a).

Step 2: Draw one box directly to the left and one directly to the right of the first box; both should be 1" wide × 4" tall. The top and bottom of the new boxes should line up with the top and bottom of the first box (Figure 6-4b).

Step 3: Draw another box 2" wide and 4" tall directly to the right of the existing three boxes (Figure 6-4c).

Step 4: Label each box *left, front, right,* and *back*. These boxes now represent the "material surface" and, in this case, represent an ice block measuring 20" × 40" × 10" (Figure 6-4d).

Step 5: Using a photocopier, resize the original design to fit within the box labeled *front*. Now trace the original design into the box (Figure 6-4e).

Step 6: Determine which of the features from the original drawing will be visible from the right and left sides. With a pencil and a guide ruler, draw a light

Figure 6-4a.
Step 1

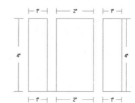

Figure 6-4b. Step 2

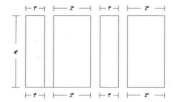

Figure 6-4c. Step 3

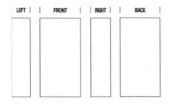

Figure 6-4d. Step 4

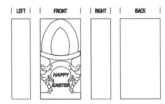

Figure 6-4e. Step 5

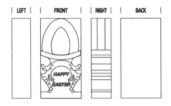

Figure 6-4f. Step 6

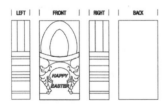

Figure 6-4g. Step 7

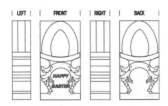

Figure 6-4h. Step 8

line from the top and bottom of the components that will be visible from the right side of the sculpture through the right box (Figure 6-4f).

Step 7: Repeat the same procedure with the left box, only drawing lines from components visible from the left view. **Note:** Use these lines to show the exact positioning of these features on the two new side views now being created. A three-dimensional model or actual pictures of these new side views may be necessary to fill in the blanks (Figure 6-4g).

Step 8: Fold the tracing paper so that the *front* and *back* view drawings line up. The sculptor must keep in mind that he is creating the back view drawing. This means that even though the silhouette will be the same, he may need to add or eliminate certain lines depending on the configuration of the subject matter (e.g., positioning of limbs and other detail work) (Figure 6-4h).

MASTER TEMPLATES

When sculpting, ice artisans regularly use paper templates to transfer designs onto ice blocks. The process involves wetting the ice block and laying the paper template against it. With a chain saw or router tool, the artist traces the template's pattern; the paper template is destroyed in the process.

Often the sculptor is trying to perfect a specific sculpture, or he has a favorite pattern he frequently sculpts. In either case he repeats the same design, or one very similar, on a regular basis, and it is convenient to have a master pattern from which to trace. A **master template** is one which is not destroyed and on which small variations, improvements, and sculpting directions can be noted for future reference. It is not unusual for a sculptor to have between five and ten generations of templates that originated from one master template.

Saving the template for future reference and modification makes it the *first draft master template*. Future alterations to the design will be noted on the *master template*.

Creating a Master Template

The following method is commonly used to create a template:

Step 1: Cut four pieces of paper to the actual size of each side template needed:

    2 each 10" × 40"

    2 each 20" × 40"

Step 2: In a room that can be darkened, tape one of the pieces of template paper to the wall. If you are using the outside wall of a galvanized steel freezer, use magnets to secure the paper. Magnets are preferred, since they reduce potential damage caused when readjusting the paper.

Step 3: Using an opaque projector, project the drawing so that the outside box of the original drawing lines up perfectly with the outside edges of the paper on the wall.

Step 4: Trace all lines. When you have finished, take a moment to make sure all lines are traced before moving the projector or actual template. One way to check is to turn on the lights and compare the template to a photocopy of the design being enlarged. *Do not remove the design from the projector for comparison.* Exact repositioning can be difficult.

Step 5: Remove the template from the wall and place the next full-size piece of paper in its place. Continue this procedure with each side view, making sure to label each one.

Note: It is very important to keep the projector angle and distance as consistent as possible in relation to the template. The projector should be at a perfect right angle to the paper to prevent distortion. Care should be taken to mark the surface of the table where the projector is sitting to ensure consistent distance from the wall.

Production Templates

Master templates are used to trace **production templates**. Tracing the master template can be done using a light table or a window with light behind it. In either case, make sure that both the master template and the paper on which the design is being traced are secured so they will not move during tracing.

Production templates are destroyed during design transfer. They are applied to the raw block, and then cut as the design is traced onto the block. Any remaining paper can be ground off using a circular sander.

Sub Templates

Sometimes the details of a certain area of the design may be lost when removing bulk ice during the initial rough-cuts. In these areas, **sub templates** can be used. Sub templates are smaller templates that contain only the detail needed for a small area of the design, such as a face, wings, or hands. Like production templates, sub templates are usually destroyed during the sculpting process.

APPLYING PAPER TEMPLATES

After the artist has created a paper template, he has to apply it to the ice. Successful transfer of designs from paper templates to ice, as demonstrated in this text, can only be achieved when the temperature of the ice block remains below freezing.

The ideal conditions for attaching a paper template, etching the pattern, and sculpting the piece would be in temperatures below freezing from start to finish. This happens in the great outdoors of the North Country on a cold winter's day, or within the confines of a spacious walk-in freezer. (Thermoshock, as discussed in Chapter 2, only occurs when the temperature outside the block varies from that inside the block.)

However, we realize it is likely that many people will not be sculpting in sub-freezing conditions. For them, a few adaptations can be made. Templates can be applied to the raw block before it leaves the freezer, or immediately upon removing it from the freezer. Either way, the trick is to apply the template quickly to the frozen block.

To set a paper template, the artist sprays cold water onto the ice, then immediately applies the paper and slides it into position. The edges of the paper should be squared evenly to ensure proper alignment.

Figure 6-5. Applying a template using a water bottle

Templates will tend to tear less by using a chain saw than by using a die grinder. Once the outlines are marked onto the block, approximately $\frac{1}{4}$" deep, the template can be removed and the block allowed to temper (when sculpting at above freezing temperatures) to the ideal stage for sculpting.

ARTIST PROFILE

Meet the Artist—Mac Winker

Many ice artisans consider Mac Winker to be the "father of template ice sculpting." In 1989, Mac and his wife Claire published their text, *Ice Sculpture: The Art of Ice Carving in 12 Systematic Steps*, which gained wide acceptance within the ice sculpting community, especially regarding the use of design templates. Mac, one of eleven Master Club Managers in the world, is Owner/Operator of The Racquet Club of Memphis, and manages an ATP men's and WTA women's tennis event in Memphis. Among his many ice-related accolades, Mac was captain of the U.S. Ice Sculpture Team, representing the NICA at the Fairbanks, Alaska International Exposition in 1989. He is a certified ice-carving judge for both the ACF and NICA. Mac Winker has been asked to do many unique pieces, including the LPGA U.S. Open's Championship Trophy, and, most recently, the 2002 Ryder Cup in Belfrey, England, where the ice replica was featured.

Ask the Artist

Q   Where did you get the idea of sculpting ice with templates?

A   *After struggling to do a perfect vase or the neck of the swan every time, I was fortunate to receive a gift of* The Agony and the Ecstasy *by Irving Stone, one of the books about Michelangelo. After discovering that he used line drawings and sketches extensively, including when working on the Sistine Chapel, I developed many drawings of animals, fish, birds, etc. into Winker Design Templates.*

Q   You have been very successful in ice sculpting; do you sculpt full-time?

A   *No, certainly not. For me, ice carving is a hobby that I dearly love. There have been weeks when it seemed full-time, when I was carving between 20 and 40 sculptures in a week, with several for charity. I still practice this exciting art form, but now I usually only sculpt for my business interests, demonstrations, charitable causes, social occasions, and high-end sporting events such as the Ryder Cup.*

Fusing: Joining Ice to Ice

OBJECTIVES

After reading this chapter, you will be able to:

- Define the process of fusing ice to ice
- Discuss fusing with aluminum in detail
- Describe flat fusing
- Describe natural peg fusing
- Describe weight on pressure/handsaw fusing
- Describe nail-board fusing
- Discuss various techniques used in fusing
- Discuss the benefits of horizontal fusing over vertical fusing

Key Terms and Concepts

fusing

raw block

natural peg fusing

flat fusing

weight on
  pressurc/handsaw
  fusing

instant fusing

nail board

nail-board fusing

primary sculpture

Fusing is a method where one or more pieces of ice are welded together. It allows you to expand the finished sculpture beyond the limitations of the original dimensions of a block of ice. The size and shape of an ice block should not dictate the ultimate dimensions of the artwork, nor limit the creativity of the sculptor. The design, quantity of ice available, and—*most importantly*—safety considerations, should define the ice sculpture's final form.

The fusing process may be applied when creating single or multi-block sculptures with dimensions beyond those of a standard block of ice. Appendages and accessories, such as arms, legs, wings, tails, swords, and shields, can be sculpted separately and joined to the **primary sculpture** later.

These additions are normally carved from the scrap ice removed from the negative space that remains after completing the primary sculpture. Sculptors consider possible uses of the scrap ice when designing their templates to best utilize the entire block.

During fusing, the sculptor should try to join pieces where natural curves or existing lines will help mask the joint. The skilled artist will blend the fuse with details applied to represent feathers, muscle tone, fish scales, or similar finish work. The locations for the fuse joints are decided during the designing and mapping of the templates.

When working on large, multi-block designs, it is wise to avoid stacking ice walls for carving substantial sculptures whenever possible. By placing block on block, straight lines or seams will show throughout the finished piece. To eliminate this unwanted appearance, it is usually best to design the sculpture in modular units, and then assemble the units to hide the fuse lines. This modular approach will result in less waste and less unnecessary lifting.

FUSING WITH ALUMINUM

Aluminum has completely changed the way most of today's best sculptors approach joining multiple pieces of ice. Before the use of aluminum was introduced, peg fusing, heavy applications of slush, or time consuming sanding were how all sculptors assembled their ice pieces. Applying aluminum allows the carver to polish both surfaces of the ice, thereby forming a tight seal.

When ice melts it, of course, turns to water. When water flows over ice it erodes the surface. The warmer the water, the more drastic and defined this erosion can be. Since ice tends to begin melting at 32° F, an aluminum sheet warmer than 32° F will melt the ice with which it has contact. If the goal is merely to remove subtle imperfections in an already prepared piece of ice, then the aluminum only needs to be between 40° and 60° F, reducing any excess run-off of water.

The other problem that may occur when using overheated aluminum is that it will raise the temperature of the ice to which it is being applied, further impeding the freezing process. Obviously, the aluminum will cool down quickly once it is placed on the ice, often at uneven rates, depending on the temperature at which the sculptor is working. The colder the working conditions, the faster it will cool down. The solution is to either keep reheating the aluminum or to alternate between two or more pieces of aluminum. The sculptor should note that overheating the aluminum results in uneven erosion and warming of the ice.

Although aluminum has made fusing much easier, there are several considerations that sculptors should address to ensure a perfect fuse:

- Using the proper piece of aluminum is very important. A piece $\frac{1}{2}$" thick, or more, will be less flexible. The rigidity of the straight edge will increase the integrity of the flat surfaces on both sides of the aluminum. The aluminum piece should also be larger than the surfaces being leveled. This allows the sculptor to rub the aluminum against the ice in a circular motion without gouging the surface. This process allows the melting ice to dissipate evenly while preventing water from pooling between the aluminum and ice, which would make the surfaces uneven.
- Aluminum is most affordable and most commonly found in flat sheets. However, aluminum can be customized to attach pieces together in curved lines or "V" shapes.
- Aluminum can be heated in several ways. The most affordable and most commonly used is a standard, no-frills clothes iron. This method is preferred over the use of blowtorches and heat lamps.

Figure 7-1. Using warmed aluminum to flatten and smooth ice prior to fusing

OTHER METHODS OF FUSING

There are several additional methods of fusing ice, including *flat fusing, natural peg fusing, weight on pressure* or *handsaw fusing*, and *nail-board fusing*. These methods all have their benefits, and for the most part, were the procedures followed before *fusing with aluminum* was developed. They are still used, but their applications are more limited.

Flat Fusing

Flat Fuses are used where two pieces are joined at a line, such as a belt or between several slate rocks, to conceal the fuse. When using this method, both surfaces of the ice pieces that will be joined must be perfectly smooth; *it is very important to make sure that both sides are as flat as possible.* Sculptors often use an electric iron, marble cutting board, or thick sheet of aluminum for this purpose. They are rubbed over both surfaces to be joined in a circular motion, as if the sculptor is waxing the ice, to ensure that the joint ends are perfectly flat.

When the pieces are assembled there should be no gaps in the joint. Gaps appear as either pockets of water or air between the pieces of ice. After inspecting for gaps, the sculpture is placed in the freezer and allowed to harden.

Instant Fusing

Between the 1940s and the 1970s, ice sculptors used sheets of wet cheesecloth or a sprinkling of salt between blocks to create a rough exterior. This roughing of the ice would aid in bonding the two surfaces together. However, each process had its faults. Cheesecloth created a visible seam, and salt hastened the deterioration of the ice. Better methods are available today.

Pressing a slightly softened, warmer piece of ice against a very cold piece of ice results in **instant fusing**, as the two join instantly. This method is most commonly used in conjunction with, and during, *flat fusing*. Both surfaces must be perfectly flat and free of all debris, such as slush or ice chunks, prior to fusing.

Note: *Never use salt!* Using salt in the fusing process is a bad method that tends to be taught frequently in ice-carving books and classes. Salt actually causes pitting in the ice while softening it. The use of salt can help in the initial freezing process under the correct conditions, but salt residue will be trapped in the joint, causing the ice around the seam to melt first. The use of salt during fusing only weakens the joint.

Natural Peg Fusing

Figure 7-2. Section of ancient stone column with peg hole

The great Grecian and Roman architects have been lauded over the centuries for their ability to construct massive temples and aqueducts, with columns rising high into the sky, capable of supporting substantial weight. Considering the lack of advanced technology, construction equipment, and adhesives, how did they build their tall columns of stone? The answer is **peg fusing**.

Stonecutters chiseled out massive, but movable, pieces of marble, granite, and limestone. Each section was roughed out to approximately the same height and width, and then flattened until smooth on both the top and bottom. The stonecutters would then chisel a square depression or slot, about 4" deep, into the center of each flattened side.

After determining that the ground was level, or by creating a level base as described in Chapter 4, a large foundation block was placed where the architect wanted to place a column. A rectangular stone peg, approximately $7\frac{1}{2}$" long, was then placed into the 4" slot. The next stone was placed on the first stone, with the stone peg inserted into the bottom of the top stone, and so on until the column was the desired height. The structure was secured from movement by its own weight, centered on the stone pegs linking each section, creating a solid monument that has stood the test of time.

Figure 7-3. Stone columns of the Parthenon

To finish the column, and to give the illusion of a monolithic stone pillar, the stonecutters chiseled vertical channels around the length of the column. Additionally, for stability, the architects would often reduce the diameter of sections of the column as it rose, creating a larger diameter at the base that gradually tapered to a smaller diameter near the top.

In ice sculpting, *natural peg fusing* is used to make pieces fit together in a place where a natural curve or line exists. This technique makes the fuse almost impossible to detect, as it blends in with the naturally flowing lines of the sculpture. Extensive study of composition, as well as considerable practice in pegging, is needed to properly execute this method.

When attempting natural peg fusing in a warm and melting environment, the sculptor should allow both pieces to freeze separately. This will stop the ice from melting and prevent water from dripping into the fuse holes. Water running into the fuse holes will expand when re-freezing, and could cause the ice to crack. It is important not to use any more water than is absolutely necessary.

Weight on Pressure or Handsaw Fusing

Weight on pressure fusing, otherwise known as **handsaw fusing**, is often employed when making multi-block displays. For this method, it is imperative that both surfaces being joined are perfectly flat. However, it is not usually necessary to use marble, an iron, or aluminum since the sculptor will be using raw blocks. New **raw blocks**, which have not been cut, normally have

Figure 7-4. Diagram illustrating the natural fuse lines of The Great Seal of the United States

smooth sides formed during the making of the ice block. If the surfaces to be joined are not perfectly flat, it may be necessary to use a **nail board** to level out any uneven areas.

To achieve a successful fit after one block has been stacked upon another, it is often necessary to guide a handsaw between the blocks. This improves uniformity between the contours of both surfaces being fused together. The sculptor may need to run the saw through several times before the two blocks mesh together properly.

Cool water is then poured slowly over the blocks to fill some of any remaining gaps. Caution must be observed when applying the water, as it may cause the blocks to crack if they or the applied water were not properly tempered. The water should also be applied very slowly and in small quantities. It is best to pour the water onto the ice slightly above the seam, allowing it time to chill as it cascades down the ice before actually entering the seam. It may require several passes for the water to freeze to the ice.

There should be no gaps around the outside edges, as these gaps often become much larger as the block melts. Although this is usually not a major issue, it is wise to inspect each piece after it has been displayed, to become familiar with the changes that occur during melting. Some snow may need to be added around the seam to aid in the initial freezing process. Later, the snow may easily be removed while finishing the sculpture.

Nail-Board Fusing

Nail-board fusing is one of the most recent developments in the evolution of ice sculpting, although it has its faults. The process involves roughing the facing edges of two ice blocks with a board that has many nail points protruding

Figure 7-5. Nail board used for roughing ice

evenly through one side. After scoring the ice with the board, the two blocks are laid upon each other with a spacer, such as a screwdriver, between them. Freezing water (32° F) is poured between the blocks as the screwdriver is removed. The frozen water cements the grooves of ice together.

One benefit of this method is that it can be done without a heat source or electricity. And its seam does not dissolve after long exposure to the sun's rays. But although the bond between the two blocks is very strong, it produces arguably the least attractive of the joints created by fusing. When safety and strength are paramount, nail-board fusing is a good method. However, if the piece were for competition or for a presentation centerpiece, this would not be the preferred method.

NOTES ON FUSING

One thing to keep in mind when working at below-freezing temperatures is that the pieces of ice must be attached immediately. Otherwise, the melted ice on the surface that was just planed will re-freeze, creating a weak and uneven surface. To be safe, the best thing to do is to wipe off the melted surface after planing it with the hard, flat edge of a concrete trowel or similar tool.

In some cases, when fusing ice at temperatures above freezing, it may be necessary to chill one or more of the pieces to be fused. Before doing so, the sculptor needs to make sure that the areas to be attached are smooth and free from debris prior to letting them set. This will reduce the time the ice piece will need to be in contact with the warm aluminum.

Gum remover and/or dry ice may also need to be applied to the area being fused, to speed up the freezing process. While any of these are being applied, it is *very important* that the pieces being frozen together do not move during any fusing process.

The larger the surface area at the point of attachment, the stronger the bond becomes. If the surface area needs to be small for design reasons, it is wise to fuse the two pieces together as larger, rough-cut pieces, and then finish shaping after the bond is secure. This method will also result in a much cleaner fuse line. When fusing two pieces together, the sculptor will notice a slight indentation around the external edges of the lines where they come together. This is almost impossible to avoid, so the best way to eliminate the problem is to make the pieces wider than needed. This way, the sculptor can cut the piece down. He will find that the point at which the two pieces come together is much more precise and no longer contains the indentation.

Horizontal Versus Vertical Fusing

When fusing ice, regardless of the method used, it is best to work in concert with the forces of nature. Gravity is the natural force that secured the great columns of the Parthenon. It can be both the agent and the enemy of the sculptor. Obviously, it is best to let the gravitational forces of nature work for the sculptor whenever possible.

To ensure a quick and secure fuse in the exact location desired between two ice pieces, it is imperative that they remain still. With this in mind, *it is best to fuse ice sculptures horizontally*, stacking one piece upon the other. This is both safe and easy.

However, not all joints are destined to be horizontal. Quite often wings, arms, hands, and other extended appendages require fuses on the side of the primary sculpture. Still, it is best to fuse sections horizontally, even if the sculpture will eventually be exhibited vertically. This will require some extra handling of the ice block, but the improved fusing may actually result in time saved overall.

ARTIST PROFILE

Meet the Artist—Michael Vosburg

Michael Vosburg is the owner and operator of Ice Sculptures Unlimited, Inc., an independent, full-service vendor of ice sculptures of all sizes and configurations. Based in Richmond, Virginia, his company serves the metropolitan areas of Richmond, Washington, D.C., Williamsburg, Virginia Beach, and Charlottesville. Michael began his business in June 1997 after a 20-year career as a chef. His company averages approximately 40 sculptures a month, sometimes producing more than 150 sculptures during the month of December. Chef Vosburg has produced sculptures for a variety of clients, including ESPN and ABC's *Monday Night Football*.

Ask the Artist

Q How did you get into the ice sculpting business?

A *I was working as a chef at the Bull & Bear Club in 1992, when the general manager mentioned how nice he thought it would be to have an ice sculpture as the centerpiece for an upcoming buffet. I volunteered, although I had never done one. So I bought a book and a chain saw, and made a pretty mediocre cornucopia. But by the time I was an executive chef a little while later, I was doing around 70 sculptures a year. I decided to give it a try full-time, and have never lost money since I went into this business.*

Q What do you think is so important about fusing ice?

A *Well, I have to tell you that I had my struggles with my sculptures frequently breaking when I first started out. It happened during ice sculpting competitions and while doing sculptures for my clients. Learning to fuse was often my only way to have a finished sculpture. I've learned a lot over the years about the benefits of fusing ice.*

III

Managing The Ice

The Studio

OBJECTIVES

After reading this chapter, you will be able to:

- Discuss the artist's studio, and what design elements should be included
- Define movement and proximity, and describe how they affect the sculpting process
- Identify the elements of a well-designed walk-in freezer
- Discuss the concept of the stage, cutting zone, and safety zone and the relationship between them
- Discuss the proper storage of equipment and gear
- Describe how ice and sculptures should be stored at all stages

Key Terms and Concepts

mise en place	**proximity**	**safety zone**
artist's studio	**cutting zone**	**raw ice**
movement	**sculpting stage**	

Mise en place means "everything in its place," from French. One of the first rules a student culinarian learns is *mise en place*. All things have their place, and to be efficient one must be organized. Organizational guru Robert Townsend said, "All organizations are at least 50 percent waste—wasted people, wasted effort, wasted space, and wasted time."

The professional sculptor must be organized, for there is a great investment of time, money, and talent when a person chooses a career as an ice artisan. The orderliness of the studio is paramount to long-term success as a sculptor.

THE ARTIST'S STUDIO

Successful artists have always designed and built spaces that were conducive to the production of their craft. The **artist's studio** is the place where sculptors conduct their business of creating sub-zero art. The sculpting environment, including the equipment and relationship to other workspaces, affects the artist's ability to work efficiently and safely.

Proximity to Work

Because ice is extremely fragile, yet heavy and temperature-sensitive, sculpting should be done as close as possible to the freezer. Every time the ice is moved there is risk of damage. When planning a studio, the sculptor should consider **movement** and **proximity**.

As discussed in Chapter 2, "Understanding the Medium: The Science of Ice," ice can be sculpted either inside a freezer or in a safe area protected from sunlight, wind, and rain. Most people who sculpt only sporadically set up just outside their kitchen door. They do so because this location is otherwise used for different activities and doesn't require an additional investment of space and equipment, when only used on a limited basis for sculpting. It is also closest to the freezer, but is outside the general pattern of foot traffic of staff and out of earshot of the customers. After tempering the ice, this location can work reasonably well.

An example of a more permanent arrangement is found at Grand Rapids Community College (GRCC) in Michigan. When the Applied Technology Center was first constructed at GRCC, an ice-sculpting studio was integrated into their covered loading-dock area. The sculpting studio is located on a portion of the large receiving dock that is enclosed, heated, and well lit. Its facilities include three Clinebell Ice Block Makers, a dedicated walk-in freezer with custom shelving for holding finished sculptures with the raw blocks stored underneath, and an equipment storeroom for holding chain saws, die grinders, safety gear, and display trays, along with countless other parts and pieces of equipment. Insulated extension cords with GFCI circuitry are suspended from the ceiling from retractable cord reels, compressed air and water lines are mounted on a nearby wall, and individual sculpting platforms include heavy rubber matting mounted on custom designed stainless steel tables.

When completed, the sculptures can either be stored within a few feet of where they were sculpted, rolled down the hall to the four banquet rooms and restaurant for use and display, or wrapped and packed for transport off-site. *Movement* and *proximity* were addressed in the design.

The additional investment in ice-making equipment, freezer space, and equipment storage is justified because the Culinary Arts program teaches four elective sections of ice sculpting classes annually. Additionally, an instructional module on ice sculpting is taught in their Banquets and Catering course, and the department also sponsors an ice sculpting competition team, "the Chain Gang." The arrangement allows for a large number of students to safely sculpt on a regular basis without disrupting other activities.

Those individuals who sculpt regularly often have a studio arranged within the protected environment of a walk-in freezer. This arrangement allows for minimal movement of the ice and reduced chances for accidental damage. Such proximity to the work also benefits the sculptor who has multiple components to be fused.

At the sculpting studio of Ice Sculptures, Ltd., Derek Maxfield and Randy Finch have created a highly productive environment for their team of employees. With ten Clinebell Ice Block Makers, two walk-in storage freezers, and one freezer dedicated as a sculpting studio complete with an Iceculture 5200 router, they produce several hundred sculptures a month. Their building includes a loading dock, business office, CAD design office, ice-block room, equipment room, and several storerooms for packing supplies and shipping containers. Again, *movement* and *proximity* were addressed in the facility design.

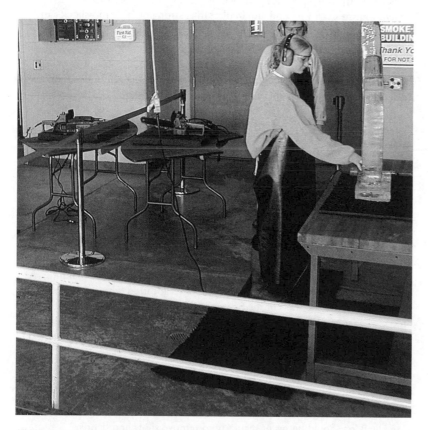

Figure 8-1. Sculpting studio arranged on a loading dock

FREEZER LAYOUT AND DESIGN

A walk-in freezer is vital to sculpting ice on a regular basis. Because of size and temperature requirements for storing multiple raw ice blocks, a walk-in freezer is the only practical option for storage. Some operations have dedicated freezers to warehouse only raw blocks and sculptures, and some even have sculpting studios within their dedicated freezer. Most operations, however, share the functional space of the freezer between ice and the other foodstuffs.

Access and Separation from Foodstuffs

The ideal situation is to have a freezer specifically designated to store ice, thereby reducing the chances of breaking the sculptures. In most cases this is not practical or economical. When creating a space for ice within a shared walk-in freezer, the sculptor should consider the following:

- Choose an area with a minimum of foot or cart traffic, possibly in the rear of the freezer.
- Use Ethafoam, or some form of plastic, underneath the ice to keep it from freezing to the floor.
- Whenever possible, do not place ice in the direct path of fans, where temperatures can vary and air circulation is strongest. Thermo-shock can occur due to a sudden drop in temperature, and air circulation increases the rate of sublimation.
- When using shelving, be certain that it is structurally capable of handling the weight of the ice. Any sculptures or components stored in boxes on shelves should be well labeled.

Flooring

The flooring of a modern walk-in freezer is either raised or flush with the floor outside. When a floor is raised, it indicates that the walk-in was built directly onto the poured-concrete floor without any recessed insulation. After constructing the walls of the freezer, several inches of insulation are laid onto the floor and covered with stainless steel or galvanized aluminum. A short ramp is built just inside the doorway. This method is commonly used for freezers that are installed after a building has been constructed.

The preferred method of construction requires more advance planning. A recessed area of the floor is created on the exact location where the freezer is to be built. After the walls of the freezer are erected, insulation is laid into the recessed area and covered with metal sheeting. This method is more difficult and is often expensive, but it is more convenient to the end-user since no ramp is required and more wall space is available for storage.

In either case, ice blocks will be dragged across the floor for storage. Ideally, the floor would be covered with Ethafoam to prevent shocking and chipping the ice. Short of that, plastic and a large rubber pad are suitable. *Do not use cardboard*, as it is absorbent and will stick to the ice.

The floor should be swept regularly to remove snow and debris.

Shelving

Shelving can be added to a walk-in to store ice. However, most commercial shelving is not designed to hold the weight of block ice for extended periods of time.

At GRCC, custom shelving was constructed from stainless steel sheeting and attached to three sides of the freezer walls. The 24" wide shelving was installed approximately 45" off the floor, allowing sufficient space to slide raw blocks under the shelves and stand unfinished works and completed sculptures on the shelves. Even though sculpted blocks weigh less than raw blocks, which weigh about 300 pounds, they still require a sturdy shelf on which to rest.

Moving ice in and out of this freezer is now safer for the sculptures, as their delicate appendages are out of harm's way. The finished sculptures are also easier to pick up since they are stored at waist height. Large, bag-covered blocks are slid on slick, non-porous sheeting under the shelf, and are arranged in a compacted way to allow for maximum storage and minimum sublimation. Capacity and accessibility are increased due to complete use of vertical storage space.

Figure 8-2. Walk-in freezer with stainless steel shelving

Temperature

When storing ice, an important factor is the temperature of the freezer. Temperature within a walk-in freezer should be maintained between 20–28° F. At this temperature, the ice is less brittle and less susceptible to chipping and breaking. We have found between 26–28° F to be the ideal temperature for storing and sculpting ice. The ice is both pliable and compact at this temperature and the risk of thermo-shock when moving the ice to a warmer area for transportation or display is reduced.

There are many good reasons for holding the ice at this temperature. Among them:

- The ice is less brittle, and less susceptible to chipping and breaking.
- The risk of thermo-shock is reduced when moving the ice for transportation or display.
- Less time is needed to temper the ice, specifically when carving at room temperature.
- The ice is protected from sublimation during the freezer's defrost cycle, if the ice is being stored at too warm a temperature. (However, keeping it properly covered also affords protection.)

THE CUTTING ZONE AND SCULPTING STAGE

The **cutting zone** is an imaginary circle that radiates 6' around the sculptor, *where others may not trespass.* In this area, the sculptor should be alone and free to wield power tools without endangering others. It is generally located around the **sculpting stage** where the sculptor is working on the ice piece. As the artist moves, so does the cutting zone, always keeping a safe distance between operating power tools and other people. *Maintaining the cutting zone is one of a few hard and fast rules in the ice-sculpting business.*

The Safety Zone

The **safety zone**, mentioned in Chapter 4, "Safe Practices and Procedures," must be clearly established before sculpting. Unlike the cutting zone, the safety zone is not imaginary. It is a clearly defined perimeter established to keep casual onlookers and passersby away from the sculpture and sculptor. It can be a medium-sized room, as part of a larger studio, or it can be a sectioned-off space of a much larger area. At the center of the safety zone is the sculpting stage, where the ice sculpture rests on a workbench or rubber mat. Like the safety zone, the sculpting stage does not move during the sculpting process.

It is necessary to establish such zones because ice sculptures tend to be magnets for inquisitive onlookers. The artist can be unaware of the attention drawn by the sculpture as she remains focused on her work. Conversely, the sculptor might be working with others who are very familiar with sculpting and who might become careless due to their familiarity with the sculpting process. *The danger lies in allowing anyone, curious or careless, too close to the action.*

Establishing a safe area around the ice, in which the sculptor can move unimpeded by those around her, is paramount to safe sculpting.

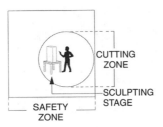

Figure 8-3. Diagram illustrating the safety zone, sculpting stage, and cutting zone

EQUIPMENT AND GEAR STORAGE

The professional and student sculptor alike must make a concerted effort to care for their equipment and gear. Failing to maintain equipment and gear properly can lead to the unnecessary expense of replacement and to unforeseen inconvenience.

Clothing and Safety Gear

Having a warm, dry area to store and dry clothing and safety gear undoubtedly enhances the sculpting experience. Clothing must be allowed to dry thoroughly and should be stored in an area with ample air circulation. When available, a heat source is desirable, as it protects against the mildew and fungus that can grow on wet clothing.

The sculptor should have multiple pairs of gloves and socks available for rotating during a long sculpting session. These clothes must be maintained properly, so they are ready and available the next time the sculptor needs them.

Additionally, rubber boots, eye goggles, earplugs, and head muffs need a home. They have a way of getting misplaced when not organized properly.

Tools

Properly dried and oiled tools can help reduce expenses by adding longevity to each tool's life. A sculpting area may not provide the best conditions; therefore, it may be necessary to create a separate storage area for tools.

The sculptor must allow adequate shelving and hooks for tools, replacement parts, and repair tools and supplies. Cabinet space, sturdy plastic tubs, and large "C" hooks work well to organize a sculptor's studio.

When laying out equipment to be used while the artist is working on a sculpture, it is recommended to allow enough room around the sculpting stage to spread tools out. This will reduce the risk of one tool damaging another, as can happen when tools are jumbled in a pile.

Lighting and Electrical Cords

As with all tools, electrical cords and lighting should always have a specific home. Improperly stored electrical cords and lighting can become damaged and create a serious safety risk. Dangling cords or cords strewn about a work area can cause an accident. Care must be taken, and habits established, to stow any electrical cords not in immediate use. The use of retractable cord reels is recommended as one convenient and effective method for storing extension cords.

Trays, Drains, and Buckets

The sculptor generally supplies the client with the equipment needed to display a sculpture. Service can also involve the delivery, set-up, and removal of the sculpture, when the size and complexity of the sculpture warrant the extra service. In any case, display trays, drainage tubing, and water reservoirs (such as 10-gallon buckets) will be needed at the time of the display.

It should be noted that these items are not part of the sculpting process and therefore do not need to be stored near where the actual sculpting process occurs. There is no reason to take up precious space near the freezer or sculpting stage to store these items.

Carts

Carts, whether two-wheel or four-wheel, are an important tool in moving ice safely from the freezer to the loading dock or banquet room. However, they tend to be a nuisance when not in use. Planning for their convenient storage is a good idea.

Ice Block-Making Equipment

When deciding on the arrangement of an ice studio with production capabilities, it is important to make the configuration as user-friendly as possible for harvesting and storing of ice. Freshly pulled blocks tend to come out of the machines extremely cold, and should not be transported through a warm area on the way to the storage freezer. This can cause thermo-shock.

Figure 8-4. New block being harvested from a circulating tank

Ice-block makers have supplemental equipment, such as hoists and cradles that are used for harvesting and handling raw ice blocks after removing them from the block maker. This equipment must be stored properly while not in use, but the storage should be in reasonably close proximity to the ice machines for convenient accessibility.

LONG- AND SHORT-TERM ICE STORAGE

Ice can be safely held in a walk-in freezer for extended periods of time when proper precautions are taken. The sculptor must consider thermo-shock, sublimation, and other damaging actions that will affect the ice when storing raw blocks, in-progress sculptures, and finished sculptures.

Figure 8-5. Bag and cardboard box protecting ice

Raw Blocks

New block ice, also known as **raw ice**, may be purchased boxed or uncovered. When received unprotected, or when made by the sculptor, the artisan should cover the blocks with a large garbage bag. Always keeping blocks, bowls, dishes, sheets, sculptures, or any other ice product covered while being stored will extend the shelf life of the ice. Additionally, the ice will be protected from the unwanted accumulation of snow, crystal formations, and whatever else may fall or form on the ice.

In many freezers, not only very low temperatures are a factor, but also limited space. Since block ice is large and heavy, sufficient floor space is a must. It is advisable to place the blocks tightly together along the wall of the freezer, keeping only a small space between the walls and the ice blocks for proper air circulation.

In-Progress Sculptures

Usually, those sculptures that are in the process of being completed will need to be accessed easily. For that reason, partially completed sculptures should be stored closest to the door of the freezer, but kept safe from being damaged by the normal traffic in the freezer.

If necessary, lighter items that are properly packed and labeled may be stacked on top of new block ice. But it is best not to stack partially or fully completed ice too high, because there is more airflow at the top of freezers from the condensing fans that send warmer air past the ice.

Finished Sculptures

When a sculpture is finished, proper storage is important so that it will be preserved safely until it is displayed. If a sculpture was carved at room temperature, it must be thoroughly cleaned with a hand brush or hosed off with water so that no slush, ice chips, dirt, Ethafoam, or any other foreign matter freezes to the finished sculpture. Be sure to remove any excess water from the recesses of the sculpture before placing it in the freezer.

Before moving the sculpture into the freezer, prepare a space in a low-traffic area with good circulation, but away from the door or condensing fans to prevent sublimation. Place something non-porous on the floor, such as a plastic garbage bag, Ethafoam, or Coroplast™, to prevent the wet sculpture from freezing to the floor.

Before covering the block with plastic, allow the ice to "set" or freeze for 10–20 minutes. If it is wrapped when wet or soft, the plastic will freeze on the ice and leave wrinkles. Once the ice has set, wrap it in plastic or cover it with a garbage bag. This will help prevent sublimation and ice crystal formation.

Ice crystals form when the freezer goes through a defrost cycle. The condenser heats up to melt excess frost or ice buildup on the evaporator. When the freezer starts back up after the defrost cycle ends, the water molecules in the air attach to anything in the freezer, forming ice crystals. Over a period of time, an exposed sculpture will be covered in ice crystals, making the surface furry and fuzzy. When this happens, the crystals can be carefully brushed away, leaving the original sculpture relatively undamaged. If storing the piece for a long period of time, placing a plastic bag and then a cardboard box over the sculpture will help. Make sure the box is labeled so no one puts something on top of the boxed sculpture.

ARTIST PROFILE

Meet the Artist—George O'Palenick

George O'Palenick is an Associate Professor at Johnson & Wales University, where he has been teaching since the early 1980s. George has served as the advisor to the "Chipper Club," the student ice-carving club. Many of his students have competed in local and national ice-carving competitions. Chef O'Palenick has also operated an ice sculpture business, Art in Ice, Inc. since the late 1980s. An active member of several professional organizations, George is currently the President of the National Ice Carving Association. Chef O'Palenick is certified to judge ice-carving competitions for both the American Culinary Federation and the National Ice Carving Association, and he represented the USA and NICA as a judge for the 2002 Olympic Arts Festival Ice Carving Competition in Provo, Utah.

Ask the Artist

Q   What do you consider to be the most important aspect of organizing the sculptor's studio?

A   *Without a doubt, it has to be safety. I have been a big proponent for safety since I've been involved with sculpting. Without organizing a proper work area, a sculptor is bound to have an accident some day. The studio must be established and organized for safe sculpting. Ground fault electrical outlets, non-skid floors, use of lifting belts and eye protection are examples of how to make your work studio safer for sculpting.*

Q   Have you seen many changes in sculpting since you started?

A   *Certainly. My first exposure to ice carving was with Joe Amendola in the late 1960s, when I was a student at the Culinary Institute of America, in New Haven. He inspired me, but the sculpting was less ornate. Back then, the ice and tools weren't as good as what is available today. The techniques in fusing used today far surpass what was done even five years ago.*

9

Methods of Transportation

OBJECTIVES

After reading this chapter, you will be able to:

- Identify the five "P's" of transporting ice sculptures
- Discuss the types of carts used in on-site transportation
- List variables that must be considered when transporting ice by ground
- List variables that must be considered when transporting ice by air
- Describe a system for maintaining cushion during shipping
- Describe methods for maintaining the proper temperature for the ice during shipping

Key Terms and Concepts

planning	portable	display cart
produced	flatbed cart	two-wheel dolly
protected	on-site	foam in place
preserved	transportation	dry ice

Having the proper tools and ice is an important part of the ice sculpting business. However, after the artist has performed her magic on the ice, the sculpture must be safely delivered to its point of display. Sculpting ice tests the artistic abilities of the sculptor, but delivering the finished product requires a whole different set of skills. All of the painstaking effort that went into planning, design, sculpting, and storage can be wiped out by a single mistake during transportation. The careful sculptor takes steps to ensure the sculpture's safe arrival.

THE FIVE "P's" OF ICE SCULPTURE TRANSPORTATION

The professional sculptor evaluates the many aspects of transporting ice before beginning the sculpture. Whether it is down the hall or across the state, the sculpture needs to be planned, produced, protected, preserved, and made portable. These are known as the **Five "P's" of Ice Sculpture Transportation**.

Planned

The **planning** process requires some up-front effort to evaluate the known and unknown aspects of the sculpting request. The object in planning is to reduce the risk involved while meeting the objectives of the service request. It's about gathering pertinent information that can help both in the planning of the sculpture and in its safe transportation and display. The sculptor determines in what form the sculpture would best be able to travel the distance required and meet the expectations of the client when it gets there.

Produced

Once the proper design has been decided upon, it is up to the sculptor to **produce** a sculpture consistent with the plan. Sometimes a plan contains only some loosely ordered ideas that seem logical in their flexibility, but are short on direction. The artist must be sure that the work that is produced meets the intended goals, including safe transportation.

Protected

After the sculpture has been completed it must be packaged and **protected** from damage. Several different invasive forces, including sunlight, heat, or physical shock, can cause damage to the sculpture. Covering a sculpture with a garbage bag and holding onto it as it is rolled down the hall may be sufficient protection for short distances. However, if the piece is being transported off-site it needs substantially more protection. Wrapping a sculpture in bubble wrap or a moving blanket will guard it against physical shock as well as heat and ultra-violet rays.

Preserved

Once the sculpture has been protected against physical shock, it needs to be **preserved** against light and heat. A sculpture will melt when placed in an environment above 32° F. Wrapping a heavy wool or moving blanket tightly

Figure 9-1. Bubble wrap used to insulate and protect the sculpture

around a sculpture that has been covered in plastic or bubble wrap is an easy and effective means of trapping cold air against the sculpture.

Portable

After the sculpture is protected and preserved, then it must become **portable**. Portability refers to the ease in which an item can be moved from one location to another. For safe transportation, the sculpture must be placed on a cart securely. The next section will discuss various options the artist has for transporting her ice art, either on- or off-site.

ON-SITE TRANSPORTATION

On-site transportation means moving the sculpture to another location within the same building. Even though there are presumably fewer obstacles to overcome and fewer unknowns to consider, a sculpture can break at any moment if treated carelessly. The following methods are generally available for on-site transportation of a sculpture.

Two-Wheel Handcarts

A two-wheel handcart, also known as a **two-wheel dolly**, is an important piece of equipment when moving raw blocks or finished sculptures. Its use will prevent the need for dragging or sliding the ice across the floor or ground, which will likely cause some kind of damage.

When evaluating a handcart, the tires are of utmost importance. They need to be large and preferably air-filled to absorb the weight and shock of rolling on bumpy surfaces and up and down stairs. Generally, a cart's capacity is a reflection of its sturdiness. Aluminum frames are lighter than steel, and generally have a 500–800 pound weight capacity. Steel frames are heavy and can rust, but they have a higher weight capacity.

Padding the frame with pipe insulation and then wrapping the insulation with duct tape will protect the ice from the metal. Securing the insulation to the handcart with duct tape will not only hold it in place, it will also prevent the ice from sticking to the insulation, which could otherwise cause deterioration and shorten its useful lifespan.

The ice block is placed on the handcart, resting tightly against the tape-covered insulation. Bungee straps are used to secure the ice to the cart before moving it.

Figure 9-2. Two-wheel dolly covered with pipe insulation and duct tape

Four-Wheel Flatbed Carts

Using a four-wheel flatbed truck, also known as a **platform cart**, will help save the sculptor time and effort if there are many items to carry. Although it is larger and wider than a two-wheel handcart, which makes it more difficult to maneuver in crowded hallways, its capacity and ease of use is beneficial.

When purchasing a flatbed cart for sculpting, it is best to find one that has large, air-filled tires capable of absorbing the shock of travel. A platform made of heavy gauge plastic that has a 1,000-pound weight capacity is preferred. Plastic platforms absorb vibrations better than metal, and they will not conduct heat as readily. Because the sculptor will likely be traveling through doorways of various sizes, it is best to purchase a cart with a 24" × 36" platform, which will fit through a standard doorframe.

It is always best to pull the cart rather than push it. Pulling the cart gives more steering control.

Figure 9-3. Flatbed cart

Display Carts

The sculptor can purchase or construct her own **display cart**, which has wheels and a platform to hold a sculpture for display. (See Chapter 10, "Displaying and Lightning for Effect," for more information on display carts.) These carts often have built-in through lighting under the Plexiglas base on which the ice sits. One obvious advantage is that the artist can arrange the sculpture for display on the cart, and then store the cart in a freezer until it is needed. The ice can then be transported from the freezer to the banquet facility with relative ease. Disposal of the sculpture is also easier since there is no need to lift anything off the display table.

Care still needs to be taken to avoid physical shock and thermo-shock when moving the sculpture initially from the freezer.

OFF-SITE TRANSPORTATION

Transporting ice safely down the hall has its challenges, but consider the prospect of delivering ice across town or to another city or state. Ice professionals do it on a regular basis, but not without taking certain precautions. The following procedures have proven to be successful.

Shipping by Ground

When shipping by ground, there are a lot of variables beyond the control of the sculptor. These include weather, traffic, and road construction. Anticipating some of these possible delays is important; planning is the solution. The following recommendations can help avoid potential problems with the delivery:

- Check the weather the night before.
- Leave early enough to allow for possible traffic delays.
- Map out the route. Use Internet travel software like Mapquest, AAA Travel, local maps, or GPS software and a laptop.
- Request directions from the customer. Most resorts, hotels, country clubs, arenas, and banquet halls have this information readily available.
- Bring your own cart, as a proper cart may not be available upon arrival. You can then safely move the ice art from the loading dock to the display area.
- It will be necessary to pack the sculpture with dry ice when shipping will take more than 3 hours.

Vehicle size requirements will vary depending on the dimensions of the sculpture. On a daily basis, Ice Sculptures, Ltd. delivers smaller pieces, such as Valentine's Day heart sculptures packed in small containers, in a mid-size car. They use a pickup truck with an insulated box and **dry ice** basket for larger sculptures. A standard box-bed truck with a freezer and compressor could be used, but the cost to purchase and operate such a vehicle is much higher.

In addition to maintaining the necessary temperature for the ice, it is important to keep the sculpture protected from wind, rain, and sun.

Shipping by Air

Shipping the ice by air is not too much different from shipping sculptures by ground. The ice needs to be designed for travel, wrapped in plastic or bubble wrap while frozen, and insulated with moving blankets.

It will be necessary to pack the sculpture with dry ice when shipping will take more than 3 hours. Equally important to the preparation for shipping with dry ice is inquiring about airline policies or restrictions. Airlines consider dry ice to be a hazardous material, as it releases carbon dioxide into the surrounding environment when it sublimates. A container with dry ice must be clearly marked, noting the quantity of dry ice originally placed in the container.

It will also be necessary to investigate the airline's policy on weight limitations prior to arriving at the airport.

MAINTAINING CUSHION AND COMPRESSION DURING SHIPPING

Figure 9-4. Insulated foam in place shipping box with sculpture

When packing ice for shipping for long distances and extended periods of time, it may be necessary to place the ice in an insulated box, such as a Styrofoam container, to better retain the cold air. It will also be likely to need insulation or filler around the sculpture to reduce the air in the cavity and create compression on the sculpture.

There are several companies that sell "**foam in place**" systems that allow the sculptor to box an ice sculpture and then apply foam around the ice. The foam fills the void surrounding the sculpture, thereby allowing the ice to maintain its own freezing temperature and eliminating unwanted movement inside the box. Another similar system uses air bags to cushion ice inside a packing container. (See Appendix E for a list of suppliers.)

MAINTAINING ICE TEMPERATURE DURING TRAVEL

There are many ways to ready a sculpture for transport, but the goal is always the same—to deliver the sculpture to the destination safely. The greatest concern is thermo-shock. Ice needs to be transported in a temperature-controlled environment to maintain a consistent temperature.

An easy procedure to ensure consistent temperature is to cover the sculpture with a garbage bag, then wrap it with bubble wrap, and finally wrap it in a moving blanket. It is recommended to pack the sculpture while in the freezer. Placing the plastic bag on the ice while it is frozen prevents wrinkles that would form if the bag were placed on the ice when it was beginning to soften. Wrapping it in the freezer also traps cold air between the ice and the insulating wrap. It is wise to store insulating blankets in the freezer to help retain cold air against the sculptures during their transportation.

Some artists use other methods of insulating their sculptures. Large, hard-sided ice chests like those used on charter fishing boats are one option, or large, soft-sided thermal bags similar to the kind in which pizzas are delivered. Depending on the physical size and number of sculptures to be delivered, there are several good choices available.

Insulated Box Method

An inexpensive but dependable method of transporting ice sculptures by truck is with an insulated box. The following list describes how to make an insulated box for transporting ice sculptures.

- Measure the inside dimensions of the pickup truck or panel van. Make sure the box will fit within these dimensions.

- Using 1" plywood, build a box at least 44" high and 44" deep. This will be large enough to accommodate up to three sculptures, but not so large that the air inside the box cannot be sufficiently chilled.

- Attach $\frac{1}{2}$" foam board insulation to all inside walls, floor, and ceiling of the box using flat-head screws and large, flat washers.

- Attach at least six u-bolts or large screw eyes to the top and bottom of each sidewall of the box for securing the sculptures. These must be well attached to the wooden box. Use bungee cords or rope to secure the sculptures during transportation.

- Make a full-sized front door with secure hinges and a hasp for a padlock.

- Suspend a perforated basket, similar to a round deep-fryer basket, from the top of the box. Cut a round hole in the top of the box over the basket. Attach a hinge and handle to the hole. The basket should be about a foot across and 8–10" inches high. This will allow you to place dry ice into the basket through the hatch without having to open the front door.

For local trips, dry ice will most likely not be needed. But for delivering the ice a fair distance from the studio, dry ice is warranted. Never handle dry ice with bare hands; always use gloves and eye protection. It is best to break the ice into several pieces, exposing more sides to the air for faster refrigeration. Cold air falls, which is why the wire basket is suspended from the top of the box.

Figure 9-5. Insulated box mounted on a truck bed

ARTIST PROFILE

Meet the Artist—Jim Nadeau

Jim Nadeau founded Nadeau's Ice Sculptures in 1980, making it one of the oldest ice-sculpting companies in the United States. It is also the largest—in a studio in Forest Park, Illinois, Nadeau's employs more than 30 full- and part-time employees whose sole occupation is the production and sale of finished ice sculptures. Jim's facility features a 2,000-square-foot walk-in freezer for raw blocks and finished sculptures, and another, smaller freezer that serves as their ice gallery for prospective clients. Nationally renowned for thinking "outside the block," Nadeau's customers come from across the country and include local and national media, sports, and corporate clients. Nadeau's also produces sculptures for local weddings and banquets.

Ask the Artist

Q   How do you handle such a large volume of ice at your operation?

A   *Teamwork! Our talented staff consistently "pulls rabbits out of a hat" for our loyal customers. We are constantly perfecting and developing new and better ways to streamline ice distribution through innovative ideas, such as our dry ice box. After more than twenty years of doing this, we have our systems in place. But, as I was building my business, I was learning more and more about ice and sculpture. I still am. There is so much to know in this business, and the art keeps getting more challenging as we learn how to do more with ice.*

Q   How do you safely transport such fragile artwork?

A   *As I mentioned, the dry ice box helps. Packaging them this way allows us to deliver more sculptures to more areas in a shorter amount of time. My staff is well trained in the methods of transporting ice, as we sell a lot of sculptures from our studio in Chicago. Over the last 22 years, we've redesigned our sculptures for better travel and longer display time, while still looking great. Of course, our refrigerated delivery vehicles are a plus when delivering hundreds of sculptures, particularly in the warm summer months in Chicago. Bottom line: don't let the ice get warm until you're at the loading dock of your destination.*

Displaying and Lighting for Effect

OBJECTIVES

After reading this chapter, you will be able to:

- Explain the conical field of vision
- Discuss the visual impact of sculptures by height, shape, and form
- Discuss the visual impact of traditional lighting and list several methods
- Discuss the visual impact of special-effect lighting and list several methods
- Identify considerations for displaying a sculpture safely
- Describe different display trays and carts
- Explain means of enhancing a display using garnitures

Key Terms and Concepts

conical field of
  vision
BTU
glow sticks

glow discs
pyrotechnic
light table
glow rope

fiber optic cable
color wheel
LED

OUTLINE

Conical Field of Vision

- Visual Impact by Height
- Visual Impact by Shape and Form

Visual Impact by Traditional and Special-Effect Lighting

- Traditional Lighting
- Special-Effect Lighting

Displaying the Sculpture Safely

- Proper Drainage

Display Trays and Carts

- Commercially Available Permanent Display Trays
- Commercially Available Disposable Display Trays
- Display Carts

Enhancing the Display with Garnitures

- Floral and Greens
- Linens and other Man-Made Objects

Artist Profile

When considering the design of an ice sculpture, the artist must think about where and how the sculpture will be displayed. Variables such as purpose, location, environment, lighting, and length of time on display must be evaluated.

Sculptures are generally seen from many perspectives and multiple points of view. They can be either the center of attention or a supporting piece of a larger exhibit. The sculptures are often enhanced by special lighting, decorated with floral arrangements, or used as a chilled vessel for presenting food. Whatever the purpose, to better understand how the work will be perceived by the viewing audience, the artist must first understand the concept of **conical field of vision**.

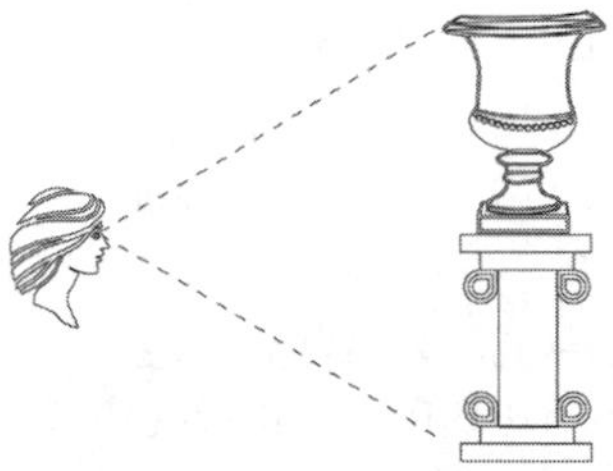

Figure 10-1. Diagram illustrating the conical field of vision

CONICAL FIELD OF VISION

When viewing any object, what we see is limited by our peripheral vision. We experience a conical field of vision that radiates from our eyes outward to infinity. We have a limited ability to observe width and size when objects are close to us, but when they are farther away, our field of vision widens. For example, when we stand ten feet from a large building, the building's corners and sides are outside the boundaries of our peripheral vision. Stand back one hundred feet, and much more of the building comes into view. This is important for the sculptor to understand when displaying a sculpture.

Even though artists often use lighting, decorations, and other special effects to highlight their works, sculptors are able to create interest in their pieces without any of these embellishments. Sculptors can create visual impact by inventive use of height, shape, and form (see *The Composition of Ice Sculptures* in Chapter 1). They can sculpt and fuse the ice to arouse interest and imagination.

Visual Impact by Height

In displays, size always makes an impression. People tend to be impressed by sculptures that are very large and prominent, or small and delicate. It is often harder to make small and delicate ice sculptures that survive the ravages of heat and light than it is to make substantial centerpieces or an impressive table display. Ice sculptures are most often used as a single, large focal point or are incorporated into an even larger display. Not coincidentally, past experience in culinary and ice sculpting competitions has proven that judges prefer sculptures that are larger and set higher relative to their field of vision.

Visual Impact by Shape and Form

When queried, judges respond that ice makes an immediate and more powerful visual statement when it is in full view. They like to see sculptures with strong primary lines that can be identified from afar, with details that are revealed upon closer inspection.

In other words, basic shapes, such as circular and oval designs, have powerful lines that create visual continuity in the sculpture. Secondary lines create depth and definition, giving the sculpture its form. An interesting sculpture needs strong lines to create an immediate impression, secondary lines for depth and definition, and negative space for interest and imagination. The whole package works together to aid in symmetry of design.

Visual Impact by Traditional and Special-Effect Lighting

Even though lighting isn't necessary to enhance a strong design, sculptors often use lighting to punch up the impact of their presentation. Sometimes the light even becomes an integral part of the sculpture, adding elements to the design. Whether soft and warm glow or bold and bright illumination— *the use of light always arouses interest in an ice sculpture.*

Traditional Lighting

In the 19th and early 20th century, candles and oil lamps were used to illuminate ice carvings. They were impractical, however, because they generated heat. During the mid-20th century, 150-watt floodlights with colored glass filters were used to light ice displays with less melting.

Until recently, ice sculptures were lit using one of three methods. These traditional methods are still widely used to light and display sculptures to dramatic effect, although other means of special-effect lighting have been introduced. Traditional methods include *stage lighting*, *back lighting*, and *through lighting*. Each method places the light increasingly closer to the sculpture.

Stage Lighting

Stage lighting, or spotlighting, is a commonly used method for highlighting many forms of sculpture. The sculpture is merely placed on a table under ceiling-mounted light fixtures, and the beams are directed toward the ice. The room is often darkened slightly to emphasize the dramatic effect of the shadowing or color given to a statue by focused overhead spotlights. However, front lighting from a distance is the least desirable means for illuminating an ice sculpture, since the light actually bounces off the ice.

Back Lighting

There are basically three forms of backlights used to highlight ice sculptures and focus attention to their design and presence. Light fixtures are placed strategically behind the sculpture, focusing light from behind the translucent sculpture. The lights themselves are not emphasized; rather, the sculpture is highlighted by the light's beam. The three light sources include:

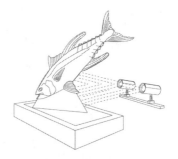

Figure 10-2. Back-lighting

- **Can Lights**—These lights use incandescent bulbs, which give off a lot of heat. Generally, the lower the wattage, the lower the **BTU**'s. They require some ventilation to exhaust the heat.

- **Fluorescent Lights**—These lights are very bright, give off virtually no heat, and are very affordable.

- **LED Lights**—This is the best type of light source, but the most expensive.

Through Lighting

There are basically two forms of *through lighting* that can be used to illuminate a sculpture from within. This form of lighting is unaffected by what surrounds the sculpture and is generally less obtrusive. The two forms are:

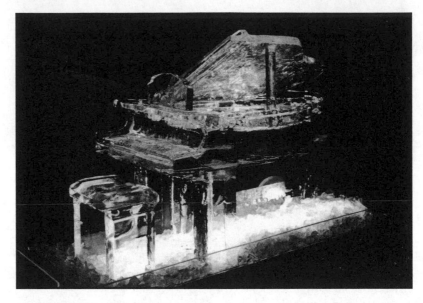

Figure 10-3. Through lighting from the bottom

- **Bottom Lighting**—This form of lighting generally originates from a lighted display tray or cart. The sculpture is placed onto the specially designed tray, which has a light fixture mounted beneath a Plexiglas barrier. Color gels are often placed over the lights to provide color enhancement to the sculpture.
- **Inset Lighting**—This system requires the light source to be embedded into the ice, usually by carving a hole into which the light (often a battery powered LED) is inserted.

Special-Effect Lighting

Recent developments in artificial lighting have allowed sculptors to show their works "in a whole new light." Artisans have been able to marry the complementary natural forces of frozen water and light waves to create fragmentations of colored light and ice. The result is a magical union of color, light, and ice theatrics.

Glow Sticks and Glow Discs

The use of **glow sticks** and **glow discs** has allowed sculptors to bring light to smaller sculptures without the need for electrical wires, making the sculptures portable and flexible. These plastic coated cylinders or discs are about the same size as a cigar or a drink coaster, and are reasonably inexpensive. The sculptor cuts a slot in the ice and countersinks the glow device, which radiates a color throughout the ice piece.

Glow sticks and glow discs are often used on individual ice serving dishes like sorbet or shrimp boats, but they also work well with table centerpieces. The sticks have a 4–8 hour "glow-life," but their glow diminishes in brilliance with prolonged exposure to cold. Artists generally put them into the ice just before an event begins.

Figure 10-4. Glow discs

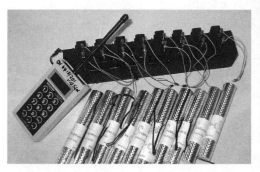

Figure 10-5. Glitzzz Super Sparkler Remote
Pyrotechnics system

Figure 10-6. Pyrotechnics

Pyrotechnics

One of the newer special effects being used with ice sculptures is the ability to detonate "cold flame" **pyrotechnic** explosions and heatless showers of sparks from remote locations. The use of these products in conjunction with large flower-filled vases made of ice, the Statue of Liberty's torch, and other festive designs can create excitement at large banquets and special awards events.

The Sparktacular remote pyrotechnics system, shown in Figure 10-5, allows the florist or sculptor to insert sparkler charges (about the same size as a test tube) into a floral arrangement or to countersink them in an ice sculpture. Through a radio-controlled system of pagers, transmitters, and charging stations, the client or sculptor can detonate each individual charge when needed, setting off an impressive shower of heatless sparks. The system can be used to punctuate award presentations and highlight special moments in an event. They make the sculptures functional, while also serving as a focal point with their dramatic element of surprise.

In addition to these high-tech devices, sculptors can use candles and sparklers with their ice displays. *However, the use of pyrotechnics requires extreme caution and a controlled environment.*

Note: As a safety precaution, the sculptor should always obtain written permission from the facility management when using pyrotechnics.

Light Tables

Light tables are a passive way to make an elegant statement for a special event. Dining or buffet tabletops are made of clear Plexiglas and are draped and skirted with standard table coverings of cotton, silk, linen, or polyester. If preferred, the sides of the tables can be skirted with opaque colors and material to prevent light from showing through the sides. The light is then directed upwards through the tabletop.

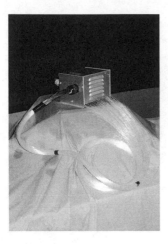

Figure 10-7. Fiber optic cable

A light source, such as an incandescent can, neon, or fluorescent light box, is placed under the table, allowing its light to glow through the cloth-covered top of the table. Centerpiece sculptures, sometimes with their own contrasting color light source, are placed on the table in small trays of clear or dark plastic. The appearance is impressive in a dimly lit room and adds to the entertainment value of the event.

Glow Ropes and Fiber Optic Cable

Glow ropes and **fiber optic cables** are an effective means to highlight the periphery of larger displays, such as ice bars and castles. Light travels through individual fibers, which are bundled within flexible outer tubing. Modular in design and sold in bundles, both cable and rope can be "built" to the desired length. There are also a variety of colors from which to select. Different products vary somewhat in function, and each shows light a little differently. Some systems pulse, alternating colors and rhythm of lights, while others are static. *Fiber optics are self-illuminating, but do not project light.*

Lasers and Projections

Ice can be used as a screen onto which logos, designs, messages, and colors are projected. Sculptors can shape ice into computer screens, television screens, and billboards onto which commercials, advertisements, and messages are projected. These specialized sculptures are most often used at trade shows and sales meetings.

Laser patterns can also be projected onto ice and fog to create an animated light show, often synchronized with music.

Color Wheels

This somewhat archaic means of lighting a display was borrowed from the Christmas tradition of lighting the tree. The process involves a **color wheel** and light projector. The wheel revolves slowly in front of the light projector, which is focused on the sculpture. As the different color panels rotate into the light, the sculpture glows in one color after another.

DISPLAYING THE SCULPTURE SAFELY

The most important aspect of displaying an ice sculpture is the safety of people around it. Ice sculptures are supposed to create a lasting impression, preferably a positive one. Misfortune can befall an event if a sculpture falls unexpectedly into the buffet, or worse, onto a passing guest. The following suggestions can help you keep your event safe:

- When planning the piece, design it for safety. Consider the length of time it will be on display, and sculpt pieces that will be stable for that period of time, given the temperature and weather environment.

- A 6" base is usually sufficient to support a sculpture for most buffets. Cut handholds into the base to help with controlled lifting, or slide heavy-duty plastic packing straps through the slots to be used as handles.

- Follow the directions as written in Chapter 4, "Safe Practices and Procedures," for safely lifting and transporting the sculpture to the space where it is to be displayed.

- If displaying the sculpture on a table, it is best to select a sturdy table that can bear more than the weight of the display. *One* raw block, before being sculpted, weighs 300 pounds. A carved sculpture generally weighs between 150 and 200 pounds. The table should be able to support at least one large adult for every sculpture in the display. Climb up onto the table to test its strength. Use milk crates or commercial dish-racks under the table for extra support, if needed.

- Select a table that is well balanced and supported by four straight or locking legs. *Never use pedestal tables to display ice sculptures.* Check to ensure that the tabletop is level.

- Select a location for the table away from both cold and warm drafts, but close to electrical outlets if needed.

- Don't display ice in high-traffic areas like dance floors, or on end tables of a buffet. Sculptures should be placed on tables that won't likely be bumped.

- Don't display ice where children have access. Ice sculptures tend to attract the curious.

- Make sure that the sculpture is set up properly for drainage. Water build-up can lead to accidental slips by staff or guests, or to damaged floors and floor coverings.

- Once the sculpture has been securely set on the table and arranged for display, it should not be moved except in emergency situations. It could tip, and water could make the floor slippery.

Proper Drainage

Sculptors must always create a proper system of water retention using a remote reservoir. Failure to allow water to drain away from the base of the sculpture will weaken the base over time and possibly cause the display to fall. The following suggestions are proven methods for draining an ice sculpture:

- Select a sturdy display vessel that is big enough to hold the ice sculpture and its melt-off.

- Drainage holes in the bottom of the display tray are preferred over holes in the side; however, the tray will have to be elevated slightly off the table.

- Securely attach the drainage hose to the hole in the display tray. Most permanent trays should have a removable hose.

- Clothe and skirt the table first to hide the drainage bucket underneath. Set the tray in the center of the table. If wrapping the ice tray with linen, *do not allow linen to drape into the ice display tray.* Linen will act as a wick and absorb water from the display, causing unwanted moisture on the table and a potential hazard.

- Always attach the drain hose securely to the drainage bucket to prevent leaks. Sculptors often use duct tape for this purpose. A 5–10 gallon bucket should be sufficient for most displays.

- Place a paper towel or cloth in the tray, directly under the ice sculpture, to prevent it from sliding around in the tray while it melts.

- Pack cubed or crushed ice or snow tightly around the base of the sculpture. This will help lock the sculpture in place and function as a filter to keep foodstuffs from clogging the hose.

- The larger the diameter of drain hose, the less likely it will become clogged.

Melting Variables

Ice that will be on display in temperatures above freezing will melt. The rate at which it melts, and also vaporizes, varies depending on several contributing factors:

- **Ice Dimensions**—The mass of the sculpture will directly affect its rate of melting. Larger, thicker sculptures melt less rapidly than slender designs.
- **Direct Heat**—Direct contact with a source as subtle as the human hand, or as intense as a branding iron or blowtorch will melt ice rapidly.
- **Indirect Heat**—Indirect contact with a source nearby, either as slight as that given off by bodies or heat ducts, or as intense as that emitted by sterno, can also increase the melting rate of sculptures.
- **Sunlight**—The ultraviolet rays of the sun work to melt a sculpture from the inside out, referred to as the "greenhouse effect," over extended exposure.
- **Artificial Light**—Spotlights using incandescent bulbs emit heat. Direct light excessively softens the ice and can turn clear ice opaque. The use of cold light, such as fluorescent or **LED**, is best.
- **Air Currents**—Moving air, particularly if it is warm, can cause a sculpture to melt more rapidly. Sculptures should not be exposed to drafts, warm or cold.

DISPLAY TRAYS AND CARTS

All sculptures need to be exhibited at some point. As mentioned previously in this chapter, of greatest importance are the safety of the viewing audience and the stability of the table array (also see Chapter 4). The sculptor has a wide variety of choices available to use as containers in which to display ice. At one extreme is an aluminum "square head," used by the military as a large roasting pan. At the other are ornate, polished silver display trays with filigree designs. One extreme is utilitarian, the other ostentatious. Both should be sturdy and functional.

Between those ends of the pan spectrum is a selection of disposable or permanent, light-free or illuminated, trays commercially available for ice display. Additionally, the sculptor can construct a custom cart that serves as both a transport device and display vessel.

The following represent a few of the vehicles commonly used for ice display.

Commercially Available Permanent Display Trays

There are a variety of commercially available display trays designed for reuse. Advantages include durability and appearance, as well as adaptability to incorporate lighting into the sculpture. They include *non-lighted, lighted*, and *rotating display trays.*

Non-Lighted Trays

Non-lighted trays were the first to be used in displaying ice sculptures. In the early days, ice was only for the most elegant events and only available for those who could afford the services of a skilled carver. Such sculptures required serviceware befitting their importance—they graced the tables of the wealthy in copper and silver display vessels. Newer permanent display trays use polished stainless steel to reflect modern times. None of these trays uses light directly, but some are mirrored to help reflect the light.

Lighted Trays

Lighted trays (also known as glow boxes) are an effective means to accent an ice sculpture, illuminating both the sculpture and the table presentation around the ice. The light source is often contained in a separate box located beneath the transparent plastic tray that holds the ice sculpture, providing *through lighting*. As with other display trays, the water drains to a reservoir in the base or through the box to another exterior bucket connected by a drainage tube. These display trays can be large or small. Larger display units are for full-block sculptures that would typically be displayed as part of a buffet. They are plugged in, with AC current powering the light. Smaller units are typically for half-block to one-third–block sculptures, and are generally used as centerpieces on individual dining tables. Battery powered lights, often hidden in the tray's base, illuminate these smaller display units.

There are several reputable companies that manufacture these types of display trays. Most of the newer tray systems use acrylics and other hard plastics in their construction, while some incorporate attractive wooden frames, metal, and even cloth slipcovers with their base boxes.

Rotating Display Trays

Rotating display trays bring an additional element of movement and theatrics, beyond colored lighting, to ice sculptures. These large, six- or eight-sided, mirrored display bases are often cumbersome but are worth the hassle for the impression they create. Slow rotation allows the guest to view all sides of the sculpture without having to walk around the display. The outside of the display unit is covered with acrylic mirrors that reflect the current surroundings. However, these plastic parts tend to chip, crack, and fall off of the base.

Figure 10-8. Through-lit sculpture on a rotating display tray

Commercially Available Disposable Display Trays

Even though permanent display trays are nice to use, a considerable disadvantage lies in their initial cost and the need to retrieve them from the location where the ice was on display. This need for recovering the tray has given rise to a market for disposable trays.

Disposable plastic trays today can even come complete with drain lines. This is a real benefit to the professional sculptor who sells her product on either a "pick-up" or "drop-off" basis. Having to return after a party has concluded is time consuming, and therefore costly, for the sculptor.

Ideally, the sculptor should find a way to use permanent display trays as often as possible. Sometimes that isn't an option. For these times, the disposable tray is a workable solution.

Display Carts

Display carts are a practical way to have an ice display ready for set-up, but still in the freezer for storage. When needed, any staff member can roll the preset sculpture out of the freezer and into the banquet hall. These carts have the same dimensions as a banquet table and white laminate tops, and

Figure 10-9. Custom-built lighted display cart being skirted

Figure 10-10. Ice vase with floral display

so they can blend into a row of tables easily, particularly if the tables and cart have been skirted. If desired, the cart and sculpture can be illuminated from within.

ENHANCING THE DISPLAY WITH GARNITURES

When arranging table displays that include ice sculptures as either functional vessels or for decoration, consideration should be given as to how to present the ice at its best. We believe that most of the time sculptures are best displayed with no exterior garnitures. That is to say, ice well shaped is its own decoration. It needs no help to be attractive or elegant.

However, there are times that ice is presented in concert with other items, generally for a specific purpose. Sufficient forethought should be given to ensure that the ice is presented well.

Floral and Greens

The use of floral arrangements has always been associated with ice sculptures. Vases are one of the most commonly sculpted pieces, and most students start their sculpting lessons making them.

When marrying these two decorative elements, the sculptor must consider the size of the arrangement that will be displayed in the ice. For practical reasons, it is best to obtain a sample of the flower base that will be used by the florist. It is easier to have a properly sized depression cut into the sculpture from the beginning than to have to adjust the sculpture on location during set-up.

Using flowers introduces theme colors into the otherwise colorless ice sculpture. The use of greens also adds a nice touch of soft color to ice displays. They are commonly placed around the base of the sculpture for their color contrast, and they also work well as camouflage when needed to hide the ice display tray.

Linens and Other Man-Made Objects

Sculptures can be dressed in linens, clothes, beads, top hats, and canes to create a campy appearance. The best advice is to never use porous materials with ice. However, if the event is best served by this indulgence, then the choice of material and its color should be carefully considered. As the sculpture melts, porous material will absorb the sculpture's melt-off. Dark colors will hide the water stains better than light colors, and thin fabrics have less capacity to absorb than bulkier fabrics. Mylar and other water-repellent cloth materials are best to use with ice.

Although a single rose, a string of colored beads, or a plate of food can look stylish with ice, the authors generally prefer to use as few of these accoutrements as possible, instead allowing the ice to be the focal point.

ARTIST PROFILE

Meet the Artist—Bruno Haenggi

Bruno Haenggi is a highly skilled pastry chef from Interlaken, Switzerland. In addition to the figurines of marzipan and chocolate that he sculpts for his customers, Chef Haenggi creates a variety of ice sculptures for the Ice Palace, one of the world famous attractions located on the Jungfraujoch–Top of Europe. Chef Haenggi discovered his love of ice in Asia while on an extensive trip across three continents. Since then, he has traveled to various points around the world to hone his skills in ice sculpture.

Ask the Artist

Q   What do you consider the most difficult aspect of your work?

A   *I think the most difficult part is determining the correct assessment of the proportions of my sculptures. For example, my sculptures in the Ice Palace are on display for extended periods of time; it is vital that they melt evenly, so the sculpture remains in proper proportion as it melts.*

Q   Do you set any limits to your work?

A   *No. I don't believe artists should set limits for themselves. Although it's not always possible to replicate natural figures exactly, I do think that we can do pretty much what we put our minds to. It's all a matter of creative thinking and proper planning.*

IV

Advanced Skills
With Ice

Custom Design Techniques and Special Event Sculpting

OBJECTIVES

After reading this chapter, you will be able to:

- Discuss the design process
- Explain how the artistic process affects the final design
- Discuss the myth of originality
- Define symbolism
- Identify characteristics of the techno-artist
- Define special-event sculpting and discuss related design ideas
- Identify several types of functional ice displays and their purposes
- Explain how transparent ice displays are made
- Discuss the pros and cons of colored ice
- Describe the Maxfield Color Method
- Describe how to make snow-filled ice sculptures
- Discuss other means for special effects with ice

Key Terms and Concepts

artistic process	vectorized	reverse snow fill technique
marcottage	logo	snow-filled design
symbolism	ice luge	Maxfield Color Method
myth of originality	shooter-block	
techno-artist	transparent display	

This chapter is a peculiar combination of questions and answers. Its focus is the custom design and creation of ice sculptures for special events. The first part of the chapter discusses the importance of the design process and examines the need for original or adapted works. Next, the chapter suggests some opportunities available in sculpting for special events and in creating functional ice sculptures.

The balance of this chapter provides information on several advanced techniques used in sculpting. They are proven methods for obtaining positive results with ice, and they will assist the sculptor in achieving customer satisfaction.

THE DESIGN PROCESS

The act of designing a sculpture is perhaps one of the most important aspects of the sculpting process. The sculptor evaluates many variables, including time, money, transportation, display environment, and purpose. But beyond that, the artist wants to advance his craft with the medium. He wishes to use this opportunity to gain yet another skill and try another method. And he wishes to grow as an artist.

Taking the time to design and create a high quality, original template cannot be stressed enough. An original design is the foundation on which the entire display will be built.

The artist must understand that the finished sculpture will not necessarily match his template, even if both the template and the execution were flawless. Haphazard or quickly created templates can lead to imperfections in the design that may not or cannot be corrected during the sculpting process.

Unlike the culinary arts, which can appeal to all five senses, sculptures appeal to only sight and touch. Often they cannot even be touched. The other senses are conveyed visually in the form of a suggestion. When a sculpture can stir an emotion it allows the viewers to personalize their experience internally.

They have not touched the sculpture, the sculpture has touched them.

The Artistic Process

The **artistic process** is a mental and physical journey that the artist takes to create his final sculpture design. The sculptor works and reworks his ideas by doing sketches until he feels that the image expresses the intended concept.

At the height of his career, many regarded Auguste Rodin as the greatest sculptor since Michelangelo. He is a perfect example of an artist who labored through the artistic process to achieve his masterpiece, *The Gates of Hell*.

Rodin used a method known as **marcottage** to create many of his more complicated sculptures. He would layer sculpture upon modular sculpture during the assembly process to achieve his total design. This technique of building a larger work by using fragments intrigued Rodin.

Inspired by Dante's *Divine Comedy* and Baudelaire's *Les Fleurs du Mal*, *The Gates* is an arrangement of hundreds of independent pieces modeled in high relief and in-the-round. Among the most popular and well-known pieces is *The Thinker*. The sculpture was designed to be the lintel (the top piece of a doorway) of an entrance portal for a never-realized Parisian museum of decorative arts, to peer over the desperate figures below like Dante dwelling over the lost souls in the *Inferno*. It has groupings that all relate to each other. *The Kiss*, also designed as part of *The Gates of Hell*, has similarities to *The Thinker*. The powerful bodies of each figure, placed on a rough unfinished mass, show the contrast of textures: skin like softness against the hard rock. Atop *The Gates of Hell* are three human figures representing *The Three Shades*, a variation of Rodin's *Adam*. Each figure is similar, but each was changed slightly by altering the positions and angles of the limbs.

Modern ice sculptors can apply the same technique. It is not necessary to reinvent the wheel every time a new piece is designed. A different twist may be added to an existing sculpture, thereby creating new and different designs.

Aiding in the Artistic Process

Sculptors typically have strong beliefs about design and approaching the process of design. The following is a short list of our design suggestions. The intent is to provide a list that illustrates methods of design and of altering already existing designs that can stimulate the artistic process.

- Even when creating a totally unique figure, whether man or beast, the sculptor should always keep muscular contortions close to reality in order for the creation to be somewhat believable.

- Ideas are manifestations derived from one's own experiences. By gaining exposure to many different types of art, the artist will increase the bank of ideas from which to draw.

- When designing a sculpture, the artist should try to capture the strength, balance, and movement of the subject. Make it natural and graceful, never with over-exaggerated features.

- Fuse lines, or unnatural seams in the design, will detract from the sculpture. The practice of natural peg fusing should be used to make the lines less obvious.

- Changing the angle of the design may provide a sense of movement or give a different perspective. The greater the difference in angle, the more impact the changes will have on the design.

- Taking the block apart and fusing it back together, like using a wider wingspan, will help expand beyond the static block figure.

- The addition of accessories related to the sculpture, including weapons, tools, or even clothing, can be used to make the design more interesting.

Several years ago, Dan Hugelier and Ted Wakar collaborated on the design of a sculpture that they planned to make for a competition. They spent several meetings considering the nature of their sculpture—its mass, primary lines, practicality—but certainly its message. Their goal was to present a piece that would not only demonstrate their sculpting prowess, but appeal to the viewer. The artistic process of planning the conceptual design paid off, as they were awarded the "People's Choice Award" and "Carver's Choice Award." (See Figure 11-1.)

THE MYTH OF ORIGINALITY

Realism is only one approach for expressing an idea in a sculpture. Artistic liberties can be taken with the subject matter to add originality. Originality is defined as creating something that is not currently in existence and that is significantly unique. Since the human mind has been conjuring up visions since the dawn of time, creating something that is strikingly new and significantly unique has become somewhat more difficult.

Figure 11-1. Dan Hugelier and Ted Wakar's award-winning design, *Aurora*

However, as the world has evolved so has human imagination, creating new ideas to satisfy new demands. Even with the continually expanding catalog of pre-existing concepts, the yet unrealized volume of untapped dreams is as infinite as the universe. It is our belief that original works can be as simple as a variation on or a blending of existing ideas, designs, or styles. Variations can be made by changing texture, positioning, size, or even proportion, as is often the case in fantasy style art.

Symbolism

Symbolism is a means of suggesting an ideal or concept. The artist can use the medium of ice to communicate a message or express a belief, in addition to providing beauty through sculpture.

A good example of the use of symbolism in art is The Great Seal of the United States, often mistaken for the Presidential Seal. It was carefully designed by the Founding Fathers to symbolize the United States. The constellation of thirteen stars over the eagle's head, thirteen olives and leaves in the right talon, a bundle of thirteen arrows in the left talon, and the thirteen vertical bars on the shield all refer to the thirteen original colonies. *E Pluribus Unum*—"out of many, one"—also refers to the thirteen colonies united into one nation.

The olive branch symbolizes peace, and is placed in the eagle's stronger right talon to emphasize its importance, with the eagle's head turned towards the olive branch. The bundle of arrows symbolizes the power of war; unity in arms is symbolized by the unbreakable nature of multiple arrows in alignment. The eagle looks away from the arrows—it is not looking for war. The shield symbolizes power and unity. The colors of the shield have their own symbolism: white signifies purity and innocence; red signifies hardiness and valor; and blue signifies vigilance, perseverance, and justice. The eagle itself is used because of its long life, great strength, majestic looks, and because it was believed to exist only on this continent.

Artistic Design Influences

For many years, the authors' pursuit of new sources of design has led them to investigate a diverse variety of art forms not usually considered when designing ice sculptures. The following examples serve to illustrate the variety of influences and resources available to the sculptor—there are many, many more.

- **Classical**—Flowing robes, Rubenesque figures, idealized figures, and heavily religious themes.
- **Tattoo Art**—Includes bold line artwork, Celtic patterns, characters, and bio-mechanical art. (*Bio-mechanical art*, a term coined by H. R. Giger, is a sometimes erotic style of art which blends the living with the mechanical, illustrating how we are all machines inside.)
- **Fantasy Art**—Artists such as Boris Vallejo, Frank Frazetta, and Julie Bell are all individuals whose works emulate and romanticize both human and animal forms, sometimes splicing man with beast to create a dreamlike scene. These artists' paintings are frequently used as an idea source for many competitors.

The Techno-Artist

Techno-artist is an expression used for artists who use computerized machinery to create their art. We are sometimes called techno-artists because we use computerized sculpting equipment. However, the use of technology and computers as an asset in designing our work far preceded our present use of machine tools for sculpting. The use of CAD programs as a means of creating, manipulating, and resizing drawings has provided us, along with many other ice sculptors, a better way to create and catalog our work for future use.

The proper use of the Internet can also speed up research and design. Search engines offer millions of photos searchable by subject. Clip art programs, with their enormous volume of ideas, are an excellent resource for designs. We recommend choosing a clip art program that will display and print designs in a **vectorized** format. The number of clip art Web sites is growing. Many of these sites require paid membership, but there are still some free art sites available.

Corporate logo artwork can usually be obtained by merely holding the mouse over the logo and then right-clicking. An option menu, which should include Copy, will appear, allowing the sculptor to save the artwork to most art software programs. Surfing the sites of ice sculpture companies is another way to see new designs that have already been tried.

SPECIAL-EVENT SCULPTING

Special-event sculpting can be described as "sculpting with purpose." There is a specific theme that the sculptor is trying to capture, and the design reflects how the sculptor interprets that theme. Sculptors generally enjoy the challenge of special-event sculpting, as it often provides an opportunity for artistic growth and creativity by having to design and create custom works outside of their normal production. The following list reflects the most common types of special events. However, it is by no means exhaustive.

Competitions

Competitions are a great opportunity if the sculptor is willing and watchful. There are competitive events at both the student and professional level. The goal of these events is to provide the entrants with an opportunity to learn while testing their prowess against their peers. The events also serve to promote the industry by creating a means for the general public to witness the skill of the sculptors as they carve. Chapter 12, "Ice Sculpting Organizations, Competitions, and Festivals," discusses, in detail, the nature of these events and how to plan and prepare for a competition.

Holiday Ideas

When it comes to designing and creating sculptures for the holidays (particularly during the month of December) it is best to generalize rather than refer to specific traditions or religions. "Happy Holidays" is often more politically correct for a December office party than "Merry Christmas" or "Happy Hanukkah."

When a sculpture is requested for a specific holiday, it requires the sculptor to become familiar with the significance of the holiday. Research on the Internet will help explain nearly everything the sculptor needs to know about the traditions and any religious meaning associated with the event. Greeting cards are another resource—cards tend to be succinct and are often visual, providing the sculptor with practical ideas for sculpting.

Wedding Ideas

Although the traditionally romantic sculptures of lovebirds, hearts, and a brace of swans (due to their monogamous characteristics) are still in demand, more personalized themes have gained in popularity. Modern brides and grooms are choosing themes that are representative of who they are, as opposed to generalized wedding themes. Customizing a sculpture to express the client's interests adds to the allure of an event.

Another approach is to use traditional wedding design elements in a nontraditional manner. Event planners and caterers often seek to provide innovative presentations that use familiar elements. The Wedding Cake sculpture depicted in Figure 11-2 was created by Ice Sculptures, Ltd. to use at weddings. Although the cake's shape is familiar, its composition from ice is unusual.

Figure 11-2. Cake sculpture on display

Logos and Corporate Events

The corporate use of ice sculptures has recently gained widespread popularity. Whether promoting a product or creating logo recognition, ice is a successful medium to add a sense of sophistication for companies worldwide. Banners and other print media are commonplace and are rarely received with the sense of wonder generated by a company logo that has been created out of ice.

However, the sculptor has a heightened responsibility when sculpting corporate logos. Since the logo design represents a company and provides name recognition for its product, a poorly reproduced ice logo will have a negative effect. For this reason, special care in producing a quality reproduction of a logo is of the utmost importance. Future business with that company, plus the opportunity for a positive referral, is dependent on quality craftsmanship. If available to the sculptor, creating a logo sculpture using a CNC router may be the best way to retain a good client.

Figure 11-3. Logo sculpture

Companies tend to be more service- and quality-oriented, and less pricesensitive. They want to be able to depend on the sculptor to provide the services as contracted, and with as little complication as possible. The aim of the professional business-sculptor is to demonstrate a sense of leadership and confidence in his ability when meeting with the client, and to meet the expectations of the client by delivering the product on time and within budget.

FUNCTIONAL ICE DISPLAYS: THE "ART" OF ENTERTAINMENT

As the popularity of ice sculptures grows, so does their function. In some cases, having an ice sculpture for pure visual enjoyment—one that "just looks pretty"—is not enough. An ice sculpture that also serves a practical purpose creates a certain amount of interaction between the guests and the sculpture. A functional display is appreciated as much for its usefulness as its entertainment value.

As with all ice, functional displays also melt. Consideration and forethought need to be given as to what the ice vessel will rest upon, and how the melted water will be contained without damage to the table and other decorations. Also, thought should be given to the nature of the products being displayed on the sculpture. Serving punch, for example, from a clear plastic liner within the ice bowl will help to slow the melting of the ice. Cocktail sauce eventually bleeds through ice, but using a lettuce cup to hold the sauce looks attractive and prevents discoloration of the sculpture.

Figure 11-4. Ice tray used as a serving dish for fresh fruit

Figure 11-5. Functional ice clam shell

Figure 11-6. Serving bowl

Figure 11-7. Ice bar

Ice Trays

Ice trays serve two purposes. One is to display food in an attractive yet practical manner, and the second is to help chill the food. Ice trays can be designed as flat containers or as multi-tiered salvers. When creating a multi-leveled tray, it is important to design one that offers ample space for and easy access to the food but is also stable enough to withstand the interaction with the guests.

Ice trays can also have depressions designed into them to serve as individual serving bowls. This is a particularly attractive way to display non-leafy salads, a variety of seafood, or caviar.

Ice Boats and Clam Shells

Ice sculptures can reinforce the theme of an event or represent items in a buffet. Clamshell and iceboat sculptures help express a nautical theme while also serving a functional purpose as service pieces. Seafood salad and peel-and-eat shrimp are commonly presented in these ice-art containers.

As an example, while working in a major center for shrimp harvesting in Florida, Chef Garlough often created shrimp boats out of ice for buffets and special events. He would create a boat design, with space in the bow for cocktail sauce and a larger area in the aft for the shrimp. Pairs of long, narrow, wooden dowels were secured close to the front and rear ends of the boat and rose upwards from holes drilled into the ice. Fish netting was suspended on the dowels, finishing the appearance of a shrimp boat.

Ice Bowls

Ice bowls are another practical and attractive means to present either chilled food or beverages at an event. A clear plastic liner placed into the bowl is helpful in reducing the deterioration of the ice and dilution of the beverage. Beverages, particularly those containing alcohol, will quickly wear away the sculpture and cause pits in the ice. The liner can be removed and cleaned for later use.

Objects such as silk flowers can be placed into the sides of the bowl as it freezes, creating an added feature to the display. Silk flowers need to soak in water before they are submerged into the ice mold or block maker. Soaking reduces the bleeding of color into the ice and helps to eliminate bubble formation around the flower.

Ice Bars and Tables

Of the innovations growing in popularity, the use of ice as a full-sized bar or serving table is one of the most popular. Even though they have been constructed since the 1950s, the use of ice bars and tables has been limited until recently. These bars are generally constructed for the purpose of serving cold beverages or food, such as sushi. The displays are normally constructed from the floor up, as opposed to being set on another table, and have a dynamic effect and tremendous visual appeal due to their size and novelty.

The design can range from the simple to the ornate, depending on the client's budget and the technical skill of the ice sculptor. Many enhancements such as logos, pillars, and lighting can be added.

Successfully creating and displaying these bars, however simplistic their design, takes a great deal of experience. These cumbersome displays are not recommended for beginner or intermediate ice sculptors, unless under the constant supervision and direction of an experienced, professional sculptor.

Ice Luges

A popular sculpture that can enhance a beverage bar is an **ice luge,** also known as a **shooter-block**. An ice luge can serve as a great conversation piece, particularly on a traditional bar or when it becomes part of a larger ice bar, although it can also be displayed on its own.

The shooter-block is another example of how the evolution of ice sculptures has recently become a revolution. For years, the shooter-block was no more than a chunk of ice, tilted on an angle with one or two grooves cut into the surface. The beverage was poured into the top of the groove and would flow down the channels to the bottom of the block. Once the chilled beverage reached the bottom of the block, it would flow into either a glass or directly into someone's mouth.

From its crude beginnings, the luge has developed into a much more sophisticated beverage dispenser. Spiral tubes, through which the beverage travels, are frozen into the ice. The ice luge, being sculpted beyond a purely functional form, has gained broader acceptance. Now they are not only featured at bachelor parties, but often appear at black tie events.

Figure 11-8. Porpoise ice luge

Ice Vases

Ice vases, although not as interactive as an ice luge or bowl, still provide great beauty and interest to an event. Vases can be low and wide or tall and narrow. They can be small or large and can serve either as individual table centerpieces or as part of substantial floral displays.

TRANSPARENT DISPLAYS

There are essentially two styles of **transparent displays**. The first incorporates a plastic transparency copy of a logo or other artistic design into the center of the ice block. The second style involves inserting foreign objects such as silk flowers or dollar bills into the ice while it is being formed.

Transparency

The "transparency style" of transparent displays can be accomplished by either of two different methods. The first method is by placing a clear plastic transparency (with logo design or message) on a flattened side of an ice block. The use of a warmed aluminum sheet works well for smoothing the block. A second smoothed and leveled block or sheet of ice is quickly placed against the first, trapping the inserted transparency between the layers of ice. If the sculptor works quickly, the warmed sides of the ice will fuse the two blocks together with little or no evidence of a seam.

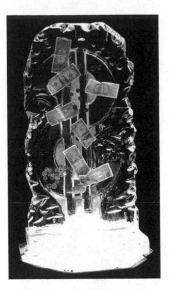

Figure 11-9. Dollars and coins encased in a transparent sculpture

The second method is by inserting the plastic transparency into the ice block as it is forming in the block maker. This is an excellent method for making a seamless transparent sculpture that requires little time or skill, but does require access to the ice block as it is forming and a few special steps.

In 1954, George Weising described a method for freezing transparent inserts in his text *Ice Carving Professionally*. Even though the first man-made plastic had been developed in 1862, polymers weren't commonly available until the late 1950s. Weising's method was to suspend painted glass panels in the metal canister ice molds while the ice formed around them. The panels were painted with waterproof paint and sealed under a coat of spar varnish. The paint took at least a week to dry sufficiently. Although there were several problems inherent with the process, the painted designs in the ice aroused curiosity among the viewers.

Objects

Objects such as flowers, toy tractors, golf balls, or playing cards can be suspended in the ice to support a theme. Items are generally positioned in the semi-frozen water during the initial stages of freezing. For the greatest effect, it is best to vary the depth and locations in which the objects are suspended. This usually requires positioning the items in the forming ice at intervals during the two to three days required for freezing the block.

Today we have silk flowers, but they weren't always available for putting into ice sculptures. Real flowers are delicate and can be difficult to work with. And extreme temperatures can affect their appearance. So, before silk flowers were used, and because plastic flowers were not very lifelike, sculptors would apply spray wax to real flowers to give them the needed strength and durability.

COLORING THE SCULPTURE

Color is often a welcome addition to a sculpture. Adding color to ice can be achieved either by coloring the light under which the sculpture is seen or by altering the natural color of the ice with dyes or color gels. We prefer to use color gels and have developed a method for using them in controlled applications.

Dye-Colored Ice

The use of dye colors in ice sculptures has both its good and bad points. The concept has been around for many decades, and it has met with some success. For example, using the colors red, white, and blue in an American flag, or green in a dragon or dinosaur sculpture, can help support and emphasize the impact.

Unfortunately, the addition of coloring agents to the process of freezing water changes the properties of the ice itself. The colorants are impurities within the water and have the same effect as other impurities on texture, melting point, and other qualities of the ice (see Chapter 2). Colored ice generally melts faster and is softer than uncolored ice—like a big Popsicle. The details of the sculpture will not be as defined as when using crystal clear ice, and they could be visually lost as a result. Colored ice also tends to stain the tablecloths around it while on display, and the sculptor during its creation.

Figure 11-10. Making colored ice

For these reasons colored ice will be more difficult to purchase, because it is not commonly used. Those sculptors who have the capacity to produce their own colored ice are more likely to try using it. However, it should be noted that the block maker will require some additional cleaning after using coloring agents.

Using Color Gels

We spent several years working on methods to incorporate color into some of our special event and custom-designed sculptures. Dissatisfied with the compromising effects of coloring agents added to water as it freezes, the team at Ice Sculptures, Ltd. created a method for coloring a logo, lettering, or portions of a sculpture. The process is now referred to as the **Maxfield Color Method**.

Prior to applying the Maxfield Color Method gels to the ice, the block must be prepared for the coloring gel. The following steps involve the **reverse snow fill technique** (see the next section on snow-filled designs), and it *requires the design to be reversed when making the template*:

- The sculptor will need to maintain a constant depth into the ice when cutting with the router. To accomplish this, the sculptor measures an inch from the tip of the desired size bit, and then wraps layers of duct tape around the bit to act as a depth guide.
- Start cutting in the middle of the area that is being hollowed out, allowing the depth guide to rest on the surface of the ice.
- Be sure to stay within the lines of the template. Keep a hand brush close to remove snow build-up.
- Once all the ice and snow is removed from the areas you intend to color, begin coloring the ice using the Maxfield Color Method.

Maxfield Color Method

The following procedural steps were developed by Derek Maxfield of Ice Sculptures, Ltd., as a means to color ice without color bleeding, shrinkage, and deterioration from the colorants. The method is considered a breakthrough for those seeking an easy and consistent means for adding color to their sculptures:

- Heat 2 quarts of water to 160° F either in the microwave or on the stove.
- Once heated, completely dissolve seven $\frac{1}{4}$ ounce (7 gram) envelopes of unflavored gelatin in the water. Allow the gelatin to soften and dissolve.
- If creating multiple colors, divide the gelatin into the appropriate number of portions.
- Depending on the color intensity you want, add one or more teaspoons of coloring agent to the gelatin. Use a non-toxic watercolor, preferably powdered tempera, which will ensure that the sculpture will be safe to use around food. (These powders can be found at art supply stores.)
- When the color mixture reaches between 65–70° F, the mixture can be applied into the ice by pouring it from a pitcher for larger surfaces, or with a squirt bottle for smaller areas. This work should be done on a level surface in the walk-in freezer, when the ice has completely set-up.

Figure 11-11. Equipment and ingredients used in the Maxfield Color Method

- Allow the color gels to freeze solid.
- Pack clean, dry snow over the color gels. Remove any excess snow, and then apply cool water to the packed snow, encasing the color mixture from behind.
- Allow the water to freeze solid before moving the ice.

If the color is poured above 70° F, the color mixture may melt the ice into which it is being applied, thereby altering the water-to-gelatin ratio. The result, upon freezing, is a frosty appearance. Additionally, if the water is too hot it might crack the ice. Start at various points within the design to spread the heating effect of the warm gels. It is best, even at 70° F, to vary the location of the warm gels as they are being applied to prevent thermo-shock. Timing is an important factor with this method, so having the *mise en place* ready is vitally important.

The gelatin suspends the color in place while it freezes. This prevents the color from separating as it freezes and prevents the color from leaking while the sculpture is displayed. Until now, the bleeding of color has been a common problem with colored ice. Additional benefits include time saved by only needing to apply one coat of colored gels, and the fact that the sculptures will be food-safe.

SNOW-FILLED GRAPHICS—FRONT AND MIRRORED DESIGNS

A **snow fill** (also known as the "front filled method") is cut into the face of the block. A **reverse snow fill** (also known as the "mirrored snow fill method") is cut on the back side of the block and is then viewed through the front, giving the *mirrored snow fill* more depth of appearance.

Snow-filled sculptures are made by cutting a line of a design or pattern as a channel, partway into the ice. A die grinder works well for this task. It is extremely important that the grooves are not cut entirely through the ice. The channel should be cleaned of debris, snow, and ice chips. The channel is then packed tightly with clean, dry snow, leaving the design line opaque white. The snow is sealed into the ice by applying a layer of very cold water over the snow pack, which eventually freezes. It is best to allow the sculpture to freeze in the horizontal position overnight to prevent run-off. A hot water bag, blowtorch, or heated aluminum can be run quickly over the area to smooth out any blemishes.

Figure 11-12. Dragster with snow-filled highlights

A reverse snow fill is made in the same manner. It is very important to keep a consistent depth throughout the design, since the design is viewed through the ice and varied depths will be noticeable. Using a depth guide will ensure a consistent appearance to the reverse snow-filled sculpture.

Using snow fill provides the sculptor with a high level of control in creating shapes, outlines, and lettering. Altering the form of a block by sculpting gives a distinct shape to the block. However, snow fill creates more defined texture and shading contrast to the sculpture, while working within the original form of the block.

Note: Sometimes when doing a reverse snow fill, sculptors will make a mixture of water and fat-free milk that is poured sparsely into the channels, creating a thin white layer. The mixture is allowed to freeze before the channel is packed tightly with clean, dry snow. This process is *not* used with front snow-filled sculptures.

SPECIAL EFFECTS WITH SCULPTURES

Enhancing a sculpture with different special effects can be achieved in a growing number of ways. In addition to the use of pyrotechnics, light, color, objects, and decorations, ice sculptures can be combined with other embellishments to attract attention. However, it is important to remember to never overshadow a sculpture with special effects.

The following are a few examples of how ingenuity can elevate a sculpture's impact on the viewing audience.

Dry Ice and Fog Machines

Dry ice and fog machines can make a dramatic impression. There is something mysterious about the wispy nature of dry ice gases and fog. Dry ice is generally used only for a temporary smoke effect. It works well, but the dry ice dissipates in minutes. Fog machines create a longer and more controlled smoke effect, but they often generate heat—so caution must be exercised with regard to their proximity to the ice.

Motorized Sculptures

Most sculptures are static in nature. They do not move without some outside force. However, with the proper use of rotating stands, motors to turn Ferris wheels, or clocks added to the face of a sculpture, motion can be infused into ice sculptures.

Animation or motion can be added to help bring the sculpture alive. The process of animating a sculpture requires a great deal of skill. If a sculpture is to have motion, where there is "ice on ice" precautions must be taken to prevent components from freezing together prior to activation. Again, this is an advanced skill that should only be attempted by experienced ice artists.

ARTIST PROFILE

Meet the Artist—Steve Brice

Steve Brice was born in Fairbanks, Alaska, where he returned in 1990 to get his first taste of sculpting ice. Steve was a stone sculptor, but found ice to be more interesting and a greater challenge. He is now a full-time sculptor. By 1996, he was heavily involved in ice competitions, traveling to various parts of the world to test his abilities in ice sculpting against some of the world's best. Steve placed first in the Olympic trials for the 1998 Winter Olympics in Nagano, Japan and for the 2002 Winter Olympics in Provo, Utah. At different world championships, Steve has had eight first-place finishes, three second-place finishes, and one third-place.

Ask the Artist

Q   What is your philosophy when it comes to creating sculptures for special events or competition?

A   *I like to push my sculptures to their limits, trying to make something that moves and amazes people. I'm satisfied when I've achieved the maximum weight on a fuse, or the perfect balance of weight, size, and motion in my designs. It's about stopping just before the "crash and burn" that happens when you've pushed the ice too far.*

Q   What do you enjoy most about the ice business?

A   *As much as I love carving, I enjoy making new tools more. To see ice carving evolve and advance is the most exciting part of what I do. There will always be a better tool and a better way to do something, especially in such a new and unexamined art form as ice carving.*

Ice Sculpting Organizations, Competitions, and Festivals

OBJECTIVES

After reading this chapter, you will be able to:

- Define and explain the concept of the "artistic eye"
- Discuss common purposes for festivals and competitions
- Identify the major groups who organize ice sculpting competitions
- Discuss the unique nature of several ice and snow sculpting competitions
- Discuss categories of competitors
- List and explain the 21 steps to successful competition
- Discuss professionalism and its role for the ice artist

Key Terms and Concepts

showpiece

artistic eye

American Culinary
Federation (ACF)

National Ice
Carving
Association
(NICA)

World Ice Sculpting
Alliance (WISA)

Competitive people who feel that a friendly contest is both healthy and rewarding view games as a means for learning and growing. In competition the competitor is judged against his peers and gains a sense of his relative skill level. However, the most lasting and beneficial rewards are the knowledge, skill, and confidence gained by planning, practicing, and executing a **showpiece** for competition and review. Medals and plaques are nice validations of one's abilities, but the true benefit lies in the experience itself.

Having competed in culinary and ice sculpting competitions, both at the student and professional level, we can attest to the benefits. The discipline and attention to detail that is paramount to success in competition carries over to daily work. We have found our own work was improved after we went through competitions. Our focus on technique and artistry, honed through years of competition, has improved our overall skill and has helped us to be successful professional chefs, ice artists, and culinary instructors.

THE ARTISTIC EYE

A common belief among food and ice artists is that participating in a competitive event forever changes one's **artistic eye**.

An individual's growth process usually includes guidance, training, and exposure to competitions and submissions by both student- and professional-level entrants. By learning about the basic rules, guidelines, and what the judges are evaluating, the student gains a sense of understanding. Repeated exposure to works of quality by competent sculptors adds to the growth experience. Simply put, learning occurs by repeated observation.

Eventually, the ice artist develops a critical eye for quality and can appreciate fine work when he sees it. Full appreciation of fine work, however, comes after also working with the medium and understanding its complexities and limitations. The *artistic eye* develops from constant practice of a critical eye and hands-on experience—and competition provides plenty of opportunity to practice both.

THE NATURE OF COMPETITIONS

Festivals of one kind or another take place throughout the year. They are often rooted in purpose by season and subject and are frequently celebrated with food and crafts. Whether it is an annual State Fair, complete with jam and jelly competition, or the festival of the autumn harvest, these gatherings provide opportunities for artistic expression and friendly rivalry. Seasonal inspiration, geographic location, ethnic and local customs, and historical significance often have an impact on the type and focus of the event.

Figure 12-1. Sculpting at a festival

Common Purposes for Organizing Competitions and Festivals

From such origins, competitions and festivals are born. People of common interest, locale, and background gather to test their prowess against their neighbors, co-workers, and rivals. These events are organized and offered for a variety of reasons and attract competitors of varying skill levels. The most common purposes for organizing competitions are:

- To celebrate a season and/or crop
- To complement or support another related activity
- As a non-profit promotion associated with a township or business area
- To highlight an art form and increase awareness of it within the general public
- To provide opportunities for artisans to hone their skills through competition
- As a for-profit promotion associated with an organization or company

Skill Levels of Participants

These events are generally organized to attract up to all three of the following skill levels of participants:

- **Professional**—Currently the highest level of competitor, usually someone who has competed at the student and/or novice levels. This category offers the greatest recognition as well as the largest prize value. Professional competitions tend to draw artists from farther away than do the novice and student categories.
- **Novice**—(neither student nor professional) This level usually is entered by those who have graduated from the student competitions, or have never attended culinary school, but have yet to compete as a professional. This is the most important stage to work with a mentor, as you do not have the benefits of having an instructor from school.
- **Student**—Either high school or college, this is typically an introduction to competition for these participants. This can be a great learning experience due to the preparation and time constraints.

It is best to compete within your appropriate skill designation, neither higher nor lower. These levels have been established out of fairness and concern for the benefit of the competitors.

Competitions exist to give ice artists opportunities to stretch the limits of their abilities. Judges willingly give of their time and expertise to help students and professionals benefit from the process. The public attends to gain insight into the profession. The competitor should be gracious and appreciative for the opportunity to learn and grow and to share in the experience with all that come forward.

ICE-COMPETITION ORGANIZERS

There are many local, national, and internationally affiliated organizations that plan winter festivals and events for their community. The following groups are the leading organizers for this sub-zero art form:

American Culinary Federation

Based in Florida, the **American Culinary Federation (ACF)** is reputed to be the oldest and largest organization of professional chefs in America. The ACF was founded in 1929 and has a membership of 25,000 members in more than 300 chapters across the United States and the Caribbean. The ACF established a standing committee, called the Culinary Competition Committee, to assist in the organization and judging of ACF-sanctioned culinary competitions.

The Culinary Competition Committee has published a *Culinary Competition Manual* that defines the rules and structure of culinary and ice-carving competitions. The ACF offers five subcategories (H 1–5) in which ice artists may compete.

National Ice Carving Association

Based in Illinois, the **National Ice Carving Association (NICA)** was the first organization in the United States devoted exclusively to the promotion of the art of ice sculpting. Consisting of more than 500 members, the organization has various categories of membership, which include Carver, Business, Associate, and Student. NICA organizes, sanctions, and judges ice-carving competitions all around North America and publishes a newsletter, *On Ice*, for its membership.

World Ice Sculpting Alliance

Established in 2001, the **World Ice Sculpting Alliance (WISA)** is among the youngest of the international professional organizations devoted to the ice-sculpting industry. WISA was founded to address the business interests of those associated with ice sculpting, equipment, and sales. (Randy Finch and Derek Maxfield, co-authors of *Ice Sculpting the Modern Way*, are founding board members.)

A SAMPLING OF FESTIVALS AND COMPETITIONS

Every year, communities and organizations work together to host ice- and snow-sculpting events. The following list, although hardly exhaustive, includes a sampling of many of the largest and longest-held events of their kind.

Colorado Ice Fest

The city of Woodland Park in Colorado is host to the annual NICA-sanctioned Colorado Ice Fest. Sculptures range in size from 300-pound single-block pieces to 2,500-pound multi-block pieces, and events are open to both individuals and teams.

Coupe du Monde de la Patisserie

Every two years, the Coupe du Monde de la Patisserie Organizing Committee invites teams of three pastry chefs and a manager from approximately twenty countries to come to Lyon, France. The event consists of two days of nine-hour live competition, with teams preparing desserts, chocolate carvings, sugar work, and ice carvings.

Fairbanks Ice Carnival and Dog Derby (AKA, World Ice Art Championship)

The Fairbanks Winter Carnival began in 1934 and has grown to become the annual Fairbanks Ice Carnival and Dog Derby, featuring both dog races and ice sculpting events. Ice Alaska, Inc. was formed in 1989 to promote artistic and educational endeavors using ice, and sponsors the annual World Ice Art Championship that attracts more than 100 international ice sculptors to its single- and multi-block competitions.

Early ice artists at the Carnival, Piestro Vigna and Ted Lambert, were famous for their complex ice sculptures of Eskimos, igloo ice thrones, bush cabins, and ice castles. The purpose of the ice thrones was to provide a background for the crowning of the Carnival King and Queen. Today, they are a focal point of the celebration.

Harbin Ice and Snow Festival (bingdeng jie)

For more then twenty years, Harbin City, the capital of the Heilongjiang province in China, has held a spectacular ice and snow festival in Zhaolin Park during the months of January and February. Many other winter sports, including sledding and skating, are available to the public as they come to use the giant ice slides. Large and small, grand and intricate, numerous ice sculptures fill the park throughout the festival. But the most spectacular sight is the city at night, when the giant ice castles and pagodas are illuminated.

Inaxi International

Held at various locations around the globe, beginning in July, the multi-week Inaxi International is the largest ice and snow festival in the world occurring during the summer months. This prestigious and elaborate demonstration, sponsored by the Dutch foodservice company of the same name, invites approximately thirty international teams of professional chefs and ice sculptors to carve individual sculptures and entire exhibitions in ice. The teams are provided with huge enclosed tents with condenser units to maintain temperatures below freezing while the teams carve and the public observes.

Internationale Kochkunst-Ausstellung (IKA)

Organized every four years by the Verband der Koche Deutschlander, the "Culinary Olympics" has been held since 1996 in German cities such as Frankfurt, Berlin, and, in recent years, Erfurt. The five-day event hosts individual, regional, and national teams from countries around the globe and attracts over 300,000 spectators. The competition features contests in hot food, cold food, and centerpiece design.

National Collegiate Ice Carving Championship (AKA, Frankenmuth)

Zehnder's of Frankenmuth, Michigan, hosts both the US Nationals Winterfun-organized State of Michigan Snow Sculpture Competition and the NICA-sanctioned National Collegiate Ice Carving Championship every year. Zehnder's invites two-person teams to compete in One Block/One Hour Individual Compulsory, One Block/Three Hour Individual Freestyle, and Three Block/Four Hour Team Freestyle events.

National Ice Carving Championship

This two-day national championship is the flagship event for the National Ice Carving Association and features one- and two-block Individual Freestyle-type competitions. To qualify for the national championship, an entrant must achieve a minimum level of points or have placed 1st, 2nd, or 3rd at a NICA-sanctioned event.

Olympic Arts Festival Ice Carving Competition

In 1988, the Canadian Olympic Committee introduced the concept of an Olympic Arts Festival in conjunction with the Calgary Winter Olympics. The new event proved so successful, the International Olympic Committee decided to include the Olympic Arts Festival in all future Olympic games. Ice-sculpting competitions have been held at every Olympics' Arts Festival ever since. Snow sculpting has also been held at every subsequent Winter Olympics except in 2002.

The Olympic Cultural Arts Council chooses a managing organization, usually from the host country, to oversee the ice-carving competition. The managing committee develops the rules, selects the international jury of judges, and invites qualified ice artisans from around the world to compete (usually at their own expense).

As of the writing of this book, the last Olympic Arts Festival Ice Carving Competition was held in February 2002 in Provo, Utah. The two-day competition was managed by NICA and invited 30 two-person teams to each sculpt ten blocks in seventeen hours. The 2006 Winter Olympic Games are scheduled for Italy, and plans are underway to hold competitions for both ice and snow sculpting.

Plymouth International Ice Spectacular

For five days every January, 400,000 pounds of block ice is transformed by high school age, collegiate, and professional ice artisans in front of 500,000 visitors in the small Michigan town of Plymouth. The event, reputed by the organizers to be the oldest and largest "ice carving only" affair in North America, attracts teams from many other countries, including Canada, Japan, Switzerland, Norway, and Russia, in addition to countless competitors from the USA.

Sapporo Snow Festival

The annual Sapporo Snow Festival was founded in 1950 in Sapporo city, the capital of Hokkaido, Japan. The weeklong event, held in early February, is considered Japan's most famous winter festival and features 300 large snow statues exhibited in three sites around the city. Over 7,500 five-ton trucks of snow are brought in from the surrounding communities to make the enormous sculptures, which are mainly the efforts of the city's Ground Self Defense Force, private organizations, and local Sapporo citizen groups. Some ice sculptures are also on display.

Figure 12-2. Derek Maxfield, Dan Hugelier, Mac Winker, and Randy Finch in front of their gold medal entry in the Team Competition at the Plymouth Ice Spectacular

United States National Snow Sculpting Competition

This annual competition is the national championship for the state winners of the U.S. National "Winterfun" competitions. Each team of three amateurs or professionals receives a cylinder-shaped mass of snow 7 feet long and 9 feet high that must be carved into a snow sculpture not to extend beyond a twelve-foot circle. Winners receive an invitation to compete at the Association International de Sculpture sur Neige et Glace.

Winterlude

The month of February is busy in the National Capital Region of Ottawa, Ontario (Canada) where Winterlude is held. Founded in 1979 by the National Capital Commission as a means of celebrating Canada's unique northern climate and culture, Winterlude attracts thousands of artists, athletes, and visitors from across Canada and around the world. It is estimated that more than 650,000 attendees take part in the three weeks of various activities. It is considered the largest winter festival of its kind in North America, with ice- and snow-sculpting competitions being part of the attraction.

WHERE TO START

Students and professionals wishing to enter competitions often debate as to where is the proper place to start their competition career. The serious contender needs to be careful with both his time and his money. Education need not cost too much money at the beginning, but time must be invested before any expectation of success can be realized. We recommend the following process to get started.

Figure 12-3. First-place entry at the NRA Team Freestyle event in Chicago, Illinois

Preparing for Competition

Many of our culinary arts students enrolled in ice sculpting classes have gone on to compete in ice sculpting at both the student and professional level. They have achieved varying degrees of success and acclaim at the local and national level. Nearly all of them started in the same manner. Their differences in achievement had more to do with their persistence and dedication to practice than their natural talent. And those who truly succeeded always prepared.

There is no substitute for preparation when competing. The following steps are presented sequentially to aid the novice competitor in evaluating where they are and where they need to be, relative to competing in ice-sculpting events.

Twenty-One Steps to Successful Competition

Competitive sculpting begins with preparation. The following steps are a guide by which a serious competitor may properly plan and practice for a competition. They are not the only means to achieve success in competition sculpting, but our experience has proven they work.

1. Get a good book to guide you through the process and serve as a reference. Read and study the information provided. If possible, take an ice sculpture

course from a competent sculptor who is also a good teacher (they are not always the same people!).

2. Get a binder to organize all of the important materials needed for practicing sculpting and entering and competing in a competition. This list of materials will include sculpting ideas and designs, to-do lists, needs lists, timed prep list, competition application, rules, and driving directions.

3. Find a mentor for direction, insight, and support. The person can be a current or former sculpting instructor, skilled chef (with ice sculpting experience), or another competitor who is both knowledgeable and generous with his time and talent.

4. Observe finished ice sculptures. Whether they are displayed on buffets, in competitions or shows, or at culinary school, looking at many different ice pieces will aid greatly in gaining perspective and understanding sculpting. (Being an assistant to a competitor is a great way to gain experience.)

5. Learn about the basics of sculpting. Understand the effect of primary lines, proportion, balance, and movement on sculptures. Work with clay models. Review books on sculpting hands, feet, and faces.

6. Learn how to use the sculptor's tools. Practice cutting, gouging, rounding, and scoring using power tools. Keep them clean, dry, and sharpened.

7. Practice making basic shapes and forms using power tools, as described in Chapter 5 of this book. All sculptures contain these shapes and forms as their foundation.

8. Learn how to make a template for sculpting. Understand the concept of scope and dimension.

9. Observe ice sculpting competitions and demonstrations. Note how the competitors have organized both their work area and their tasks. Study the rules and requirements. Observe the differences between the sculptures earning higher awards versus those gaining lower recognition. Take photographs for future reference.

10. Find an assistant who will be willing to help during practices and competitions.

11. Draw a template. Practice designs on paper before cutting into ice. Obtain a model or picture of the design, if possible.

12. Practice sculpting the piece you want to compete with in private or in an ice-sculpting class. Be self-critical, but not brutally harsh about your work. Ask your mentor for suggestions about your sculpture. Note areas for practice and improvement.

13. Take photos of each attempt to review a few days after completing the work. Look at the pictures with fresh eyes.

14. Seek opportunities to sculpt ice privately, whether for free, at cost, or for profit. Sculpting for others will help build needed confidence for sculpting in competitions.

15. Time yourself as you create a sculpture, from beginning to end. Establish a timetable for completing each segment of the work. Prepare a list of tools, equipment, clothing, and safety gear needed to sculpt off-site.

16. Adjust and refine your template based on issues that appeared during your attempts. Develop new side-view templates as needed.

17. Sculpt in public, but not in competition. Do demonstrations at festivals and other events to gain experience and confidence in sculpting in front of strangers. Master the basics.

18. Reorganize the binder paperwork to prepare for a competition. Fine-tune your step list.

19. Enter lower-level competitions. Gain experience sculpting under pressure. Improve sculpting artistry and efficiency. Gain confidence and understanding of competitions and the judging process. Learn from each experience.

20. Learn to fully utilize your assistant. Discuss the rules and steps you will follow in competition.

21. Enter higher-level competitions. Look for opportunities that test the limits of your abilities, and always seek out new challenges. Learn more by trying more. Prepare for the next competition.

These steps are a proven, methodical way to elevate your skill level from novice to master sculptor. Although competitions are not the only path to perfecting technical and artistic abilities, they serve as a useful tool. They provide a reason to focus; they are a goal with a deadline.

Sample Competition Equipment List

The following list is representative of the tools and equipment commonly used when competing. Your final list will depend on personal preference:

Chain saws

Spare and new chains

Die grinders

    Rubberizers, both grits

    Excali-bur bit

    Brice bit

    $\frac{1}{4}$" spiral 2-flute

    $\frac{1}{4}$" round rasp bit

Tools for changing chains and bits

Rotary tool with $\frac{1}{8}$" bit

2 angle grinders: 1 36-grit finishing, 1 16-grit roughing

Electric planer

Hand pruning saw

2 blowtorches with pistol ignition

Heat gun

Drill with spade bit

Ice tongs

Two-wheeled dolly, with tires slightly deflated

Hand brush

Push broom

Surge protector with splitter

Generator

Compass

Two sets of templates, for all sides

Any necessary jigs

String

Metal ruler

Bubble level

Duct tape

2 5-gallon water buckets (with water)

Small slush bucket

Hot water bags

Hot water balloons

I.V. drip bag and stand

Work table

Step ladder

Scaffolding

Canvas tarps and rope (to block the sun)

Dry ice

Gum remover

Shovel	Cooler (to store finished ice at below-freezing temperature)
Electric brush	Large display LED timer/clock
Aluminum, cut to appropriate sizes	Ice lathe
2 clothes irons	Ethafoam pads
Branding tools	Ethafoam vise
Rubber extension cords	Air compressor

Sample Timed Step List

When practicing to sculpt a piece, particularly for competition where time is restricted, it is helpful to account for the time needed for each step in the process. A *timed step list* is a useful tool for documenting how long it takes to complete a sculpture, step-by-step. While practicing, the artist can record how long each step originally took to complete. Then, if needed, the sculptor can revise the timetable and budget his time to fit the rules of the competition. The use of a timed step list during competition allows the sculptor to measure his pace against an established timeline. This will let him know whether he is moving along as planned or falling behind.

We include here a sample format a sculptor may choose to use as a model for a timed step list. It reflects the steps for the Logo sculpture in Appendix B.

Ice Sculpting

Timed Step List

Name of Sculpture: Logo

Required Tools:

Templates	Rubber extension cord
Transparency	Die grinder with $\frac{1}{4}$" end mill bit
Cool water	Heat gun
Hand brush	Blowtorch
Chain saw	Metal yardstick
Circular sander with 36-grit paper	Ethafoam
Ice pick	

Comments: Make sure that the surface area where you place the transparency is completely dry. Any water that gets between the ice and the transparency will freeze cloudy and distract from the appearance of the logo when viewing from the front.

	Steps	**Time**		
		Planned	**Actual**	**Elapsed**
1	"Z"-cut block and clean thoroughly.			
2	Apply template to both sides.			
3	Use $\frac{1}{4}$" router bit in die grinder to transfer lines.			
4	Use chain saw to transfer straight lines on both sides.			
5	Remove template with sander.			
6	Use ice pick and hand brush to clean out template paper from cut lines.			
7	Cut away the negative space around the outside silhouette.			
8	Repack all lines with clean, dry snow.			
9	Use the ice pick to carefully remove ice around inside edge of circle.			
10	Sand inside of circle to 1" depth as evenly as possible. Brush off debris in order to keep track of actual progress. Save all snow produced from sanding in a freezer for later use.			
11	Stand the ice upright and completely remove all snow debris from inside the circle.			
12	Gently melt away sander marks on the inside of the circle with heat gun.			
13	Place pre-cut transparency inside the recessed area of the circle so that the front side of the transparency is face down against the ice.			
14	Carefully pack the recessed area with clean, dry snow. Make sure the transparency does not shift position during the process.			
15	Pour cool water over the surface of the snow to glaze and seal the snow.			
16	Scrape off all excess snow, creating a level surface with the metal yardstick.			
17	Stand the sculpture upright and brush off any loose snow and ice particles, then glaze with a torch and store in a freezer.			

THE VIRTUE OF PRACTICE

The sculptor must commit energy to the process. It bears repeating that successful sculpting and competing only happen through adequate preparation and practice. Talent may be born, but perfection is only achieved by perseverance.

A famous pianist once played to a select audience of aristocrats, performing a sonata so impressively that those present could not believe his brilliance. At the end of the flawless recital, there was a moment of breathless awe, followed by a thunderous roar of approval. Stunned by the perfection of his work, the Queen of England was heard to say, "Mr. Paderewski, you are a genius!" Bowing in humble appreciation, Paderewski replied solemnly, "Before I became a genius, Your Majesty, I was a drudge."

ARTIST PROFILE

Meet the Artist—Ted Wakar

Ted Wakar earned his credentials as a Certified Executive Chef (CEC) in 2000, after working in the culinary industry for many years. Currently, Wakar is proprietor of Frozen Images, Incorporated. A respected sculpting competitor, Chef Wakar has competed in more than 70 events around the world since 1981. His greatest honor was being part of the first non-Japanese team to place 1st in the team World Championships, during the 37th Annual World Ice Sculptors Competition held in Asahikawa, Japan. His 1st place accolades have included ice showpieces at the Plymouth International Ice Sculpture Spectacular and the Fairbanks Ice Art World Championship. Ted is a certified judge for the American Culinary Federation and teaches ice sculpture classes at Schoolcraft College and Oakland Community College in Michigan.

Ask the Artist

Q   What do you think is one of the most important things a sculptor can do to prepare for a competition?

A   *Of course there are many things to do in preparation for a competition, from practicing to being well organized. But the most important thing, to me, is choosing a design. Putting effort into planning a sculpting design that will excite and challenge me is very important. If the sculptor is excited about what he or she will make, then that will motivate them to work with it until it becomes an award-winning sculpture.*

Q   Why do you participate in these ice-sculpting competitions so frequently?

A   *Every event is an opportunity for me to grow as a sculptor. My peers both challenge and inspire me. I also find pleasure in exposing the art form that I love; I am rewarded by the spectators' appreciation.*

13

The Business Side of Ice Sculpting

OBJECTIVES

After reading this chapter, you will be able to:

- Identify the responsibilities a professional sculptor must manage
- Discuss the nature and purpose of a business plan
- Describe various financial documents used in business, including budgets, break-even analysis, profit and loss statements, and balance sheets
- Discuss methods for attracting media attention and creating press kits
- Discuss the nature and purpose of service contracts and work orders
- Discuss how theme is used in creating sculpture designs
- Define functionality as it relates to ice sculptures
- Identify and discuss various practical considerations that must be made before finalizing the contract

Key Terms and Concepts

icework

professionalism

entrepreneur

risks

business plan

budget

break-even analysis

profit and loss statement (income statement)

balance sheet

press kit

work orders

suggestive selling

service contract

theme

design element

functionality

functional display

practical consideration

hassle factor

lost opportunity

cost/benefit mix

This chapter addresses some of the business-related issues affecting sculpting for profit. That said, this chapter will not tell you how to succeed in business. It merely touches on some topics relative to sales and service, customer satisfaction, and financial management that are part of good business practices. The chapter discusses some of the attitudes and tools needed to be successful in the business side of ice sculpting.

We begin by evaluating the different responsibilities a sculptor must assume when doing works for hire on a regular basis. Effort must be expended in many areas in order for the business to thrive. However, some of these areas may be new territory for the artist.

We continue by focusing on the customer's needs, and the evaluations that the sculptor must make before committing to produce the work. If a sculptor carefully considers the variables involved when planning an **icework**, a more efficient solution and a better sculpture can be expected. Both the sculptor and the customer will benefit from a thorough examination of the work being requested. There should be no surprises by either party.

The Professional Sculptor

As much as in any enterprise, the personality and philosophy of the sculptor affects the character of her business. **Professionalism** is an attitude and a way of business. It is reflected in the condition of the tools, orderliness of the work area, and demeanor of the artist. It is valued by the relationships that are established with customers and employees and evidenced in the execution of the work orders. Professionalism is everything to the sculptor, and to the customer.

In the beginning, it is typical that an individual creates works for hire as a sideline business to his or her primary employment. Not many people jump in without having at least some previous experience in making and selling ice sculptures. But at some point, a few decide to start a full-fledged business.

As with most start-up businesses, the principal owners of an ice sculpting company are involved with the three primary functions of the business: administration, sales, and production. Some of these duties include:

- **Administration**—Paying staff, paying bills, paying taxes, ordering raw products, organizing office work, computer work, ordering equipment
- **Sales**—Returning telephone calls, placing ads, meeting with customers, writing sales contracts
- **Production**—Creating designs, making sculptures, fixing tools, cleaning the studio, delivering finished sculptures

It is rare that one individual has exceptional talent in all areas. Humans generally have their likes and dislikes, their strengths and weaknesses. And an individual who has been successful in the past through above-average talent in one area may not be as successful and talented in another area of business. This has been witnessed time and again in the sports, entertainment, hospitality, and business arenas.

The professional sculptor must recognize her weaknesses and capitalize on her strengths. Each aspect of the company's business must be sufficiently addressed in order for the business to succeed. That will probably mean partnerships between people with complementary skills or hiring people to fill in the gaps.

As Artist

The professional sculptor is, first and foremost, an artist. The sculptor is drawn to the work by her creative desires. She feels a connection to the medium. So, it is important that the artistry is not forsaken by the demands of business. Compromises are part of our everyday existence, and the practical artisan should understand this point and adjust when appropriate. However, the quest for artistic expression must remain central to the company's goals for there to be joy in the work. Good art can co-exist with good business.

As Entrepreneur

To begin an enterprise of her own, the sculptor must also be an **entrepreneur,** a person with a business-like attitude. An entrepreneur is an individual who organizes a business and assumes **risks** in order to create a market for profit. Risks are the "unknowns." It is incumbent upon the savvy entrepreneur to anticipate unknowns insofar as possible and thereby reduce unnecessary risk. As Winston Churchill once said, "the price of leadership is responsibility."

The Business Plan

When starting a company, it is a good idea to formulate a **business plan**. A business plan can serve as a guideline for pertinent research, as a strategic plan for long-term goals, and as a focus for establishing short-term goals in addition to being a communication tool for investors and stakeholders.

Generally speaking, the typical business plan:

- Presents the overall vision for the business
- Sets the direction for the organization
- Communicates to stakeholders the intended sales, production, and financial growth of the company
- Discloses the organization's financial goals

Someone once said "research is cheap if you want to stay in business, expensive if you don't." A good business plan requires effort and research on the part of the owner, but the effort and research is vital to the success of the enterprise. Although there are some differences among approaches taken to prepare a business plan, the following sections are typically included in the final document:

- Company Description
- Industry Analysis
- Products and Related Services
- Target Market
- Competition
- Marketing Plan and Sales Strategy
- Operations
- Management and Organization
- Long-Term Development Plan
- Financial Data and Projections
- Supporting Documentation

Financial Management

Money is the primary language of business. Although sculptors would like to be able to focus on artistry exclusively, the art must exist within a proper business framework. This includes financial planning and controls, known as the Siamese twins of management. They are the essence of financial management.

The business-minded sculptor develops a business plan that becomes the guiding document for the company. Within the business plan, sources of expenses and revenues are identified. The sculptor must also establish a system that carefully monitors the financial activity of the company. The **budget** is one form of financial control and allows you to compare planned expenses and revenues to actual activity. It is used to set parameters for an identified period of time, such as for a single event, a month, or a year. The more detail that is included, and is therefore monitored in the budget, the closer the sculptor is to understanding the true financial health of the organization. A well-constructed budget is an important part of a sculptor's control plan.

Financial Documents

In addition to the budget, there are other financial documents that are commonly used by businesses to monitor and communicate their financial activity. Banks and investors generally require these documents to monitor their investments. However, even if there were no other investors demanding financial statements, the owner should still understand these concepts and create these documents to better understand the bigger financial picture of her business.

- **Break-Even Analysis**—A **break-even analysis** is an exercise demonstrating the relationship between costs and sales. It is a mathematical method for finding the dollar amount needed for a business to break even. Break-even analysis calculates the amount of sales and other financial activity with which the operation neither makes a profit nor incurs a loss. The exercise reveals the dollar amount of sales that must be reached above which profit can be realized, and below which losses are incurred. Mathematically, it is expressed as:

Sales Revenue – Variable Costs = Gross Profit
Gross Profit – Fixed Costs = $0.00

This exercise is beneficial to help the businesswoman determine the sales levels required to stay in business, and to plan for desired profits.

- **Income Statement (Profit and Loss Statement)**—An **income statement**, also known as a **P & L statement**, is a financial report that shows the amount of money a business has earned (net income or profit) or lost (net loss) over a given period (usually a month, a quarter, or a year). It is calculated by adding all of the revenue a business earns during a particular time period and subtracting all of the expenses incurred to earn it. One busy month may show a net profit, while a slower month may reveal a net loss. Hopefully, the company will show a net profit over the course of a fiscal year. Mathematically, it is expressed as:

Sales – Cost of Goods Sold = Gross Margin
Gross Margin – Total Operating Expenses = Net Profit or Loss

- **Statement of Financial Position (Balance Sheet)**—A **balance sheet** is a company's statement of financial position on a given day. It is the basic accounting equation (Assets = Liabilities + Owner's Equity) expressed as a formal report. The company's assets include the value of large equipment, furniture, cash on hand, accounts receivable, and inventory. Liabilities include all debts, accounts payable, and other expenses owed to creditors.

The owner's equity is the amount of financial interest an owner has in the assets of the business. In other words, what money is left after all debts would be satisfied.

As Promoter

One of the many hats a sculptor-for-hire must wear is that of promoter. An artist needs to understand the proactive nature of business. It is inherent in business to create interest in the product a company sells. The media-smart sculptor must learn to think in terms of publicity, free promotion being, of course, the best. This requires continuous effort in self-promotion and public relations. The sculptor must always be prepared for opportunities and the success that follows.

The Hook

There is always a limit to the budget anyone or any company can spend on advertising and promotion. The sculptor must seek ways of receiving free print. (This expression, of course, includes all media.) Understanding the general media and their needs, and developing a rapport with them, is a decided advantage over the competition and a boost to business. The following points are consistent with most media, anywhere:

- Media always need stories to cover. They must have something on which to report.
- Media cover a wide variety of stories, including human interest, business, education, hobbies, local people and companies, seasonal activities, and unusual jobs.
- Media like to work with flexible, quick-responding, dependable, punctual, attractive, clean, well-spoken, and affable people.
- Media like to get ideas for shows from viewers or persons seeking coverage.
- Media like press kits prepared by their guests.
- Media like to know recognized authorities (on any subject).
- Media must appear unbiased, but will report factual information.

We have used the following ideas, or hooks, successfully to attract and secure media attention:

- "Give the coolest gift you'll ever give" (A 9" × 11" heart-shaped ice sculpture with a special message etched on the surface and a rose encased in the ice, packed in a Styrofoam box for ease in distribution.)
- "What's the coolest job in the summer?" (Practically an annual feature by our local television station during extended heat waves.)
- Including brochures on all products and services that a company offers, with sculptures that are sold and packaged for delivery. (The easiest customer to attract is the repeat customer.)
- Creating Santa Claus displays, complete with reindeer and sleigh, outside the office in December.
- Sending carved pumpkins to radio disc jockeys during the Halloween season to illustrate your sculpting abilities.

- Creating large, highly photogenic displays of ice at outdoor ice and snow festivals in order to attract media on-site doing their broadcasts. These displays must have the ability to translate well on television or in print.
- Creating caricatures of local media personalities in ice, or the logo of their news station.
- Donating sculptures to help fundraising campaigns (place a transparency inside the large ice sculptures with the words: "these are the cold, hard facts").

The Press Kit

In order to make it easier for the media to feature a story about your craft and business, and to ensure accuracy in their reporting, it is best to create a **press kit** that you can give to the reporters. It can be gathered and assembled using a glossy pocket folder that has your logo and company name printed on the cover. If money is tight, attach a business card to a high quality pocket folder available in business supply stores. A *press kit* can include many things about you and your company, but the following items are standard:

- 5" × 7" color photograph of you. (It is best to have props in the picture to help tell the story.)
- 5" × 7" black and white photograph of you. (With your name, to ensure proper spelling.)
- 5" × 7" color close-up photograph of you sculpting.
- 5" × 7" black and white close-up photograph of you sculpting.
- 1–2 page biography, including information on any special achievements or awards.
- A few quotes from you that can be used in their stories.
- Fact sheet about your business, including address, Web site, range of products, and notable clients.
- Fact sheet about the industry.
- Several business cards.

CDs can also be used as press kits. When a sculptor has access to the proper computer hardware, software, and digital camera, a CD is an inexpensive way to include many color photographs, information on the sculptor and the company, and quotes that writers can use.

However, as the saying goes, "the best ad is a good product." Quality has a language of its own, and the consumer understands it.

As Office/Production Manager

Although sculptors generally feel most at home in the studio, the broader demands of business can impact the sculptor's ability to do all of the production alone. It is vital to the success of the company that the quality of the products does not suffer. Time management and the ability to allocate energy and time appropriately to the various tasks is crucial.

As the requests for sculptures and services increase, the company needs to expand its production. This growth will often necessitate hiring additional employees. The key is to hire individuals who are capable of doing work needed by the sculpting business but not necessarily requiring the skills of the primary sculptor. Proper delegation can allow the sculptor to perform those tasks that only she can do. Communication and training are key to this transition.

Work Orders

Work orders are most commonly used in larger operations, where the person selling the sculpture is not actually producing the sculpture. Work orders are an effective tool for recording and communicating specific design and production requirements and providing direction to production staff. Current software can generate printed work orders from service contracts. Or, with a little more effort and direct access to a computer, managers can generate electronic work orders that reflect up-to-the-moment specifications and other information for production staff.

As Delivery Driver

Quite often, part of the service that sculptors offer their clients is delivery and set-up of the sculpture. It is important that the driver/delivery person be dressed appropriately and courteous and respectful to the customer and surroundings. They are a representative of the sculpting business and its image.

Items should be packed in the delivery vehicle that might be needed on the job site but were not necessarily requested. These include duct tape, extra drainage hoses, assorted color gels, and extra light bulbs for display lighting.

As Sales Person

Every sale is driven by its own objectives. However, there are two objectives business-minded sculptors must establish for all sales: financial objectives and customer-satisfaction objectives. The salesperson must fairly represent the abilities of the production staff. Sculptures that cannot be made properly should not be sold. And sales that don't generate a profit should be carefully scrutinized.

That said, selling ice sculptures (like all sales positions) is an art. The salesperson has the opportunity to try **suggestive selling** and possibly expand on the items the customer was originally considering. It is up to the salesperson to teach the customer about the available products. Typically, clients such as event planners, chefs, and caterers have set budgets for their events. But most want to create something magical for their customers.

To accommodate, a smart salesperson can suggest using items like ice sorbet dishes, which could be bought with money budgeted for either china rental or food costs. They may suggest using individual table centerpieces as an alternative to more common floral displays. The point is to broaden the impact by using ice in clever ways and to get the customer thinking beyond a single display piece for a buffet.

The Service Contract

The prudent ice-artist who intends to sculpt for profit should always complete some form of a **service contract** between herself and the client. This form clearly defines and details client expectations and sculptor obligations based on evaluation of the cost/benefit mix, lost opportunity, client budget,

(Your Company Name and Address)

Service Agreement

Customer _____

Address _____

Phone: (day) _____(evening) _____Fax _____

Customer agrees to engage (your company name) to provide the following:

Ice Sculptures	Totals
1._____	$_____
2._____	$_____
3._____	$_____
Cube Ice _____ Crushed Ice _____	$_____
Dry Ice _____ Snow _____	$_____
Ice Blocks _____	$_____
Reusable Display Equipment _____	$_____ *

Optional Rental Display Equipment

Standard Glow Pan _____ Rotating Mirrored Pedestal	$_____
Rainbow Glow Fountain Glow Bubble Tubes	$_____
Fog Machine	$_____
Colored Lighting (indicate color) _____ No	$_____
Subtotal	$_____
Sales Tax	$_____
Delivery Fee	$_____
Pickup Fee	$_____
Total:	$_____

Special Provisions _____

_____

Payment Provisions

Customer agrees to pay a deposit of $ _____. The total due is $_____. The balance of $_____ must be paid in full by _____. Payment may be made by VISA, Master Card, American Express, Discover, or check payable to (Your Company Name). There will be no enforceable agreement between Customer and (Your Company Name) unless this agreement is signed and delivered with the required deposit to (Your Company Name) by_____.

Cancellations and Refunds

The delivery date, time, and location are material terms to this agreement. Any changes in the delivery date, time, or location must be agreed upon in writing signed by both parties. Customer may cancel the agreement and receive a refund of 50% of its deposit if (Your Company Name) receives written notification of Customer's cancellation at least 90 days prior to the delivery date. Thereafter, Customer is entitled to a 25% refund for cancellation notices received by (Your Company Name) between the 89th day and 45th day before the delivery date. All other cancellation notices will be ineffective, and Customer will be obliged to pay the total agreed amount. If the location of the delivery or setup area is affected by weather conditions, and (Your Company Name) determines in its discretion it is unable to safely deliver or set up the Ice Sculpture(s) due to weather conditions, (Your Company Name) will be excused from performance under this agreement; however, Customer's obligations will remain enforceable and no refunds will be given.

* This fee will be refunded if Customer returns the equipment to (Your Company Name) in its original condition.

<u>Setup and Access Provision</u>

(Your Company Name) agrees to deliver the Ice Sculpture(s) with / without Display Equipment and/or Ice Blocks, Cube Ice, Crushed Ice, Dry Ice, Snow as specified above to _____on _____, and (Your Company Name) understands that delivery and setup must be completed by_____am/pm. Customer agrees that a representative of Customer will be available on-site to direct (Your Company Name) to the setup area. For each Ice Sculpture Customer agrees to provide a display table with four locking legs with holding capacity of _____ pounds, one electrical outlet within three feet of the setup area if lighting is to be provided, and _____ long table cloth(s) to drape around the base of the display equipment (optional). Customer agrees to provide a display area that meets or exceeds the specifications listed here. If the display table and area do not meet or exceed these requirements and (Your Company Name) must make changes to the area in order to set up the Ice Sculpture(s), Customer agrees to handle and be responsible for any dispute arising with facility management or personnel because of the changes. If (Your Company Name) determines in its discretion that the display table and area do not meet the minimum requirements and no possible changes will render them suitable to setup, the lack of a suitable display area will be considered a material breach of the agreement by Customer.

Unless the agreement states otherwise, Customer shall be responsible for breaking down and disposing of the Ice Sculpture display(s), and returning the display equipment to (Your Company Name). If Customer rents the optional equipment, customer agrees to store all display equipment and make it available to (Your Company Name) by the time requested by (Your Company Name). (Your Company Name) shall / shall not pick up the equipment on _____, at _____am/pm. Customer agrees that a representative of Customer will be available on-site to permit (Your Company Name) access to pick up the equipment used in the display and setup of the Ice Sculpture(s). Customer will be billed $_____ for every _____ minutes (Your Company Name) must wait to pick up the equipment beyond the first 15 minutes.

<u>Hazard Warnings and Safety Requirements</u>

Customer acknowledges receiving and understanding (Your Company Name)'s Minimum Display and Safety Requirements information sheet. Additionally, Customer agrees to take adequate precautions to prevent electrical, mechanical, and water hazards from occurring. Customer understands and agrees that the misuse of decorations, skirting, and food or floral arrangements in or around an ice sculpture display tray may restrict or prevent the proper drainage of water, and any item placed in the display tray may cause water to be siphoned onto the display table or floor. Customer agrees to provide adequate supervision and maintenance of the sculpture display area so that no injuries or damage may result from the misuse or melting of any ice sculpture. Customer agrees to indemnify, defend, and hold (Your Company Name) harmless for any and all claims, injuries, losses, and damages arising from the use, display, and modifications of any ice sculpture display after the display is set up by (Your Company Name), and Customer agrees to be fully responsible for any consequential damage that occurs.

<u>Miscellaneous Provisions</u>

This shall be the entire agreement between these parties, and no supplement, amendment, or modification of this agreement will be binding unless it is in writing signed by both parties. This agreement shall be binding on all respective employees, officers, directors, partners, successors, assigns, subsidiaries, heirs, agents, and other representatives of the parties, as applicable. The terms, conditions, and subject matter of this agreement shall be interpreted according to the laws of the (Your State). If any portion of this agreement is invalid or unenforceable for any reason, that shall not affect the validity and enforceability of the remaining terms and conditions of this agreement. In the event there is a dispute about the terms, conditions, or subject matter of this agreement, Customer and (Your Company Name) agree to resolve that dispute in a forum located in the (Name of your County and State), and the prevailing party shall be entitled to recover from other party those reasonable costs, expenses, and attorney's fees incurred in relation to resolving the dispute.

Dated: _____   _____

                                                 Customer's Representative

Dated: _____   _____

                                                 (Your Company Name)

Figure 13-1. Service Agreement

transportation requirements, set-up needs, and any equipment to be used, among other considerations.

Figure 13-1 is an example of a partial Service Agreement that was developed by SoCal Ice Productions for sculptors to purchase as a template for their own sculpting business. Note the detail relative to payment, set-up, and other miscellaneous provisions. Also important is the Hazard Warning statement contained in the contract, emphasizing the client's obligation to maintain a safe environment for their guests. SoCal has other related products that address the client/sculptor contractual relationship.

INTERVIEWING THE CUSTOMER

Will Henry once said, "What is research but a blind date with knowledge?" Ideally, it means that one should not approach the unknown with preconceived ideas but be open to what information is presented. Research is the practice of good listening skills, among other things.

The ice artisan who wishes to stay in business can only do so by providing customers with products that meet their needs. The following topics are a few of the key elements a sculptor may wish to evaluate when working with a client.

Figure 13-2. A tropical theme

Identifying Themes

One of the first tasks is to identify and evaluate the **theme** involved. Artists and event planners always like to know if there exists a certain theme or motif to the event in which the ice will appear. Ice sculptures are usually wanted for their ability to make a strong statement or impression, so the design should complement either the theme of the event or the style of cuisine with which it is displayed, so as not to detract from the other elements.

Figure 13-2 illustrates how the catering company of My Chef, Inc., of Naperville, Illinois, uses ice sculptures to support and enhance their buffet presentations. In this case, the tropical theme of the event is complementary by the use of a snow-filled sculpture depicting a flamingo and palm tree.

Figure 13-3. Butterfly display supporting this wedding theme

Identifying Important Design Elements

Capturing both prominent and subtle **design elements** of an event is the intelligent way to match the sculpture to the event. Design elements can include patterns, colors, logos, and objects, among other things. Uniting the event's prominent elements through the sculpture is a way to satisfy the customer and create a buzz among the guests.

During the writing of this text, we created an ice display of butterflies that was featured at the wedding reception for Chef Garlough's son and daughter-in-law. The dinner event was held at the Meijer Gardens, a local botanical and sculpture garden. The bride, who has a passion for flowers and butterflies, was determined to incorporate the two design elements into their wedding and reception. The dinner tables had flowerpots as centerpieces. The wedding cake featured pulled-sugar butterflies in colors matching the bridesmaids' dresses.

As a surprise addition to the reception, we designed an array of nine variously-sized ice butterflies, some with bright hues to again support the theme and colors of the event (see the color insert for the full effect). The dynamic display of stacked, winged ice sculptures flanked the hors d'oeuvre table and greeted the guests as they entered the banquet room, making a strong impression on the guests as they arrived and creating a lasting memory for the newlyweds.

Functionality

The sculptor also needs to know the sculpture's intended **functionality**. Whether the ice is meant to hold and display food, or merely to serve as an enhancement to the event, the sculpture should be practical. The artist must have a complete understanding of the client needs, which the sculpture must fulfill.

PRACTICAL CONSIDERATIONS IN EVALUATING POTENTIAL BUSINESS

Once the intended form and function of a sculpture have been established, the ice artist must also consider the practicality of the piece. From a business point of view, the sculptor must evaluate several practical considerations before signing a contract to complete the work. The following are some of the more significant considerations.

Cost/Benefit Mix

It is most important, before any other activity, to consider the **cost/benefit mix** when contemplating work for hire. In business, the owner must evaluate the assignment of assets. These assets will include equipment and facilities, cash, staff (labor), and supplies on hand. Each has value, each is expendable, and each is finite. The ultimate goal of management is to invest these assets where there is likely to be the greatest return on the investment.

However, most businesses are cyclical, and there are different variables to consider throughout the year. What is worthwhile one day might not be on another day. This is cost/benefit at play. The business-minded sculptor must evaluate the losses and gains of each job offer. Will the time and talent invested by the sculptor, plus equipment and supplies expended, be compensated appropriately, given the other variables affecting this decision?

Experience, and a practical understanding of Profit and Loss Statements, clarifies the answer. Often work is done because it is profitable beyond all costs, and its value is an overall profit to the company. And sometimes work is accepted, not because it is profitable beyond costs, but because it helps with cash flow, making payroll and promoting the business.

Lost Opportunity

Another consideration related to cost/benefit is the concept of **lost opportunity**. The business-minded sculptor, as mentioned before, has a finite amount of time and labor to expend. Agreeing to take on sculptures of little financial, public relations, or promotional value may make some sense when nothing else is scheduled. However, should a more profitable opportunity arise that cannot be realized because of prior commitments, then the sculptor experiences lost opportunity. Unfortunately, there is no crystal ball for such decisions, but experience is a good teacher.

Budget and Pricing

Knowing a client's budget constraints will help the sculptor to focus appropriately on the design aspect of the job. Creating designs beyond the client's budget will ultimately cost the sculptor in wasted time. Creating a design below the client's budget will likely cost the sculptor additional profits. A set budget, or range of budget for the work, must be established at the beginning of the discussion.

A business-oriented sculptor must also establish his desired pay rate per hour, the length of time required for sculpting a piece, the cost of consumable supplies, and the profit percentage applied to costs. The sculptor then considers all costs, including labor and supplies, plus the desired profit to establish the asking price for the sculpture.

Should the client wish to discuss or debate the asking price with the sculptor, the cost/benefit consideration comes into affect.

Transportation

Sculptures must be designed for portability. That is to say, the sculpture has to survive the trip in acceptable display condition to be of value to the customer and, ultimately, the sculptor. Depending on the distance between where the finished sculpture is stored and where it will be displayed, the sculptor must make some design decisions. One important consideration may be to assemble and finish the sculpture on site.

Sometimes, it may be necessary to make certain artistic concessions in order for the ice works to be structurally sound enough to transport. The safe arrival of the piece is vital to a successful business relationship with the customer.

Set-Up

From a business point of view, the transportation, set-up, and tearing-down of the sculpture must also be considered in the selling price. We consider these as "add-on services" and price them in addition to the base price of a sculpture. Depending on the size and complexity of the sculpture, the customer doesn't always need this service. Yet, sometimes, extraordinary services are needed. We have flown with sculptures to remote locations and have driven truckloads of them across the country. The nature of the service provided, and final price, will vary with the function's requirements.

We have an expression for service requests that go beyond the basic service and products generally offered. We call this type of added request, the **hassle factor**. (Our rates for catering at My Chef, Inc., and for creating ice pieces at Ice Sculptures, Ltd., are often affected by the hassle factor.) We take pride in our customer service and strive to build positive relationships with all of our clients through competitive pricing, high quality products, and attentive service, yet we must ask for appropriate compensation for those services that exceed the norm. The hassle factor rate is applied to those events.

Equipment Required

The attentive sculptor evaluates the equipment that is required to complete, transport, and exhibit a sculpture. It is important to design within one's means. Sometimes the sculptor needs to rent or purchase additional equipment to support a job order. Generally, rentals or purchases are considered "pass through expenses" and they are merely added onto the bill with little or no mark-up. Research into these costs in advance of quoting a price is paramount to preventing unforeseen losses.

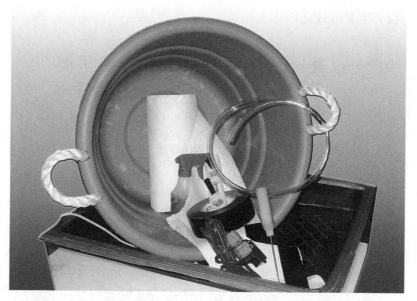

Figure 13-4. Setup equipment

PROFESSIONALISM: A REQUIREMENT AT ALL LEVELS

In addition to all of the practice an aspiring sculptor needs to learn the skills required to be considered a talented artisan, there remains an equally important virtue. It has been said that artistic temperament is a disease that afflicts the amateur. One can be a great artist but lack the substance to be a true professional.

It would be negligent of us to omit the context in which the knowledge required to become an ice artisan ought to be obtained. Knowledge is a gift to be appreciated and shared. It is acquired through study and experience, by watching and listening, in small doses and in large bundles. However, it only comes when the student is ready, and the professional appears.

The student sculptor must strive to behave professionally at all times, with all people, under all circumstances. Criticism is often difficult to accept when a sculptor has labored long and hard on a project, investing emotion and love for the art. But it is during these times of anxiety when passion must yield to professionalism. It is incumbent upon a would-be professional ice artist, and those who call themselves professionals, to solicit input and express appreciation for any interest taken in their work. This includes contact with members of the public, the media, judges, and other ice artisans. After all, art is not only for the artists.

Ice sculpting is a quest for the professional, at all levels.

ARTIST PROFILE

Meet the Artists—Randy Finch and Derek Maxfield

Ice Sculptures, Ltd. began in 1994 when co-founders Randy Finch and Derek Maxfield pooled their resources to start a business. The company's modest holdings began with one Clinebell ice-block maker and a 10' × 10' walk-in freezer, located in a converted warehouse. Prior to formalizing their business, they each sold sculptures on the side while working full-time as chefs. The company is known for taking a different approach to ice sculpting and the ice sculpting business. Central to the goal of the company is to improve the standards of sculptures, and the sculpting industry, by being actively involved in education and the advancement of sculpting technology. Their company and professional philosophy requires that they keep an open mind to new ideas and share ideas with others interested in the art of ice sculpture.

Ask the Artist

Q How should the approach differ from selling sculptures as a sideline business, versus working as a full-time ice artisan?

A *It shouldn't! Unfortunately for the sculpture industry, part-time sculptors are underpricing their works. They often are employed full-time somewhere else where they receive medical benefits, sufficient pay, and often the use of the company's tools and facilities. These costs are not initially considered when pricing their sculptures. Later, when the individual leaves their full-time job in pursuit of a career as a sculptor, they have difficulty adjusting their established rates to the necessary level of compensation for their work.*

Q How have you been able to stay in business this long? What is your secret to profitability?

A *Our company's desire to establish Ice Sculptures, Ltd. products as a "brand name" for sculpted ice has driven us to create a niche market within the greater niche market of selling ice sculptures. We have increased our sales by crossing over into other budget categories, by educating the public as to what qualities to look for in a sculpture, and by designing sculptures around our clients' individual needs, as opposed to our own existing repertoire. The use of technology has allowed us to create products that are unique and to offer hybrids of traditional sculptures.*

APPENDICES

Prelude to Appendices A, B, and C

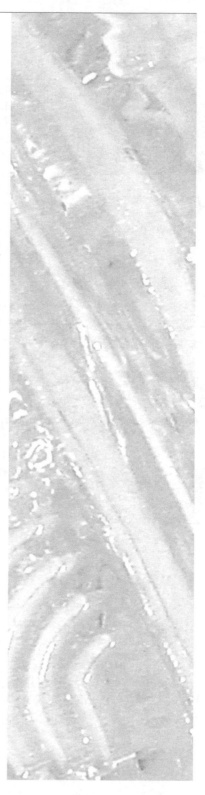

Before Sculpting

The following is a stepped-out, methodical approach to completing the 18 sculptures included in Appendices A, B, and C. We have organized these procedures to lead you through the steps of creating a sculpture without "getting lost" during the process. These steps are based on our experience and have been proven effective for both students and professionals. However, the processes outlined here are not the only possibilities; students are encouraged to find their own best process.

The following designs were chosen for their practicality and marketability. Another advantage of these pieces is that they can easily be enhanced or altered by adding additional detail in order to conform to the reader's style. All the sculptures presented here have been commissioned works, produced and sculpted by Ice Sculptures, Ltd.

Snow is used extensively in these designs as a way to add contrast. Sculptures incorporating snow also tend to hold their original appearance and detail longer during the melting process. It is best to use clean, dry snow, stored in a freezer immediately after collection.

Snow can be created from cutting ice with a power tool; in most cases, enough is produced during the normal process of sculpting. However, it may be necessary to cut scrap ice specifically to create extra snow for packing.

Note: The proportions of some sculptures depicted in these photos have been altered slightly to create a better visual description for the reader.

Tips

Keep the following tips in mind while producing each sculpture:

- Trace all of your sub templates from your main template before beginning to sculpt.

- Make sure the bottom of your ice block is flat and level. If necessary, trim the base until the block is level before you begin.
- When making reference cuts, allow the chain saw to penetrate the ice deep enough so that these reference cuts will remain visible even after the front silhouette is cut away. Be careful that these cuts are not too deep in areas that will not be removed. Make sure all of your cuts stay in the negative space.
- Ice should be cut away from the sculpture beginning at the top, working towards the bottom.
- Large sections should always be removed in small portions, thus reducing the risk of breakage.
- Keep your work area clean and free of scrap ice at all times.
- Continually brush off excess snow and ice debris from the sculpture. Scrap ice and snow left on the sculpture will begin to freeze in place if not removed immediately.
- Occasionally step back to get an overall view of your work.
- When you are working on a component, try to focus on that part alone. Don't let yourself get overwhelmed by thinking about the entire sculpture or what needs to be done next. Take it one step at a time.
- Don't overwork your sculpture.
- Etch all detail lines 1" deep unless otherwise specified.
- Use a hand brush, moving from the center outwards, to remove air bubbles and wrinkles in the template.
- A heat gun may be used to peel and lift the template, should it need to be repositioned.
- Glazing will sometimes compact the snowfill. It may be necessary to repack the lines after the first glazing.
- When transfering lines through the template to the ice it is best to work from the center of the design towards the outside edges.
- When cutting in deep score lines, it is very important to keep the lines as straight as possible.

Master Tool List

The following tools are needed for all the sculptures in these appendices:

> Templates
> Cool water
> Hand brush
> Chain saw
> Ice pick
> Rubber extension cord
> Ethafoam
> Circular sander with 36-grit paper

Additional tools are listed with each sculpture as needed.

Beginning Sculptures

Sorbet Dishes

SAFETY TIP

Using GFI plugs and circuits is paramount in working safely around water.

SCULPTOR'S TIP

Store each dish in a freezer as soon as it is polished with the aluminum to keep the corners sharp.

Required Tools

- Master tool list
- Drill with $1\frac{1}{2}$" spade bit
- Aluminum
- Clothes iron

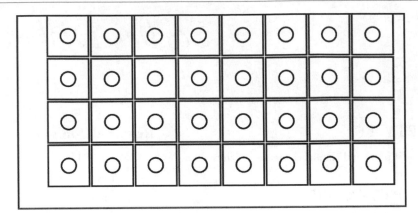

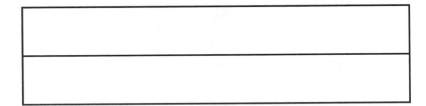

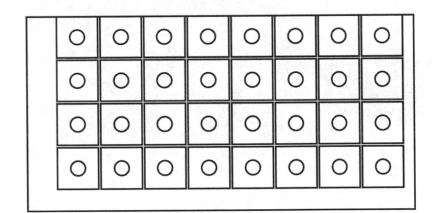

1. Apply the left and right side templates. Slice the block into three sheets, 3" × 20" × 40", then store two of the sheets in the freezer until needed.

2. Lay the first sheet down and freeze the template to the top.

3. Use a $1\frac{1}{2}$" spade drill bit to drill holes 1" deep into the sheet. You should now have holes approximately 1" deep and $1\frac{1}{2}$" in diameter.

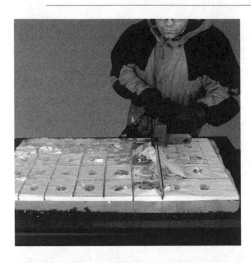

4.   Score your cut lines with a chain saw.

5.   Gently remove the remaining template paper with a sander.

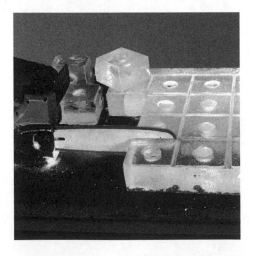

6.   Cut out each sorbet dish square with the chain saw, beginning in one corner.

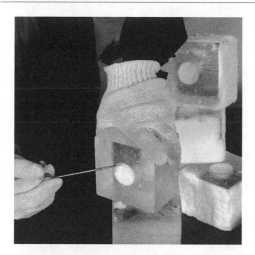

7. Clean out any template paper from the detail etches with an ice pick and brush.

8. Smooth each surface and create sharp edges by touching each side to warmed aluminum. Store each dish in the freezer on a flat piece of plastic or Ethafoam so the dishes can set up.

Ice Tray

SAFETY TIP

Establish the habit of always turning power tools off after use, and before unplugging them. Conversely, always check to ensure tools are turned off before plugging them into a live electrical circuit or power cord.

SCULPTOR'S TIP

When rounding items on warmed aluminum, always keep them moving while they are touching the aluminum.

Required Tools

- Master tool list
- Die grinder with $\frac{1}{4}$" bit
- Aluminum
- Clothes iron
- Drill with $\frac{1}{4}$" spade bit

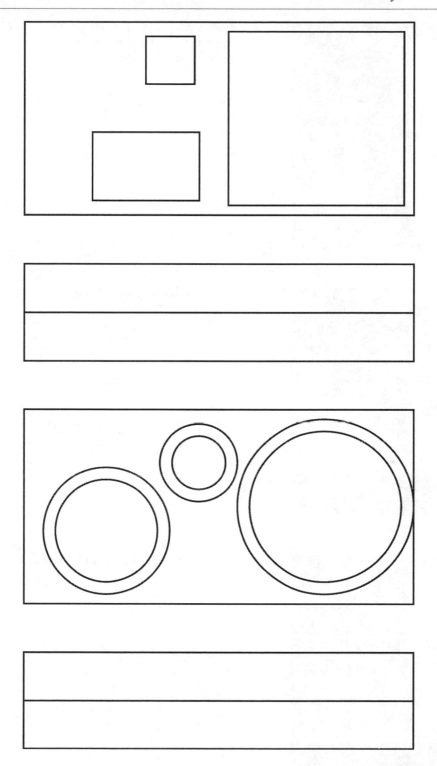

1. Apply the left and right side templates. Slice the block into two 5" × 20" × 40" sheets, and store one of them in the freezer until needed.

2. Apply the first template and etch in the circles with a die grinder and $\frac{1}{4}$" bit.

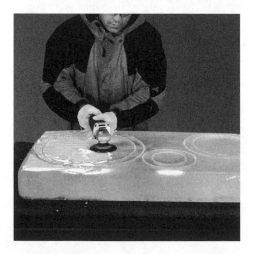

3. Remove the template paper with a sander.

4. Using an ice pick, carefully chip ice from around the inside edge of the traced circles.

5. Use a sander to recess the insides of the circles evenly.

6. Use a chain saw to cut out the silhouette of each circle. Completely clean and then store these pieces in the freezer.

7. On the other half-block, apply the second template and etch in the squares with a chain saw.

8. Remove the template paper with a sander.

9. Use the chainsaw to cut out the silhouette of the rectangular pieces. Store these in the freezer until needed.

10. Smooth the outer surfaces of the circles by rolling them on warmed aluminum.

11. Add grooves by pressing the edges of the circles against the edge of the warmed aluminum.

12. Drill a hole angled downward from the inside of each tray completely through to the outside, to allow for drainage.

13. Using the warmed aluminum, polish the surfaces to be attached, and begin assembling pieces from the bottom up.

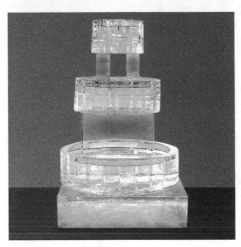

14. If this sculpture needs to be transported some distance, you may wish to assemble the pieces at the display site.

Snow-Filled Snowflake

SAFETY TIP
Always use two hands when using a rotary grinder. Also, the sharper the bit the easier it will be to control.

SCULPTOR'S TIP
When cutting away the silhouette, start at the top and work towards the bottom.

Required Tools

- Master tool list
- Die grinder with $\frac{1}{4}$" router bit
- Heat gun

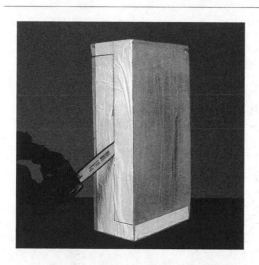

1. Apply the left and right side templates. Using a chain saw, "z-cut" the block to create two equal ice sheets with bases.

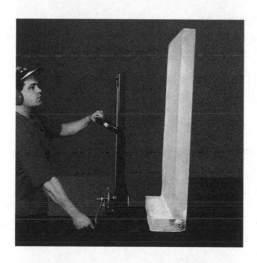

2. Using a hoist, lift one sheet onto a carving table lined with Ethafoam. Store the second sheet in a freezer until needed.

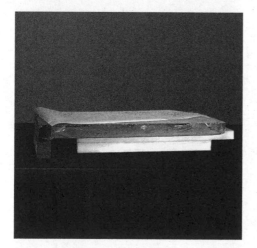

3. Lay the ice sheet flat with the base edge down, using a sufficient amount of Ethafoam to properly support the ice without distressing the base.

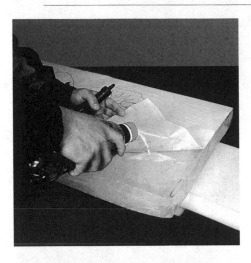

4. Apply the snowflake template with water and a hand brush.

5. Working from the center of the design towards the outside edges, carefully trace all the lines with a die grinder and $\frac{1}{4}$" bit.

6. Using the sander, gently remove any remaining template paper.

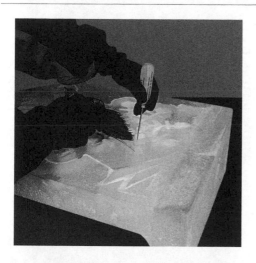

7. Clean out any template paper from the detail etches with an ice pick and brush.

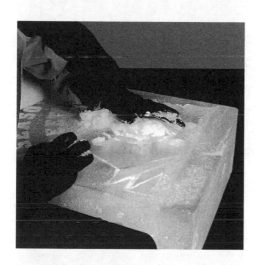

8. Pack the cleaned grooves with clean, dry snow. Thoroughly brush all excess snow from the surface of sculpture.

9. Apply cool water over the entire sculpture to glaze the surface, and allow several minutes for the water to penetrate.

10. Stand the sculpture on its base. Using the chain saw, remove excess ice to shape the silhouette. Remove debris and snow by brushing the ice sculpture with a hand brush.

Vase

SAFETY TIP

Organization can affect the outcome of a sculpture. If a person's work area or tool table is cluttered and disorganized, the sculptor will work less efficiently, and there is greater potential for an accident.

SCULPTOR'S TIP

When making deep cuts, such as those used to cut the outside silhouette, it is easier to keep control of any power tool by beginning with shallow cuts. Continually making these shallow cuts deeper each time will reduce the resistance.

Required Tools

- Master tool list
- Die grinder with $\frac{1}{4}$" bit, $\frac{1}{8}$" bit, and "V"-shaped bit
- Blowtorch

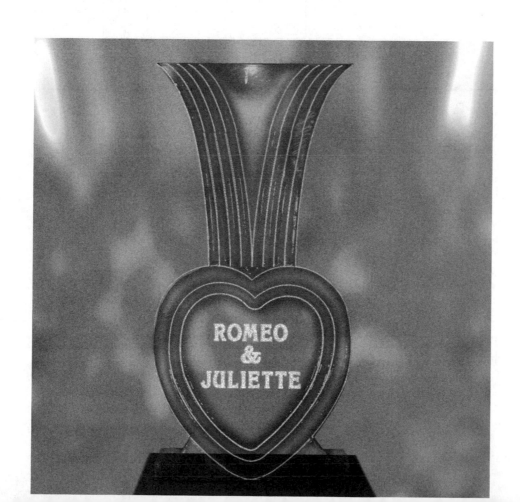

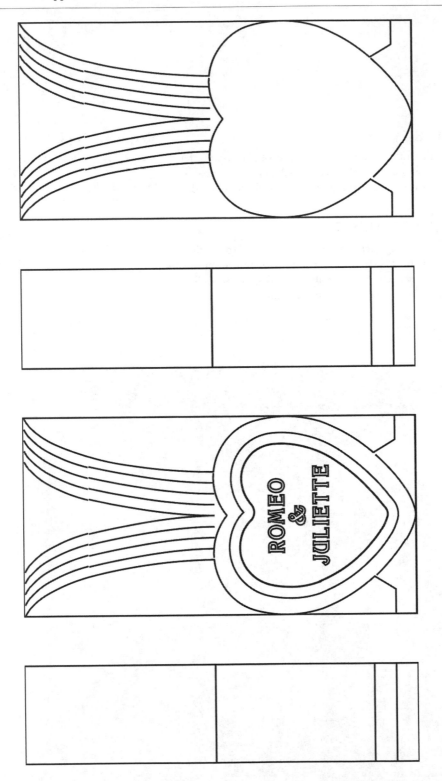

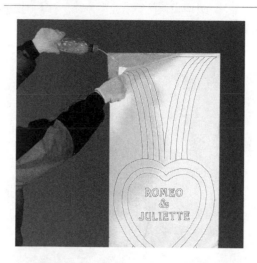

1. Apply templates to all four sides.

2. Using the $\frac{1}{4}$" bit and die grinder, carefully trace all lines into the ice.

3. Sand away the template paper.

4. Re-score the detail lines at the top of the base using a "V" bit and a die grinder.

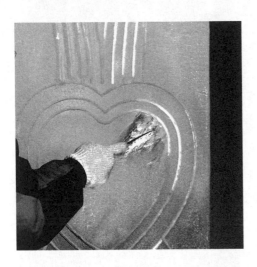

5. An ice pick or chipper may be used to clear away the ice inside the heart. Be sure to stop short of the actual desired depth.

6. Continue to recess the inside of the heart to the desired depth using the sander. It may be necessary to use the $\frac{1}{4}$" bit with the die grinder to finish areas not fully accessible with the sander.

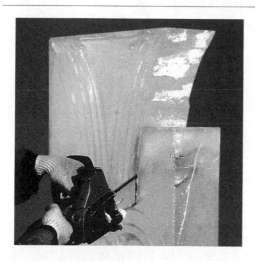

7. Using the chain saw, cut along the outside edge of the vase. Be careful to stay outside the lines to create the silhouette.

8. Insert a pre-cut sub template inside the recessed area of the heart, apply cool water, and freeze.

9. Carefully etch in lettering using a $\frac{1}{8}$" bit and die grinder.

10. Sand off sub template.

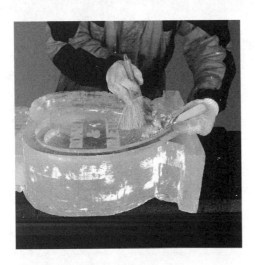

11. Clean out any template paper from the detail etches with an ice pick and brush from the recessed area.

12. Pack the letters with clean, dry snow.

13. Glaze the letters by saturating the snow with cool water.

14. At the top of the vase, cut a 4" × 6" × 3" deep 'well' for a floral brick. The depth of the well depends on what the vase will be used for (i.e. for long stem flowers, etc.).

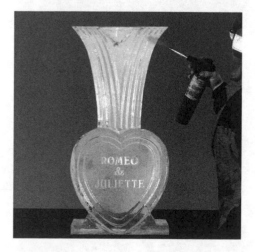

15. Brush off and torch or rinse the sculpture.

Note: You may want to drill a hole through the back side at the bottom of the well to prevent water from pooling during display. (See the Basket step list.)

SAFETY TIP

Electrical cords must not become tangled and allowed too close to the cutting blades.

SCULPTOR'S TIP

When removing large pieces of ice such as the inside of the handle, it is better to remove in several small pieces to reduce the risk of breakage.

Required Tools

- Master tool list
- Die grinder with $\frac{1}{4}$" end mill bit
- Rubberizer or rasp
- Drill with $\frac{1}{4}$" spade bit
- Hot water bag

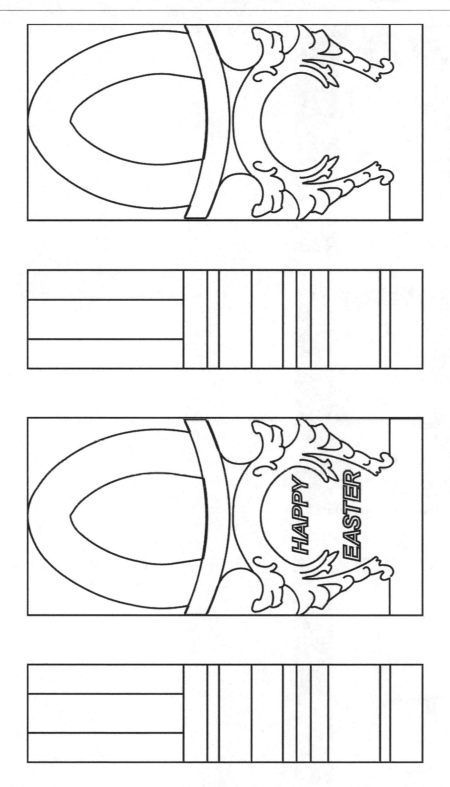

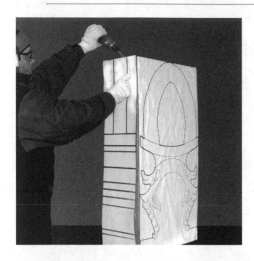

1. Apply templates to all four sides of the ice.

2. Score lines on the left and right sides, deep enough so that they remain visible after front view silhouette is cut out.

3. Etch in all detail from front and back templates.

4. Sand away remaining template paper.

5. Cut away the outside silhouette from the front view.

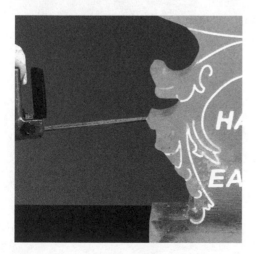

6. Clean up tight areas with the tip of the chain saw.

7. Clean up any chain saw marks or rough edges on the outside of the leaves with the rubberizer or rasp bit.

8. Remove snow and template scraps from the detail areas.

9. Pack all detail lines with clean, dry snow.

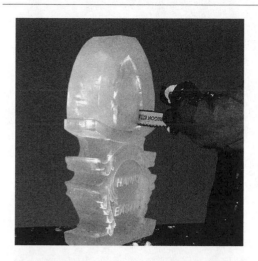

10. Remove ice from the inside of the handle. Remember to keep all cuts in the negative space only. It is helpful to remove this in several small sections to reduce the risk of breakage.

11. Using the guide cuts from the original side templates, cut away negative space from in front and in back of the handle.

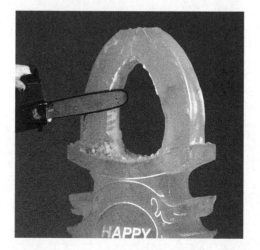

12. Use the chain saw to begin rounding the handle. Approach this in the same manner as you would a cylinder (see Chapter 5).

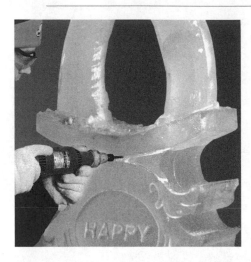

13. With a $\frac{1}{4}$" bit and die grinder, recess the area just below the basket rim on both sides.

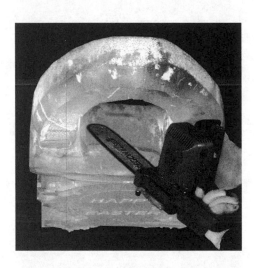

14. Use the chain saw to cut a V-shaped pocket under the handle to hold props such as flowers or eggs.

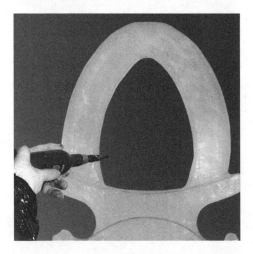

15. Finish rounding the handle with the rasp or rubberizer. Be sure to use smooth strokes and apply very little pressure against the ice.

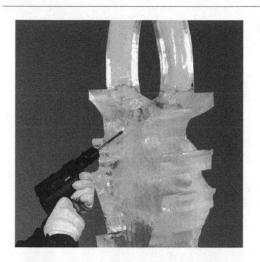

16. Drill a hole angled down for drainage in the back side of the basket.

17. Carefully clean the sculpture.

18. Finish polishing and rounding the handle with a hot water bag.

Yin/Yang Table Centerpieces

SAFETY TIP

Different glove materials serve various purposes, and the sculptor may wish to have different gloves available for their different uses. It is also recommended to have multiple pairs of the same types of gloves, for rotating into dry gloves as needed.

SCULPTOR'S TIP

When hollowing out details, such as the hearts, it is important to continually keep the template free of snow debris in order to keep track of cutting lines.

Required Tools

- Master tool list
- Die grinder with $\frac{1}{8}$" end mill bit
- Clothes iron

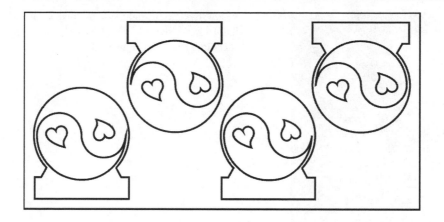

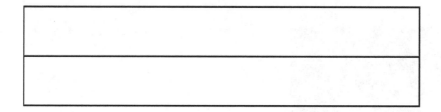

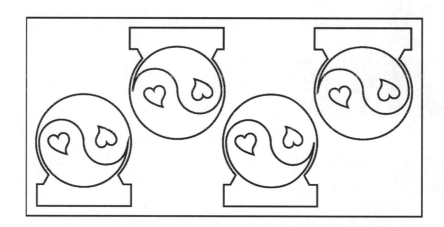

1. Apply the left and right side templates. Slice the block in half to make two 5" × 20" × 40" sheets, and place one sheet in a freezer until needed.

2. Lay the first sheet on its face and freeze the template on.

3. Using a $\frac{1}{8}$" bit and a rotary tool or die grinder, etch in the detail shapes and only hollow out one of the two paisley shapes.

4. Remove template paper with a sander.

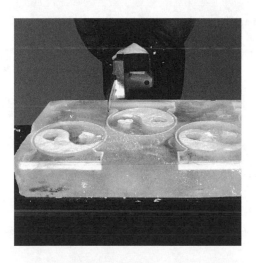

5. With a chain saw, cut away as much of the silhouette as possible without disconnecting pieces from the sheet.

6. Use the chain saw to cut out the remaining silhouette shapes and detach each centerpiece from the whole sheet. Make sure you always cut in the negative space.

7. Cut away any remaining negative-space ice that was not accessible while all the pieces were attached.

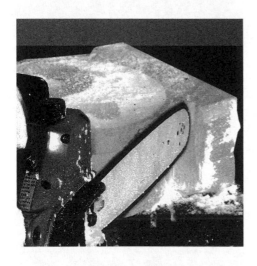

8. Sand and shape by gently dragging the side of the chain saw bar in an up-and-down motion against the outside of the silhouette.

9. Clean out any template paper from the detail etches with an ice pick and brush.

10. Pack all of the detail shapes with clean, dry snow, and brush off any excess.

11. Saturate the snow fill with water.

12. Use a clothes iron on very low temp to smooth and define the outside edges of each centerpiece.

13. Flatten the front and back of the centerpiece with the iron. Stand centerpieces upright in a freezer to set.

Intermediate Sculptures

SAFETY TIP

Ear protection is needed primarily to insulate the eardrum from the loud decibels and high-pitched noises that emanate from the motors.

SCULPTOR'S TIP

Make sure that the surface area you place the transparency on is completely dry. Any water that gets between the ice and the transparency will become cloudy when it freezes and will detract from the appearance of the logo when viewing from the front.

Required Tools

- Master tool list
- Transparency
- Die grinder with $\frac{1}{4}$" end mill bit
- Heat gun
- Blowtorch
- Metal yardstick

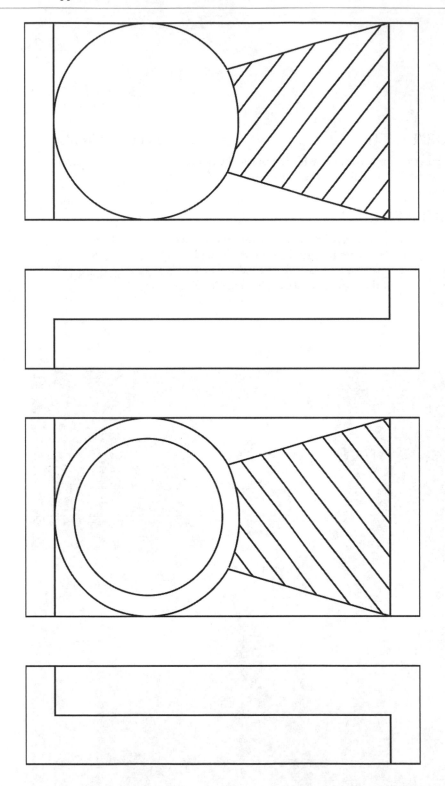

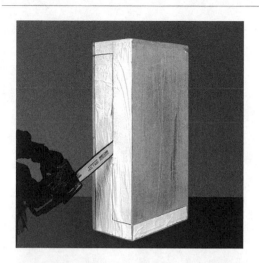

1. Apply the left and right side templates. Using a chain saw, "z-cut" the block to create two equal ice sheets with bases.

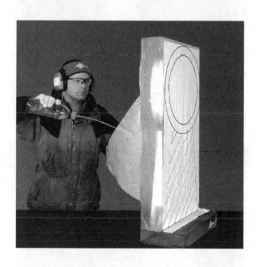

2. Apply the front and back templates.

3. Use a $\frac{1}{4}$" router bit and die grinder to transfer curved lines on both sides.

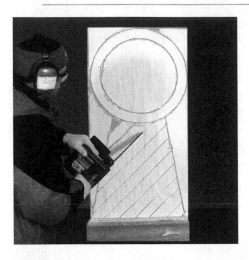

4. Use a chain saw to transfer straight detail lines on both sides.

5. Remove the template with a sander.

6. Clean out any template paper from the detail etches with an ice pick and brush.

7. Cut away the negative space around the outside silhouette.

8. Lay the block flat. Pack all detail lines with clean, dry snow.

9. Use the ice pick to carefully remove ice around inside edge of circle.

10. Sand inside of the circle to a 1" depth as evenly as possible, occasionally removing snow to keep track of your progress.

11. Stand the ice up and completely remove all snow debris from inside the circle.

12. Gently melt away sander marks on inside of the circle with heat gun.

13. Place pre-cut transparency inside the recessed area of the circle so that the front side of the transparency is face down against the ice.

14. Carefully pack the circle tightly behind the transparency with clean, dry snow. Make sure the transparency does not move during this process.

15. Pour cool water over the surface of the snow to glaze and seal the snow.

16. Scrape off all excess snow, creating a level surface with a metal yardstick.

17. Stand the sculpture upright and brush off any loose snow and ice particles. Then glaze the piece with a torch and store in a freezer.

New Year's Eve Display

SAFETY TIP

We recommend using only three-pronged, brightly colored, heavy duty, insulated, rubber-coated extension cords for ice sculpting with power tools.

SCULPTOR'S TIP

Make sure your gloves are clean when packing detail lines.

Required Tools

- Master tool list
- Rotary tool with $\frac{1}{8}$" bit

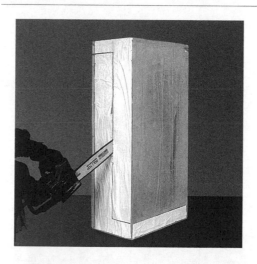

1. Apply the left and right side templates. Using a chain saw, "z-cut" the block to create two equal ice sheets with bases.

2. Lay the ice sheet flat with the based edge down on Ethafoam to properly support the ice. Apply the front template.

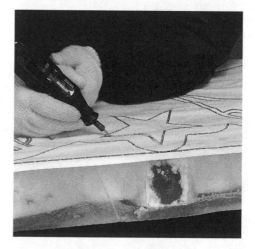

3. Working from the center of the design towards the outside edges, carefully trace all the detail lines with the rotary tool and $\frac{1}{8}$" bit.

4. Using the sander, gently remove any remaining template paper.

5. Clean out any template paper from the detail etches with an ice pick and brush.

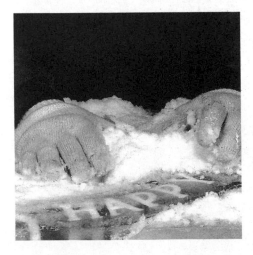

6. Pack the cleaned groves with clean, dry snow. Thoroughly brush all excess snow from the surface of the sculpture. Apply cool water over the entire sculpture to glaze the surface. Allow several minutes for the water to penetrate.

7. Stand the sculpture on its base. Using the chain saw, remove excess ice to reveal the silhouette.

8. Remove debris and snow with a hand brush.

Wedding Bells

SAFETY TIP

A loss of focus can quickly lead to an accident, just as poor judgment can. One should always work within the safe limits of the situation.

SCULPTOR'S TIP

It may be helpful to place the level on top of the aluminum when polishing off the base piece to make sure you are melting it evenly.

Required Tools

- Master tool list
- Aluminum
- Level
- Clothes iron
- Scriber or metal ruler
- Rotary tool with $\frac{1}{8}$" bit

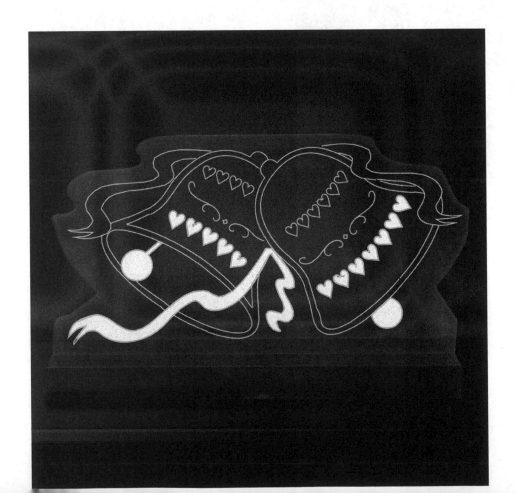

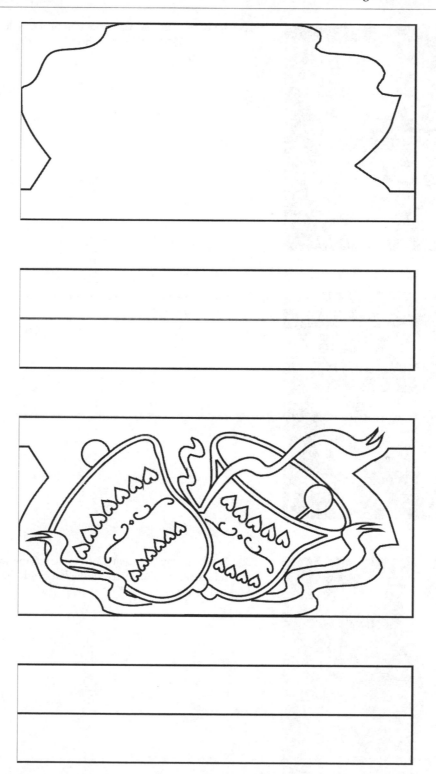

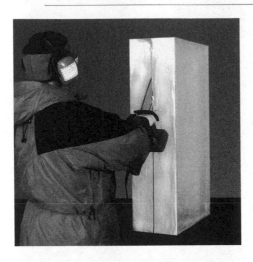

1. Apply the left and right side templates. Split the block into two 5" × 20" × 40" sheets. Store the second sheet in a freezer until needed.

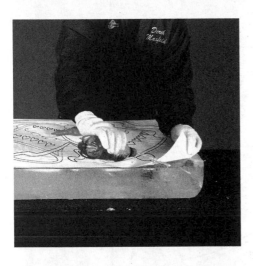

2. Lay the block on its side, apply the front template and freeze with cool water.

3. Working from the center of the design towards the outside edges, carefully trace all the lines with the rotary tool and $\frac{1}{8}$" bit.

4. Using the sander, remove any remaining template paper.

5. Clean out any template paper from the detail etches with an ice pick and brush.

6. Pack the cleaned grooves with clean, dry snow. Thoroughly brush all excess snow from the surface of the sculpture. Apply cool water over the entire sculpture to glaze the surface. Allow several minutes for the water to penetrate.

7. Stand the sculpture on its side. Using the chain saw, remove excess ice to reveal the silhouette.

8. Remove debris and snow by brushing ice sculpture with a hand brush.

9. On the second sheet of ice, use a ruler or a scriber to mark off a 10" × 40" portion of the ice for a base.

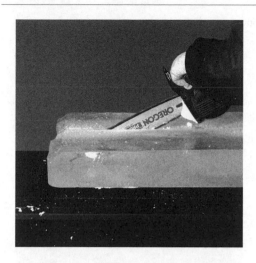

10. Using the scribed line, divide the sheet into two equal portions.

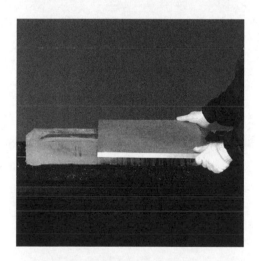

11. Use warmed aluminum to polish off the surface of one of the 10" × 40" sheets. Remove any excess water from the surface.

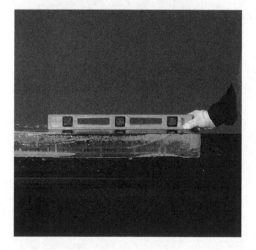

12. Check the polished section to ensure that it is level.

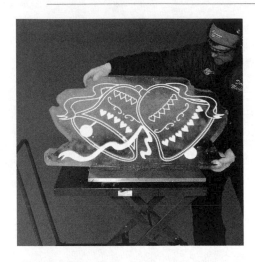

13. Polish the bottom of the bells section.

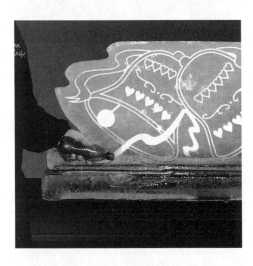

14. Place the bells section in the center of the 10" × 40" base section and add cool water around the seam.

15. Use a sander to bevel off the base edges.

SAFETY TIP

Proper lifting and handling of the ice will reduce or prevent unnecessary back strain.

SCULPTOR'S TIP

Make certain the initially shaped sculpture is sufficiently cold to allow the sub template to adhere securely to the ice.

Required Tools

- Master tool list
- Scissors
- Rotary tool with $\frac{1}{8}$" bit
- Hot water bag

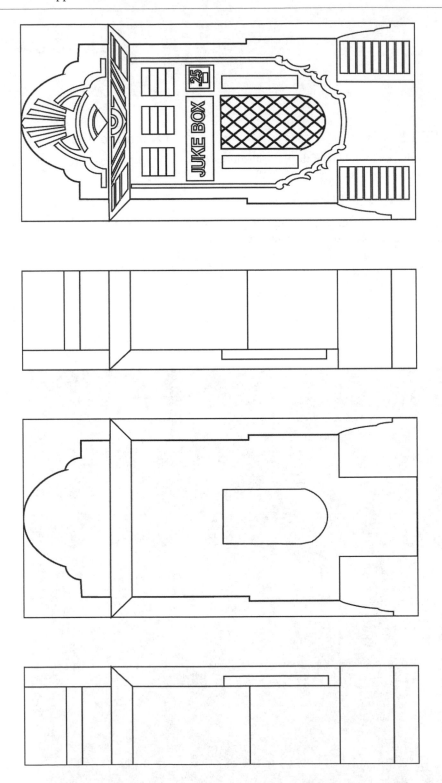

1. Apply all four templates. Be sure that the detail lines are properly aligned.

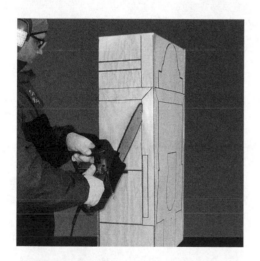

2. Cut score lines from the left and right side templates.

3. Transfer detail lines from the front template. These larger lines may be easier to transfer using a chain saw.

4. Cut away the front view silhouette.

5. Using the score lines as a guide, cut the negative space away from the profile silhouette.

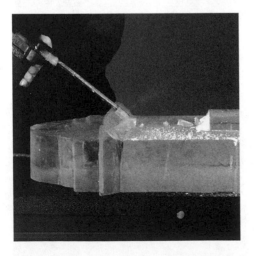

6. Taper the underside of the shelf so that it slopes inward as it does on the left and the right sides.

SORBET DISHES

ICE TRAY

**SNOW-FILLED
SNOWFLAKE**

VASE

BASKET

YIN/YANG TABLE CENTERPIECES

LOGO

NEW YEAR'S EVE
DISPLAY

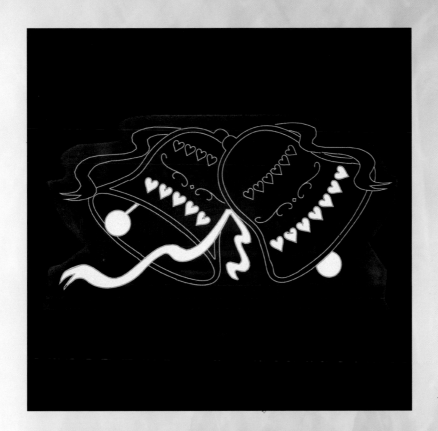

WEDDING BELLS

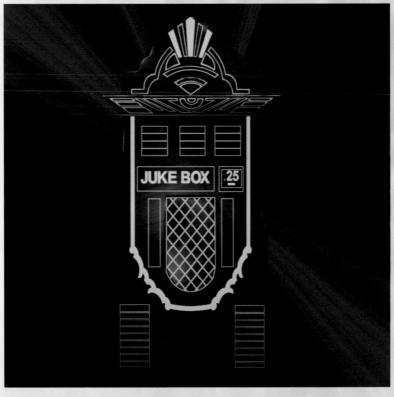

JUKE BOX .25

JUKEBOX

Castle

Cornucopia

GIBSON GIRL

BUTTERFLY

TUNA

CANNON

PEGASUS

GOOSE

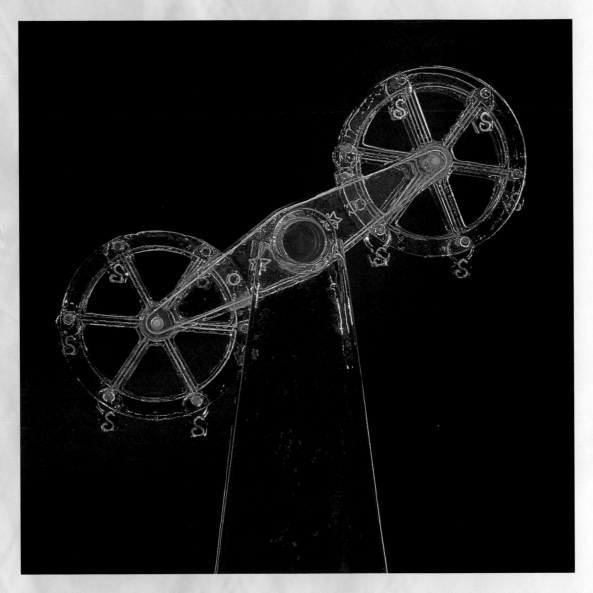

DOUBLE FERRIS WHEEL. This sculpture incorporates a small motor that drives the wheels. The seats are free-moving.

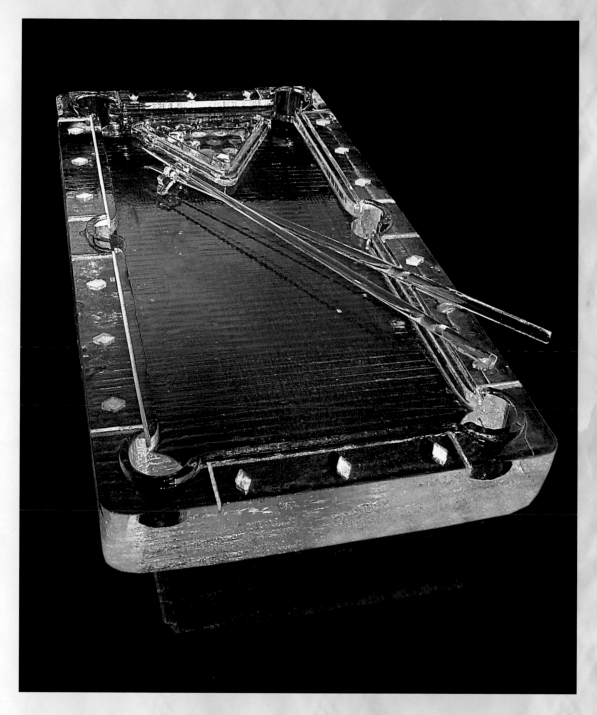

POOL TABLE. This full-size, fully-functional pool table was designed and assembled over a five-day period.

FILL TECHNIQUES. The Easter Egg and Bride and Groom on the right demonstrate color- and snow-fill techniques, respectively.

SCULPTURE IN THE ROUND. The Dolphin below demonstrates the impact a simple design can have when translated into three dimensions.

BUTTERFLY DISPLAY. This multi-piece display was designed to support the theme of a wedding (see page 158 for a photo with the bride and groom).

STATUE OF LIBERTY. The green comes from back lighting reflected on the surface of the ice, which has been textured using a small drywall-style saw. The sculpture was created from 22 blocks of ice.

PATRIOTIC DISPLAY. This sculpture was designed for an outdoor winter festival and was assembled from 40 individually sculpted components.

FIREPLACE WITH ARTIFICIAL FIRE. Cold flame, pyrotechnics, or illusory lighting can have a powerful impact when used in harmony with the overall design.

7. Smooth the surface with a sander.

8. Stand the ice up to more easily clean away the snow and scrap ice. At this point it may be necessary to place the ice back in the freezer so that the secondary template adheres better.

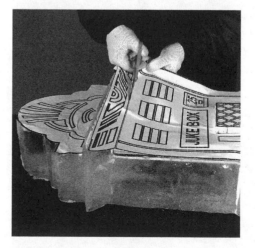

9. Lay the block on its back. Cut secondary template into appropriate sections to fit onto the ice.

10. Apply the secondary templates, using cool water and a hand brush to make sure they are securely frozen to the ice.

11. With a $\frac{1}{8}$" bit and rotary tool, transfer all detail lines.

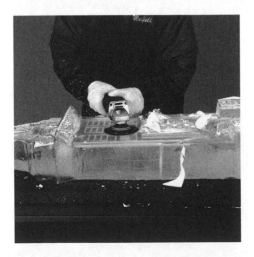

12. Sand off the secondary template.

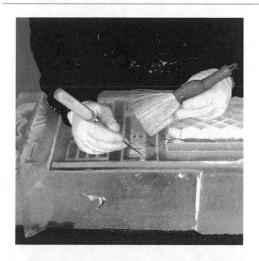

13. Clean out any template paper from the detail etches with an ice pick and brush.

14. Pack all detail lines with clean, dry snow.

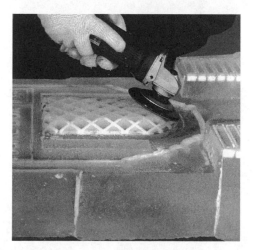

15. Use the sander to round the edges of the center speaker and clean off excess snow.

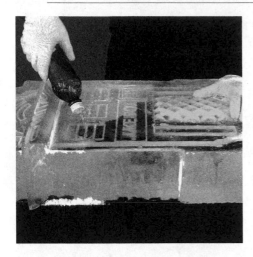

16. Glaze over the snow-packed lines with cool water.

17. Stand the jukebox up and polish the top section with a hot water bag.

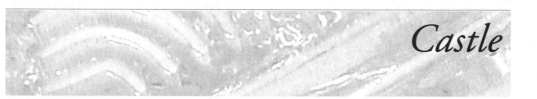

Castle

SAFETY TIP

Sculptors must be aware that they are using electrical tools around water. Proper grounding of electrical lines, and routine inspection of all electrical cords, will help to ensure a safe electrical environment.

SCULPTOR'S TIP

Remove any excess water from the surfaces of the front and back of the castle when fusing together. Trapped water may crack the piece when frozen. (Water expands when freezing.)

Required Tools

- Master tool list
- Rotary tool with $\frac{1}{8}$" bit
- Die grinder with a taped off $\frac{1}{4}$" bit
- Clothes iron
- Aluminum

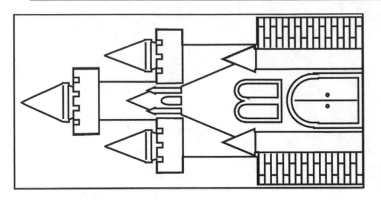

(This panel shows the assembled piece.)

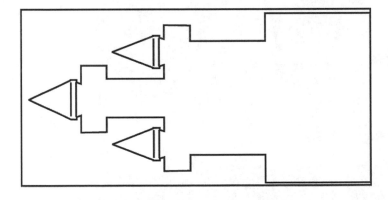

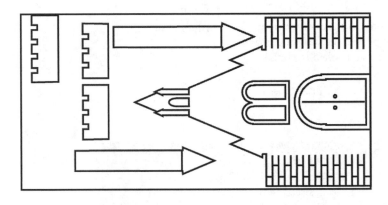

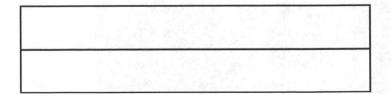

1. Apply the left and right side templates. Split the block into two 5" × 20" × 40" sheets.

2. Apply the *front* template on one sheet and the *back* template to the other sheet. Transfer the lines with a $\frac{1}{8}$" bit and rotary tool.

3. Using the sander, remove the template paper.

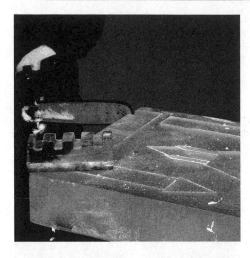

4. With a chain saw, cut grooves into each rook top while they are still attached.

5. Hollow out the window sections to a depth of 1" with a $\frac{1}{4}$" bit and die grinder.

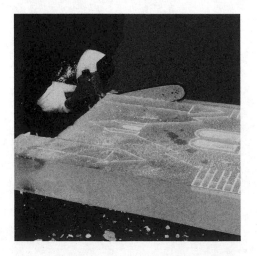

6. Carefully cut and remove towers from the *front* section.

7.   With the chain saw, cut the silhouettes out on both sheets.

8.   Remove all snow debris from each component.

9.   Clean out any template paper from the detail etches with an ice pick and brush.

10. Pack cleaned groves with clean, dry snow. Brush all excess snow from the surface.

11. With warmed aluminum, polish the front surface of the *back* sheet and the back surface of the *front* sheet, and remove any excess water from the surfaces.

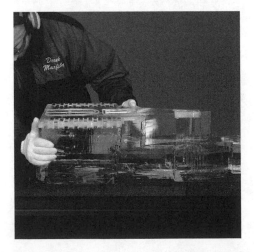

12. Fuse the *front* section to the *back* section by carefully lining up the bottoms and sides.

13. Polish the back sides of the rook sections.

14. Fuse the rook tops to the *back* section towers.

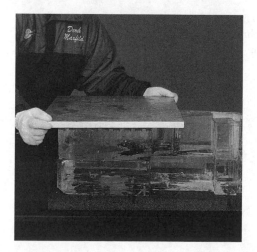

15. Polish the *front* section with the aluminum and remove excess water.

16. Polish the individual towers and fuse them onto the *front* section by lining up the tower peaks.

17. Make sure all the pieces are frozen together, then slice $1\frac{1}{2}''$ off the front surfaces of the rook tops and front towers.

18. Carefully stand the castle upright. Brush or rinse off any snow or debris. Using an iron, bevel the tower pinnacles and the front tower corners.

Cornucopia

SAFETY TIP

A proactive attitude towards safety will greatly reduce accidents.

SCULPTOR'S TIP

Before polishing the sculpture with a hot water bag, make sure it is completely free of all snow and ice debris. When you polish a piece that is not clean you run the risk of remaining scrap ice and snow freezing to the sculpture.

Required Tools

- Master tool list
- Heat gun
- Die grinder with $\frac{1}{2}$" and/or $\frac{1}{4}$" bit
- Rubberizer or rasp
- Power brush
- Hot water bag

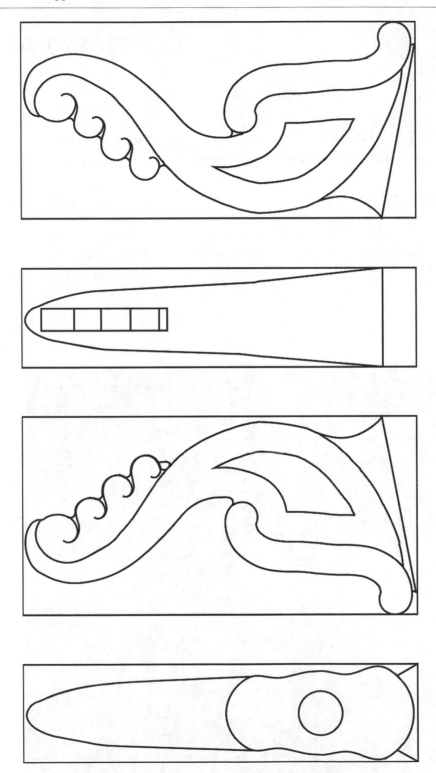

1. Apply the templates to all four sides. Make sure that the side templates line up to all corresponding lines on the front template.

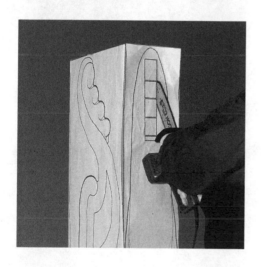

2. Cut score lines from the side templates deep enough so that they remain visible once the front silhouette is cut away.

3. Using a $\frac{1}{4}$" bit and die grinder, transfer all of the detail lines on the front and back templates.

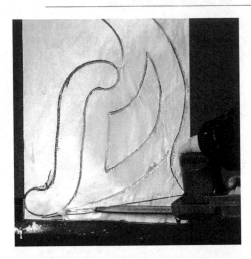

4.   Use a chain saw to etch the base line straight.

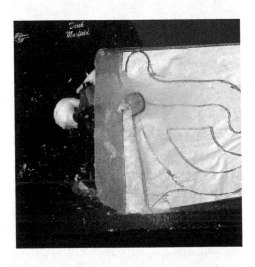

5.   Lay the block on its back, and cut the base on an angle.

6.   Remove the template with a sander.

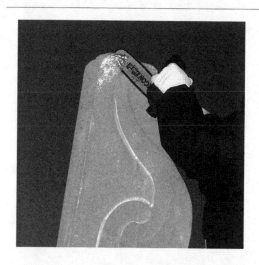

7. Stand the cornucopia up on its new base and cut away the outside silhouette.

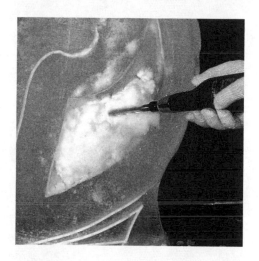

8. Recess areas on each side 1" deep with a $\frac{1}{4}$" or a $\frac{1}{2}$" bit and die grinder.

9. Beginning at the top of the horn, remove the area in front and in back of the waves.

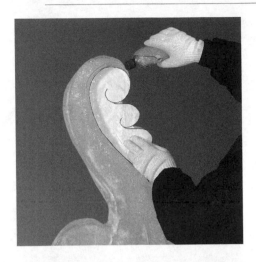

10. Apply the secondary template to the wave area.

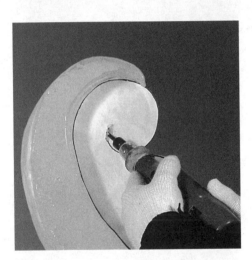

11. Using a $\frac{1}{4}$" bit and die grinder, etch detail into waves.

12. Sand away the secondary template.

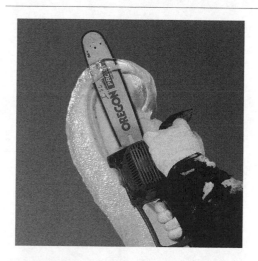

13. Taper off the top edges of the cornucopia.

14. Round off the front edges by sanding with the side of the chainsaw blade.

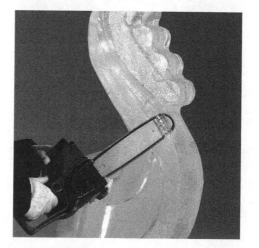

15. Remove the back corners of the cornucopia with the saw.

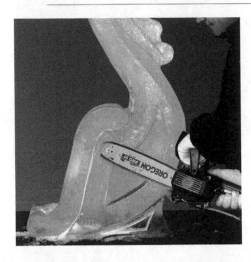

16. Round and shape the area behind the rim with the tip of the saw.

17. Taper the outer edges.

18. Hollow out a hole in front with a $\frac{1}{4}$" or $\frac{1}{2}$" bit and die grinder.

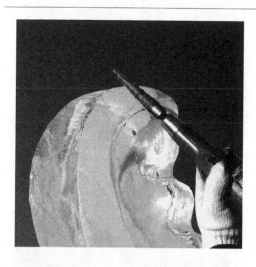

19. By applying light pressure with the rasp or rubberizer bit while following the contour, round the top portion of the cornucopia.

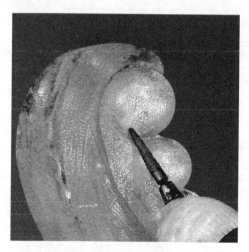

20. Round the edges and shape the waves with the rubberizer or rasp.

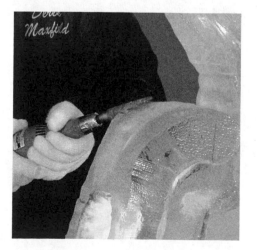

21. Use the rubberizer or rasp bit to blend the front and side silhouette view of the bottom lip.

22. Round the edges of the indented profile areas.

23. Use the power or hand brush to clean out any snow in the front pocket as well as on the entire piece.

24. Finish smoothing the entire sculpture with a hot water bag.

Advanced Sculptures

SAFETY TIP

Eye protection, whether a person normally wears eyeglasses or not, is a very important but often overlooked necessity. Ice chips, slush, and water fly off of grinder pads and chain saw blades at tremendous velocities.

SCULPTOR'S TIP

This procedure produces the best results when the entire sculpture is done in a freezer.

Required Tools

- Master tool list
- Rotary tool with $\frac{1}{8}$" bit
- Die grinder with taped off $\frac{1}{4}$" end mill bit
- Squeeze bottle
- Pitcher
- Knife
- Supplies for the Maxfield Color Method

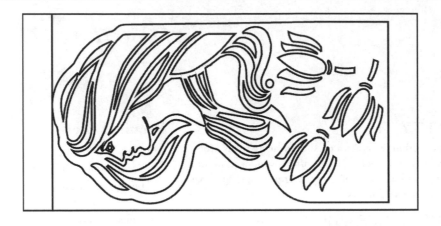

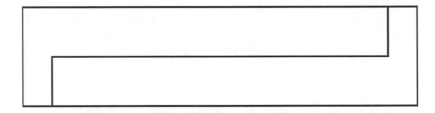

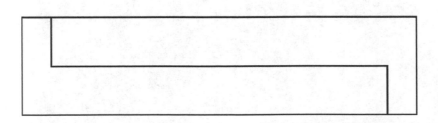

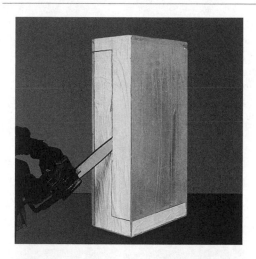

1. Apply the left and right side templates. Using the chain saw, "z-cut" the block to create two equal ice sheets with bases.

2. Lay one "z-cut" sheet onto a carving table lined with a sufficient amount of Ethafoam. Etch in all the lines with the $\frac{1}{8}$" bit.

3. Sand off the template paper.

4. Hollow out the negative space in each section with the $\frac{1}{4}$" bit. To keep a constant depth, measure an inch from the tip of the bit and wrap duct tape around the bit, leaving 1" of the cutting surface exposed. This will be your depth guide. Start in the center of the negative space and work to the edge of the traced lines. Keep a brush close to remove snow.

5. Cut away the outside silhouette.

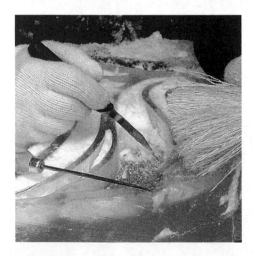

6. Using an ice pick, knife, and brush, carefully remove all snow from pockets. If available, an air compressor is ideal for this.

7. Place in freezer to set. Lay on a flat, level surface, and pour color mixture into each small hollow area using a squeeze bottle. Follow the Maxfield Coloring Method (see Chapter 11). For larger areas, a pitcher can be used.

8. Let the color freeze completely. Repack detail lines with clean, dry snow. Brush all excess snow from the surface and then glaze the surface with cool water.

9. Stand the block upright and brush off any excess debris.

Butterfly

SAFETY TIP

The artisan must take personal responsibility for his actions, be organized in his work, and always adhere to safe practices.

SCULPTOR'S TIP

When shaping with a rubberizer, remove a little at a time. Whittling away at the ice will give you more control in creating an evenly-shaped surface.

Required Tools

- Master tool list
- Rotary tool with $\frac{1}{8}$" bit
- Rubberizer or rasp
- Hot water bag

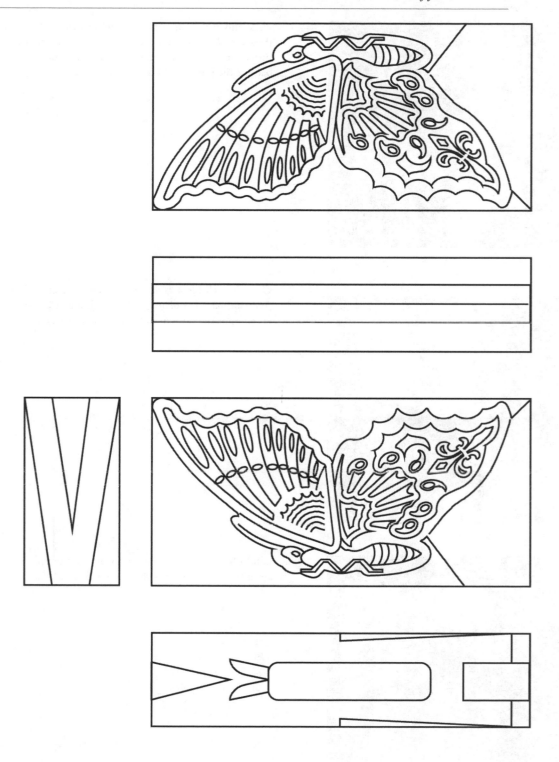

1. Place only the *left* and *right* side templates on the ice. Use these templates as a guide to angle both the front and back surfaces of the ice. Cut out a V-shaped section from the back of the butterfly, between the wings.

2. Once your ice block is shaped properly, you can attach the *front* and *back* templates to the ice. Using a $\frac{1}{8}$" bit, transfer all template lines onto the ice on both sides.

3. Sand off the template and clean out any template paper from the detail etches with an ice pick and brush.

4. Cut out the front view silhouette.

5. Taper the edges of the wings by removing all square edges so that the outside edges are thinner than the part of the wing nearest the body. This will make the wings appear delicate, yet leave them durable for transportation and display.

6. Use the chain saw to taper the lower wings under the bottom of the upper wings. This will help to give them the appearance of overlapping.

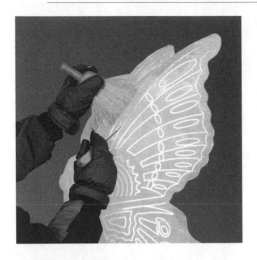

7. Carefully remove all template debris from detail lines and pack them with clean, dry snow.

8. With a rubberizer, create concave areas behind each of the indentations on the back of the wings.

9. Use the rubberizer or round-end rasp to round off and shape the body.

10. With a $\frac{1}{8}$" bit, etch in details of the head and lower body.

11. Brush off the sculpture completely and polish the surfaces with a hot water bag.

Tuna

SAFETY TIP

Tools must be properly selected for their use, maintained adequately, and used according to the manufacturer's design in order to produce good results safely.

SCULPTOR'S TIP

After cutting away both the front and the side silhouettes you need to clean the ice off completely.

Required Tools

- Master tool list
- Rotary tool with $\frac{1}{8}$" bit
- Rubberizer
- Handsaw
- Hot water bag

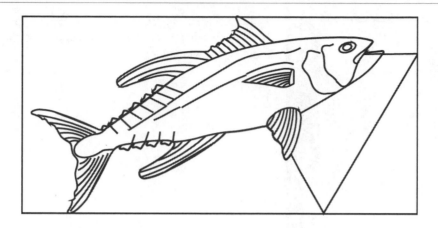

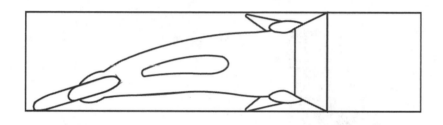

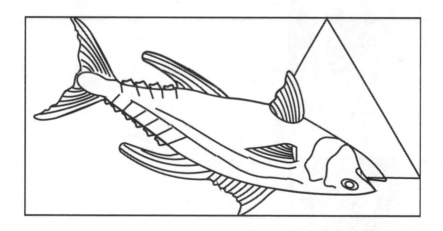

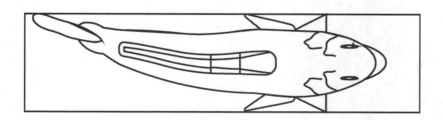

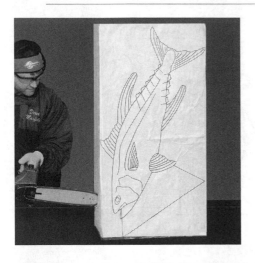

1. Apply all templates, being certain to line up with all corresponding lines on the *front* template. Make score cuts from both sides.

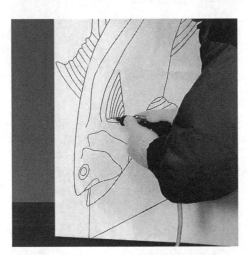

2. Use the $\frac{1}{8}$" bit to transfer lines onto the ice.

3. Sand away the template paper.

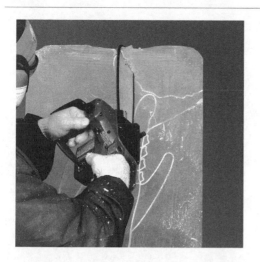

4.   Cut away outside the *front* silhouette.

5.   Lay the block on its back to cut away the *bottom* silhouette.

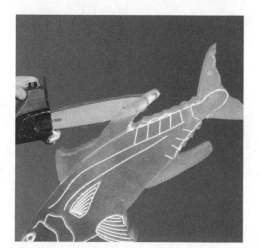

6.   Stand the block upright on its new base and finish the *side* silhouettes, using score cuts as your guide.

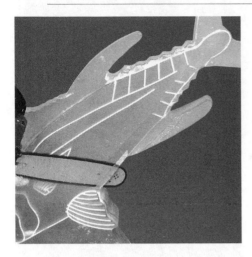

7.   Trim off all the sharp corners.

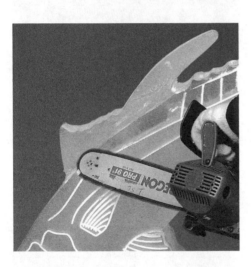

8.   Round the body by blending together the *front* and *side* silhouettes.

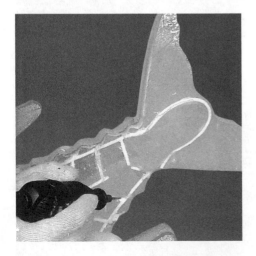

9.   Define the details near the tail.

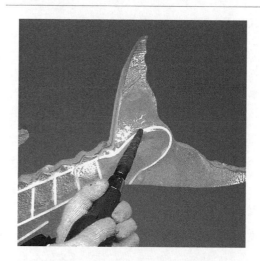

10. Round the center section of the tail.

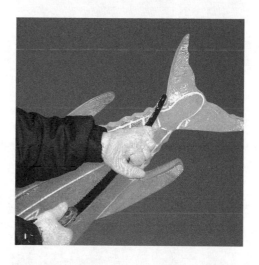

11. Gently shape and blend the surface of the body with a handsaw.

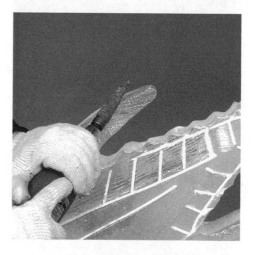

12. Taper the outside edges of all the fins using the rubberizer.

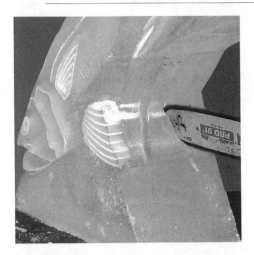

13. Divide the dorsal fins with the chain saw.

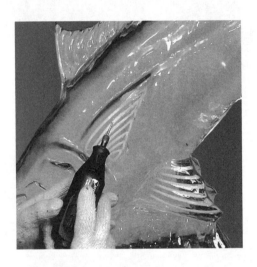

14. Etch in detail lines on the fins.

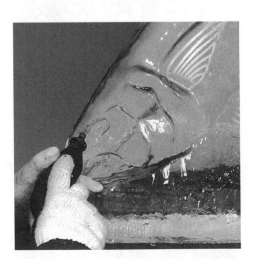

15. Define the details of the face and gills using the $\frac{1}{8}$" bit.

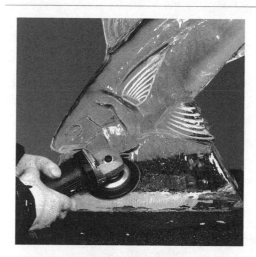

16. Sand the base below the face.

17. Clean all debris and snow from the sculpture. Carefully smooth and blend the contours of the body and face using a hot water bag.

Cannon

SAFETY TIP

When dismantling the sculpture, lay the entire block down so that when the base is cut off it won't fall.

SCULPTOR'S TIP

Remember not to overheat the aluminum. Room temperature is warm enough, and overheated aluminum will erode the finished surface.

Required Tools

- Master tool list
- Aluminum
- Die grinder with $\frac{1}{4}$" and $\frac{1}{8}$" bits
- Clothes iron
- Hot water bag

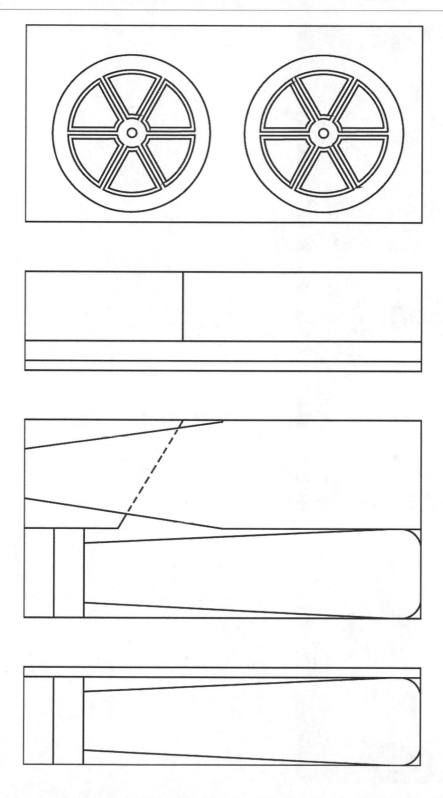

1. Remove a 1" slab from the full surface of the 20" × 40" block.

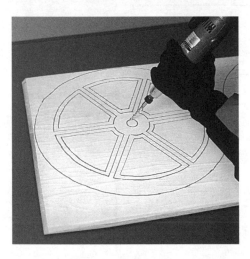

2. Lay the 20" × 40" × 1" sheet on an Ethafoam surface. Apply the *wheel* template. Working from the center of the design toward the outside edges, carefully trace all lines with the $\frac{1}{4}$" bit. Be sure to etch no more than $\frac{1}{4}$" deep into the ice.

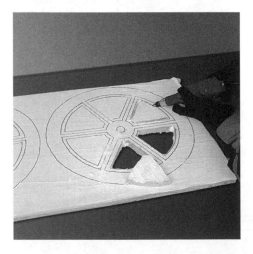

3. Using the $\frac{1}{4}$" bit, cut and completely remove the triangular sections of ice between the spokes of each wheel. After the negative-space ice from both wheels has been cut and removed, trim the outer circle of each wheel with a chain saw.

4. Sand away the template paper.

5. Clean out any template paper from the detail etches with an ice pick and brush.

6. On the remaining ice, apply the *plank/cannon front* template. Also apply the *left side cannon barrel* template, lining up all corresponding lines with the *front* template.

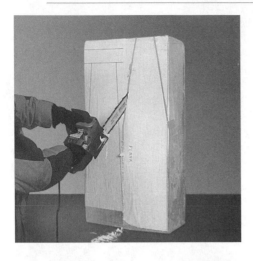

7. Cut 1" deep along the outside silhouette of the *plank* template. Be careful to stay outside the lines and inside the negative space of the block.

8. Following the *plank* outline, slice a 1" slice from the side of the block to form the plank. Be careful not to cut into the area of the *cannon barrel* template.

9. Apply the *base* template at the top of the surface area now exposed by removing the plank, and cut and remove the *base* from the block. Remove all but a 3" base from the remaining ice below where the base was cut to expose the entire right side of the cannon barrel.

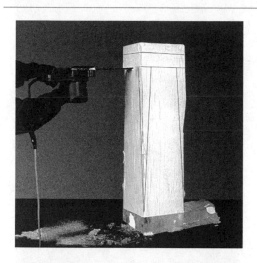

10. Apply the *right side cannon barrel* template to the newly exposed ice surface. Cut all lines to 2" deep.

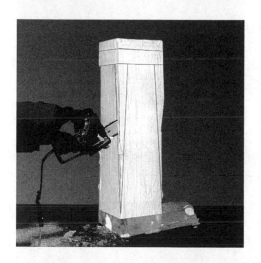

11. Cut away the *cannon barrel side* silhouette.

12. Cut away the *cannon barrel front* silhouette.

13. Remove the four corner edges to form eight sides of the cannon barrel (see Chapter 5). Use the saw blade to round and smooth the exterior of the cannon barrel.

14. Finish rounding the surface of the barrel using a hot water bag.

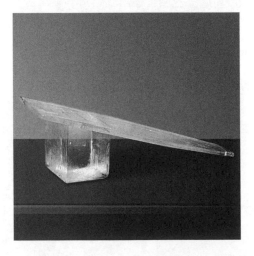

15. Fuse the base and plank pieces together (see Chapter 7).

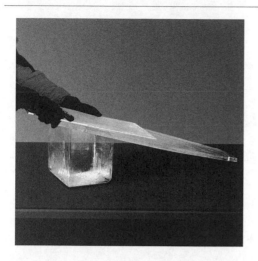

16. Polish the top surface of the plank with warmed aluminum.

17. Using the warmed aluminum, plane down one surface of the barrel $\frac{1}{2}$" to create an edge at the center of the barrel.

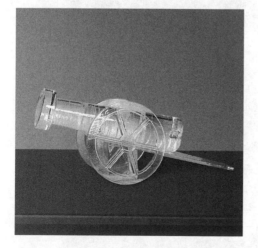

18. Attach the barrel to the plank, lining up the flattened edges. Fuse the wheels to each side of the barrel.

Pegasus

SAFETY TIP

In step 5, it is best to lay the sculpture on its side when removing the head.

SCULPTOR'S TIP

By cutting the base of the block on a very slight angle before standing it up, you can make your Pegasus lean forward, adding to the overall dimensions.

Required Tools

- Master tool list
- Die grinder with $\frac{1}{4}$" bit and course rubberizer
- Aluminum
- Rotary tool with $\frac{1}{8}$" straight bit
- Clothes iron
- Hot water bag

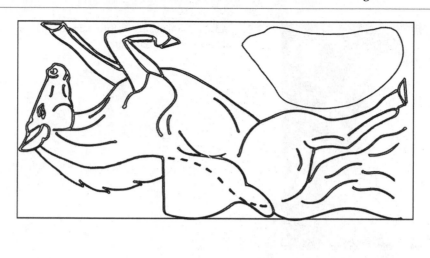

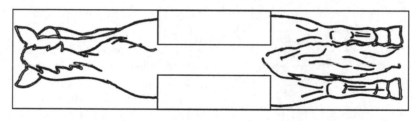

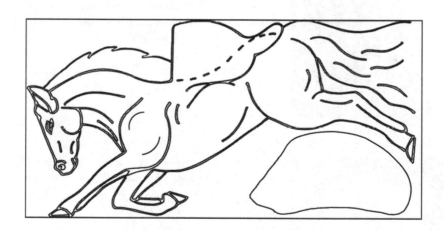

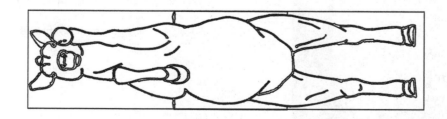

1. Apply templates to all four sides of the ice. Use reference lines to line up templates.

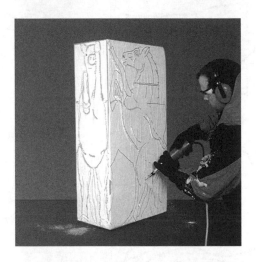

2. Working from the center of the design towards the outside edges, carefully trace all lines with a $\frac{1}{4}$" bit. Etch each template according to the following depths:
   a) Joint muscle details: 1" deep
   b) Leg muscle details: $\frac{1}{2}$" deep
   c) Behind the back leg (using a chain saw): 2–3" deep
   d) Face details: $\frac{3}{4}$"; and cheek details: 1"
   e) Stomach details: 1"
   f) Wings details: 1"

3. Make reference cuts to indicate the depth of each piece of the sculpture. Note the following cautions:
   a) Head—around the ears and head, be careful not to cut into the foreleg.
   b) Neck—do not hit the foreleg.
   c) Shoulders—through behind the horse's mane, expose a flattened shelf to support the upper section of each wing.
   d) Forelegs—make punch marks through the block.

4. Using the wing portions of the *front* and *back* side Pegasus template, carve a silhouette of each wing while they are still attached to the block. Remove each wing section from the block and set aside.

5. Using the chain saw, remove negative-space ice from the front and back sides of the template, exposing a perfect silhouette. Carefully slice off the head by cutting directly on the guiding line of the template.

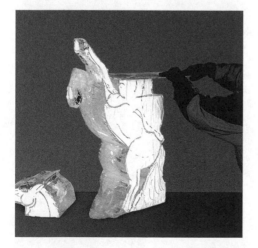

6. Flatten the exposed neck area of the main sculpture with warmed aluminum.

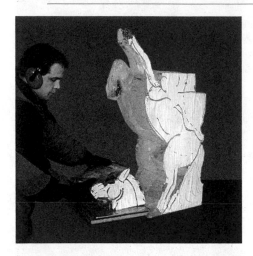

7. Flatten the bottom of the head with warmed aluminum.

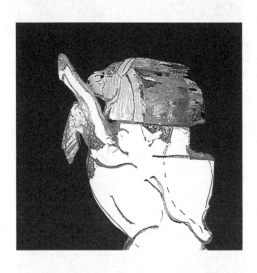

8. Fuse the head to the body with the head directed away from the raised leg.

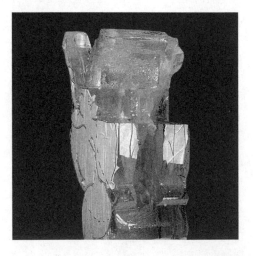

9. Make a separation cut between the two bottom sections of the wings still attached to the body, leaving a 3" gap.

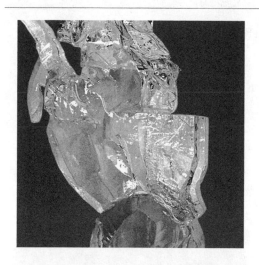

10. Separate the upper and lower forelegs by following the reference cuts on the template. Remove all template paper.

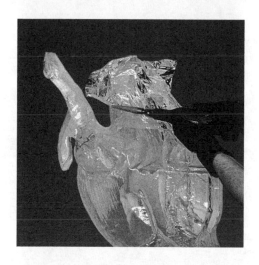

11. Using the chain saw, first blend the head and neck area to remove excess ice. Then, using the rubberizer, smooth and blend muscle tone around the entire sculpture.

12. Using a $\frac{1}{4}$" bit, etch primary detail lines into the head, mane, and tail.

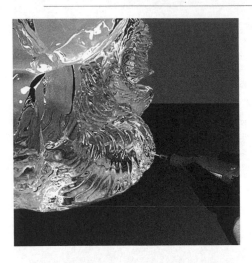

13. Using a $\frac{1}{8}$" bit, cut finer, secondary detail lines into the mane and tail.

14. Using a $\frac{1}{8}$" bit, cut finer, secondary detail lines to create facial features, hooves, and additional tone over the sculpture.

15. Using a slightly warmed iron, flatten wing shelves.

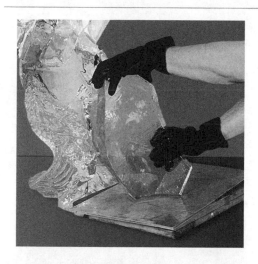

16. Flatten the wing joint using warmed aluminum.

17. Set the first wing in place and allow it to fuse and harden.

18. Set the second wing in place.

    Note: Snow may be applied to joint areas to strengthen the fuse. Allow wings to adhere to the body before beginning next step.

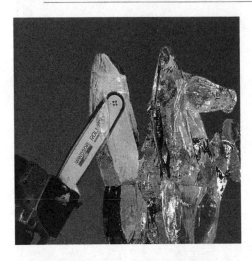

19. Blend wings to the body and to each other. Taper edges and angles to create a softened but distinct shape to each wing.

20. Clean out any template paper and ice debris from the detail with an ice pick and brush. Smooth all surfaces with a hot water bag.

Goose

SAFETY TIP

Each sculptor must recognize when he is fatigued or unable to safely operate the chain saw and other power tools, and be willing to rest as needed.

SCULPTOR'S TIP

This sculpture was designed for an outdoor display and is not easily moved once finished unless the support ice (step 28) is left between the inside of the wings.

Required Tools

- Master tool list
- Die grinder with V-shaped bit
- Aluminum
- Rotary tool with $\frac{1}{8}$" straight bit
- Clothes iron
- Rubberizer

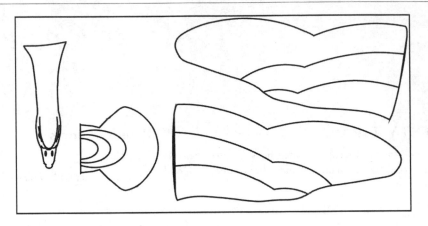

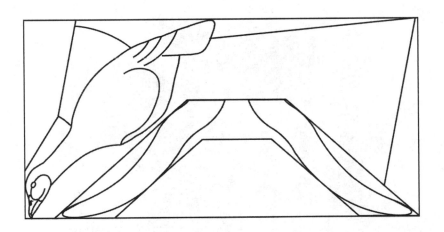

1. Apply the front template. Transfer lines using a $\frac{1}{8}$" bit.

2. Sand off the template.

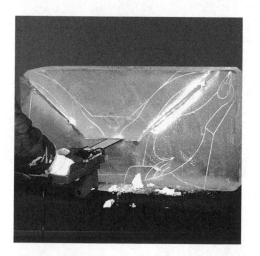

3. Lay the block on its side and remove the V-shaped wing section.

4. Remove negative-space ice to form the base the goose will sit on.

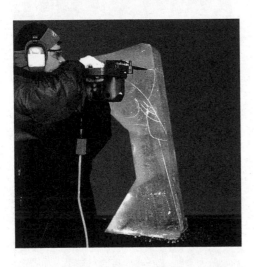

5. Stand the main piece upright and finish cutting out the silhouette.

6. Flip over the V-shaped section and remove the remaining negative-space ice.

7. Polish off a flat surface on top of the goose with warmed aluminum.

8. Polish off the bottom of the wing section with warmed aluminum.

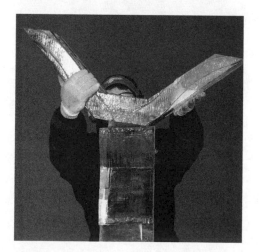

9. Fuse wing section to main piece.

10. Pour cool water over the section to fuse it.

11. Finish cutting out the rear silhouette of the wings.

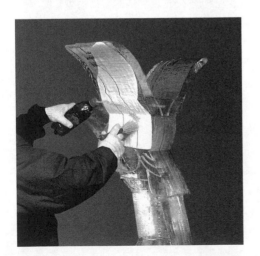

12. Place sub templates on the wings.

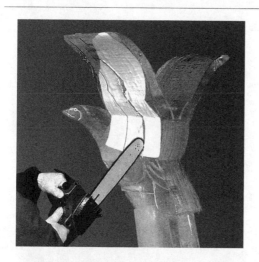

13. Etch in the outlines of the feathers on the wings.

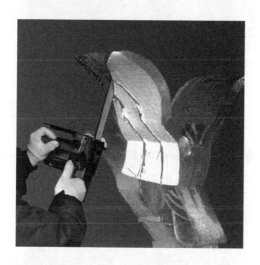

14. Cut away the silhouette of the wings.

15. Taper the rows of feathers so that they appear to overlap.

16. Taper the outer edges of the wings.

17. Etch in the feathers on the wings.

18. Attach sub template to the tail and transfer all lines with a $\frac{1}{8}$" bit.

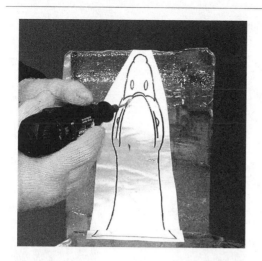

19. Attach sub template to the head and transfer all lines with a $\frac{1}{8}$" bit.

20. Remove ice on both sides of the head and neck.

21. Round and blend the neck and body so that they flow together.

22. Finish shaping the tail.

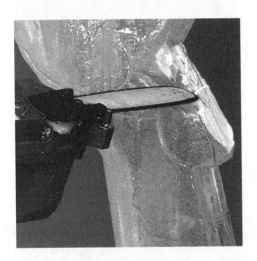

23. Taper the rows of tail feathers.

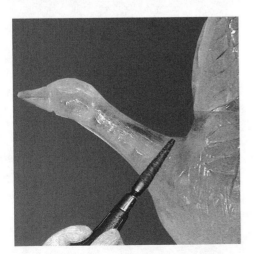

24. Smooth and round off the neck with the rubberizer.

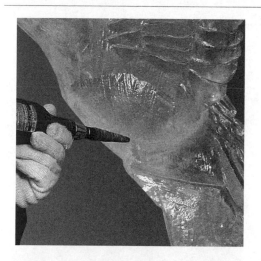

25. Smooth and round off the underbody with the rubberizer.

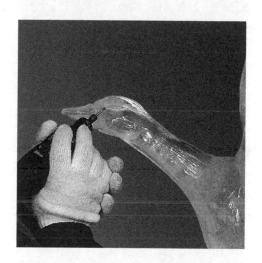

26. Redefine facial detail.

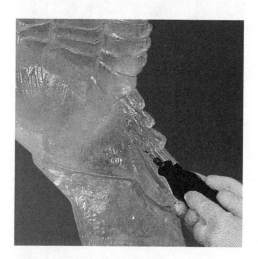

27. Etch in the tail feathers with a $\frac{1}{8}$" bit.

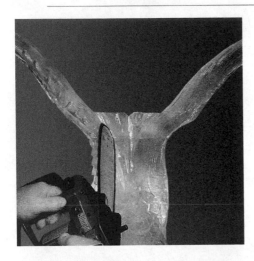

28. Carefully remove remaining support ice from between the wings.

29. Brush off any remaining debris.

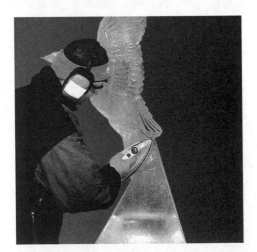

30. Polish all flat surfaces with the iron.

APPENDIX D

Additional Templates

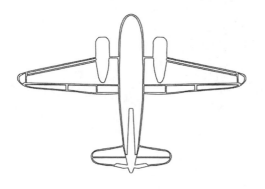

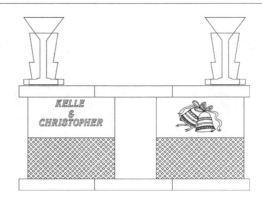

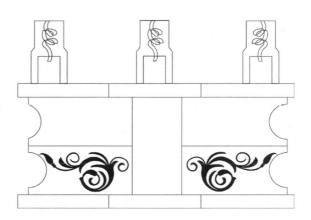

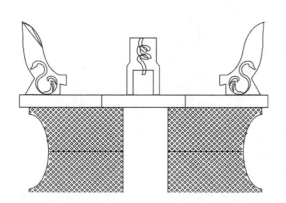

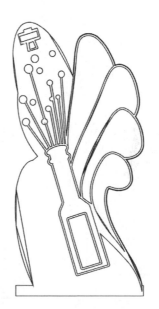

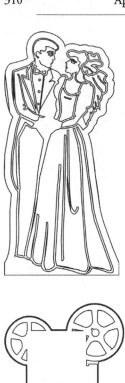

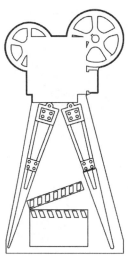

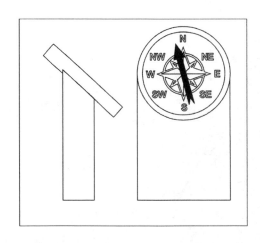

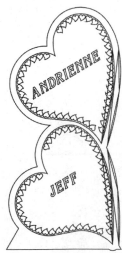

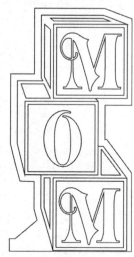

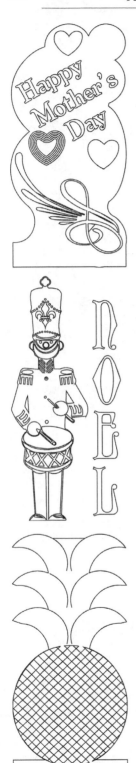

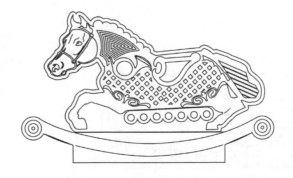

Resources and References

SUPPLIERS

Baumer Industries Corp.
114 W. 26th St.
8th Floor
New York, NY 10001
Tel: 212-414-1550
Fax: 212-924-0261

Glow box lighted display carts

Steve Brice
stevebrice@mosquitonet.com

Educational sculpting seminars

CA Safety Products
Division of Chlorine Accessories, Inc.
4780 136th Ave.
P.O. Box 8096
Holland, MI 49422-8096
Tel: 616-399-2693
Fax: 616-399-8737
www.casafety.com

Safety equipment, clothing, eye and
ear protection

Celebration Lighting
Tel: 800-859-8814
www.Celebrationlighting.com

Fog, bubble, snow, and foam machines
Lighting packages, Merlin and Chauvet
effects lights

Chemical Light, Inc.
595 N. Lakeview Pkwy
Veron Hills, IL 60061
Tel: 800-367-4569

Glow-in-the-dark products

Clinebell Equipment Co., Inc.
890 Denver Ave.
Loveland, CO 80537
Tel: 970-669-8100
or: 800-699-4423
Fax: 970-669-5707
brenda@clinebellequipment.com
www.clinebellequipment.com

Ice block-making equipment

Conical Tool Company
3890 Buchanan Ave. SW
Grand Rapids, MI 49548
Tel: 888-531-8500 (USA only)
or: 616-531-8500

Custom bits and end mills

Duende Ice Division
C/O Racquet Club of Memphis
5111 Sanderlin Ave.
Memphis, TN 38117-4398
Tel: 901-767-0313
Attn: Mac Winker

Reusable templates

Edmund Industrial Optics
101 East Gloucester Pike
Barrington, NJ 08007-1380
Tel: 800-363-1992
www.edmundoptics.com

Optics and optical instruments

Engineered Plastics, Inc.
P.O. Box 227
211 Chase St.
Gibsonville, NC 27249
Tel: 800-611-8466
or: 336-449-4121
Fax: 336-449-4121
Epi@netpath.net

Ice trays, light boxes, and bowls
Glo-Ice trays

FakeFire.com
P.O. Box 4575
Santa Barbara, CA 93140
Tel: 866-966-9566
help@fakefire.com

Vulcan Fire artificial flame systems,
bubble and fog machines

Grainger Industial Supply
www.grainger.com
Tel: 800-473-3473

Industrial and commercial equipment

Harbor Freight Tools
3491 Mission Oaks Blvd.
Camarillo, CA 93011-6010
Tel: 800-423-2567

Industrial and commercial equipment

C.J. Hummul Co.
P.O. Box 522
Nescopeck, PA 18635-0522
Tel: 570-752-0936
Fax: 570-752-0938
mail@hummul.com
www.hummul.com

Woodcarving supplies and catalog, tools,
books, and patterns

Ice Age Equipment Corporation
827 Glenside Ave.
Wycote, PA 19095
Tel: 610-292-8807

Lighted ice trays and display boxes

Ice Crafters
P.O. Box 2664
Glen Ellyn, IL 60138-2664
Tel: 630-871-0739
Fax: 630-871-0839
Icecrafter@aol.com
www.icecrafters.com
Attn: Alice Connelly

Ice block-making equipment,
tools, display trays, template paper,
custom bits

Iceculture Inc.
P.O. Box 232
81 Brock St.
Hensall, ON
N0M 1X0 Canada
Tel: 519-262-3500
or: 888-251-9967
Fax: 519-262-2492
Info@iceculture.com
www.iceculture.com

Clinebell ice blocks, carvings,
    tools, display trays, 5200 CNC,
    lathes

Ice Sculptures, Ltd.
188 Wealthy St. SW
Grand Rapids, MI 49503
Tel: 616-458-6005
Fax: 616-458-6030
Iceguru@aol.com
www.iceguru.com

Ethafoam, brochures, endmill bits,
    ice molds, boxes, sculptures,
    seminars, posters, coroplast

Ice Sculptures Ltd.
33 St. James Road
Little Paxton, St. Neots,
Cambs PE 196QW UK
Tel: +44(0) 1480 213245
www.ice-distribution.co.uk

Ice molds

J.B. Prince Co., Inc.
36 E. 31st St., Floor 11
New York, NY 10016-6821
Tel: 212-683-3553
Info@jbprince.com
www.JBPRINCE.com

Tools, display equipment,
    chain saws, die grinders

J & L Industrial Supply
Tel: 800-521-9520
www.jlindustrial.com

Industrial and commercial equipment

L.E.D. Effects
11390 Sunrise Gold Circle
Rancho Cordova, CA 95742
Tel: 916-852-1719
Fax: 916-852-1740

LED tube lighting

Magline, Inc.
503 South Mercer St.
Pinconning, MI 48650-9310
Tel: 1-800-624-5463
Fax: 989-879-5399
Marketing@Magliner.com
www.magline.com

Two- and four-wheel hand carts

Nadeau's Ice Sculptures, Inc.   Miscellaneous ice equipment products
7623 W. Roosevelt Road
Forest Park, IL 60130
Tel: 708-366-3333
Fax: 708-366-3378
icebiz@aol.com
www.nadeauice.com

ReNu Electric   Chain saws, die grinders
20163 John R
Detroit, MI 48203
Tel: 313-366-1570

Rubbermaid Home Products Division   Tubs, buckets, containers
1147 Akron Road
Wooster, OH 44691-6000
Attn: Consumer Services
Tel: 888-895-2110

Samaurai Sharpening   Ice-carving tool sharpening and
P.O. Box 44   restoration
Golden, CO 80402-0044
Tel: 303-423-6560
Attn: Michael Pizzuto

Sealed Air Corporation   Foam-in-Place systems, bubble cushioning,
Packaging Products Division   air-filled packaging systems
301 Mayhill St.
Saddle Brook, NJ 07663-5303
Tel: 1-800-648-9093
Fax: 201-712-7070
www.sealedair.com

Sculpture House   Books, tools, supplies
155 W. 26th St.
New York, NY 10016
Tel: 212-645-9430

SoCal Ice Productions   Legal service agreements
5644 Kearny Mesa Road Ste. B
San Diego, CA 92111   The Spider & Octopus
Tel: 858-565-0200   (Holding system for arranging
studio@socalice.com   items in blocks or bowls)
www.socalice.com
Attn: Mark Donovan

Sparktacular   Glitzzz Super Sparkler,
5460 State Road   remote pyrotechnics
84 Bay #12
Ft. Lauderdale, FL 33314
Tel: 954-792-1101
Fax: 954-792-1837
www.sparktacular.com

T&S Equipment Co.   Hoists, lifting equipment
900 Growth Parkway
Angola, Indiana 46703
Tel: 260- 665-9521

Uline   Shipping supply products
2200 S. Lakeside Drive
Waukegan, IL 60085
Tel: 800-295-5510
www.unline.com

Varta Batteries, Inc.   Wholesale batteries
601 Rayovac Drive
Madison, WI 53711
Tel: 800-431-2504
Fax: 800-832-9287
Cust_serv_order@rayovac.com

Weitech, Inc.   Diamond lights
P.O. Box 1690
601 North Larch Street
Sisters, OR 97759
Tel: 541-549-0205
Fax: 541-549-8154
www.weitech.com/customer_service.htm

Wood Carvers Supply, Inc.   Woodcarving accessories
P.O. Box 7500
Englewood, FL 34295-7500
Tel: 800-284-6229

ORGANIZATIONS

American Culinary Federation
10 San Bartola Drive
St. Augustine, FL 32086
Tel: 904-824-4468
Fax: 904-825-4758
Acf@acfchefs.net
www.acfchefs.org

American Hotel and Motel Association
1201 New York Avenue, NW Suite 600
Washington, DC 20005
Tel: 202-289-3100
Fax: 202-289-3199
www.ahma.com

Club Managers Association of America
1733 King Street
Alexandria, VA 22314
Tel: 703-739-9500
Fax: 703-739-0124
www.cmaa.org

Confrerie de la Chaine des Rotisseurs
444 Park Avenue South, Suite 301
New York, NY 10016
Tel: 212-683-3770
Fax: 212-683-3882
www.chaineus.org

Contemporary Sculptors Association, Inc.
117 Vere Street
Abbotsford, Victoria 3067
Australia

Council of Hotel and Restaurant Trainers
P.O. Box 2835
Westfield, NJ 07091
Tel: 800-463-5918
Fax: 800-427-5436
www.chart.org

Council of Independent Restaurants of America
304 West Liberty Street, Suite 201
Louisville, KY 40202
Tel: 502-583-3783
Fax: 502-589-3602
www.indrest.org

Council on Hotel, Restaurant, and Institutional
Education
2613 North Parham Road, 2nd floor
Richmond, VA 23294
Tel: 804-346-4800
Fax: 804-346-5009
www.chrie.org

Foodservice Educators Network International
www.feni.org

Friends of Sculpting
677 Port Kent Road
Dickinson Center, NY 12930
Tel: 518-856-9509
Frostie@northnet.org
web.northnet.org/friends_of_sculpting

International Association of Culinary Professionals
304 W. Liberty, Suite 201
Louisville, KY 40202
Tel: 502-581-9786
Fax: 502-589-3602
www.iacp-online.org

International Caterers Association
1200 17th Street, NW
Washington, DC 20036
Tel: 888-604-5844
www.ncacater.org

National Association of Catering Executives
5565 Sterrett Place, Suite 328
Columbia, MD 21044
Tel: 410-997-9055
Fax: 410-997-8834
www.nace.net

National Ice Carving Association P.O. Box 3593
Oak Brook, IL 60522-3593
Tel: 630-323-6696
Fax: 630-871-0839
www.nica.org

National Restaurant Association
1200 17th Street NW
Washington, DC 20036-3006
Tel: 202-331-5900
Fax: 202-331-2429
www.restaurant.org

U.S. Personal Chef Association
481 Rio Rancho Blvd., NE
Rio Rancho, NM 87124
Tel: 800-995-2138
Fax: 505-899-4097
www.uspca.com

World Association of Cooks Societies
Fedics House, 4th Floor
308 Kent Avenue
Randburg, South Africa
Tel: 011-27-11-787-4113
Fax: 011-27-11-787-4153
www.wacs.co.za

World Ice Sculpting Alliance
188 Wealthy Street, SW
Grand Rapids, MI 49503
Tel: 616-458-6005
Fax: 616-458-6030
www.iceguru.com

COMPETITIONS

Note: This list is not exhaustive. There are other events, some new since the printing of this book, which may have been omitted. The authors are merely attempting to provide a representative list of events for the reader. At the time of printing of this book, the following competitions and festivals were being held on a regular basis. It would be advisable to contact the organization listed to confirm that the event is still running.

Fairbanks Ice Carnival and Derby (World Ice Art Championship)
Ice Alaska
P.O. Box 83134
Fairbanks, Alaska 99708
Tel: 907-451-8250
www.icealaska.com

International Snow Sculpture Championships
Russia 614039, Perm,
K. Marx Street -49

National Collegiate Ice Carving Championship (AKA Frankenmuth)
Frankenmuth Chamber of Commerce and Convention and Visitors Bureau
635 S. Main Street
Frankenmuth, Michigan 48734
Tel: 989-652-6106

Olympic Arts Festival Ice Carving Association
C/O NICA
P.O. Box 3593
Oak Brook, Illinois 60522-3593

SELECTED BIBLIOGRAPHY

There are many fine books and articles on the subjects of ice, art, sculpting, and ice sculpting. The following references have been useful to the authors in their study of the art of ice sculpting.

Amendola, Joseph. *Ice Carving Made Easy.* 2nd Edition. New York, NY: John Wiley & Sons, Inc., 1994.

Bayley, Julian. *Ideas That Work.* Hensall, Ontario, Canada: Author, 2002.

Breithaupt, Herman A., and Betty L. Herring. *How We Started Students on Successful Foodservice Careers.* Boston, MA: Cahners Publishing Co., 1972.

Bridgeman, George B. *Bridgeman's Life Drawing.* New York, NY: Dover Publications, 1971.

Cantor Foundation. *Rodin: Sculpture from the Iris and B.* Gerald Cantor Collection. Beverly Hills, CA.

Chang, Ramond. *Chemistry.* 7th Edition. New York, NY: McGraw-Hill, 2002.

Cole, Alison. *Eyewitness Art: The Renaissance.* New York, NY: Dorling Kindersley, 1994.

Croft, Terrell et al. *American Electrician's Handbook.* 10th Edition. New York, NY: McGraw-Hill, 1981.

Durocher, Joseph F. Jr. *Practical Ice Carving.* New York, NY: CBI/Van Nostrand Reinhold Company, 1981.

Enstice, Wayne, and Melody Peters. *Drawing: Space, Form and Expression.* Upper Saddle River, NJ: Prentice Hall, 1996.

Forster, August. *Fancy Ice Carving in Thirty Lessons.* Chicago, IL: Northwestern Printing House, 1947.

Hammond, Lee. *How to Draw Lifelike Portraits from Photographs.* Cincinnati, OH: North Light Books, 1995.

Hasegawa, Hideo. *Ice Carving.* Carlsbad, CA: Continental Publishing, Ltd., 1974.

Haskins, Jim. *Snow Sculpture and Ice Carving.* New York, NY: Macmillan Publishing Co., 1974.

Hill, Dewey D., and Elliott R. Hughes. *Ice Harvesting in Early America.* New Hartford, NY: New Hartford Historical Society, 1977.

Jones, Joseph C. Jr. *America's Icemen.* Olathe, KS: Jobeco Books, 1984.

Lanteri, Edouard. *Modelling and Sculpting Animals.* Mineola, NY: Dover Publications, 1985.

Lauer, David A. *Design Basics.* New York, NY: Holt, Rinehart, and Winston, 1979.

Mariani, John F. *The Dictionary of American Food and Drink.* New Haven: Tichnor and Fields, 1983.

Matsuo, Yukio. *Ice Sculpture: Secrets of a Japanese Master.* New York, NY: John Wiley & Sons, Inc., 1992.

Paillasson, Gabriel. *Art Ephemere.* Saint-Fons, France: Author, 1995.

Shiring, Stephen B. Jr. et al. *Introduction to Catering.* United States: Delmar, a division of Thomson Learning, 2001.

Slobodkin, Louis. *Sculpture Principles and Practice.* New York, NY: Dover Publications, 1973.

Vallejo, Boris. *Fantasy Art Techniques.* New York, NY: Simon & Schuster, 1987.

Weising, George P. *Ice Carving Professionally.* Fairfield, CT: Fairfield County Publications, Inc., 1954.

Wilkins, David G. *Art Past, Art Present.* New York, NY: Harry N. Abrams, Inc., 1990.

Winker, Mac, and Claire Winker. *Ice Sculpture: The Art of Ice Carving in 12 Systematic Steps.* Memphis, TN: Duende Publications, 1989.

Glossary of Terms

A

Amperage   The strength of an electric current in amperes.

Amperes (Amps)   The standard unit for measuring an electric current, equal to 1 coulomb per second.

Aprons   Usually made of rubber, aprons are often worn by the sculptor to repel ice shavings and to remain dry while sculpting.

Artisan   Term used for a person who is skilled with a medium such as ice, bread, clay, or stone.

Artistic Process   The creative process of working and finalizing a concept while designing art.

Artist's Studio   The area established and organized by the artist in which he works to produce his art. Usually includes specific environmental requirements, equipment, and tools.

Assets   Items of value owned by a company. These include cash-on-hand, accounts receivable, land, large equipment, buildings, and inventory.

B

Balance   The harmonious proportion of elements in a design.

Balance Sheet   A company's statement of financial position on a given day.

Baseline   A horizontal line etched near the bottom of an ice block to identify where the sculpture ends and the support base begins.

Bits   Attachments to rotary tools, die grinders, and drills; bits come in a variety of designs for different uses.

Block   A rectangular mass of ice, prior to being cut. Usually measures 20" L × 10" W × 40" H and weighs approximately 300 pounds.

Blocking-In   To cut away at the block to reveal the basic form of the sculpture. Also known as *roughing-in*.

Blowtorch   Tool used in place of a heat gun or hair dryer to quickly melt the surface of the ice, it can crack the ice by exposing it to intense temperature change.

Borrowed Technology   Using the tools, methods, or science from one industry to meet the objectives in another industry.

Branding Tools   Used to emboss the ice by heating the brand end of the metal tool and quickly pressing the design into the ice.

Break-Even Analysis   A mathematical method for finding the dollar amount needed for a sculpting business (or any business) to break even financially.

BTU   Acronym for *British Thermal Unit,* which is a system of measurement used to gauge heat. The quantity of heat required to raise the temperature of 1 lb of water 1° Fahrenheit.

Budget   A financial plan of anticipated revenues and expenses for a specific period of time, used for making managerial decisions.

Business Plan   A financial document, detailing the scope and nature of a planned business, used as a communication tool for obtaining investors. Also serves as a guiding document for running the business.

C

CAD   Acronym for *Computer-Aided Design.*

Capacity   All that can be contained. Can also mean maximum output.

Capacitor   A device for storing an electrical charge.

Carbide   A binary compound of carbon with a more electropositive element, often used to coat cutting surfaces (such as chainsaw teeth) for increased strength and sharpness.

Carve   To cut into desired shapes or along specific lines.

Celsius   A metric unit of measurement for temperature. To convert degrees Celsius to degrees Fahrenheit, multiply the Celsius temperature by $\frac{9}{5}$ and add 32 to the result. At sea level, water boils at 100° Celsius or 212° Fahrenheit.

Center of Gravity   That point in an ice sculpture around which its weight is evenly balanced.

Centimeter   A metric unit for measurement of length, equivalent to 0.394".

Centerpiece   An ornamental object, such as an ice sculpture, that is displayed prominently on a table near its center.

Chain Saw   Gas or electric powered portable tool that has teeth linked together to form an endless chain. Originally designed for cutting and shaping wood, electric chain saws are now the primary cutting tool for ice sculptors.

Chipper   A 3-, 4-, 5-, or 6-pronged hand tool used for cutting or chipping ice. Also used to provide texture and design.

Chisel   A metal edged hand tool used for sculpting ice, wood, or stone by shaving or gouging it into the medium.

Circuit   The path or line of an electric current.

Circuit Breaker   A device that automatically interrupts the flow of an electric current.

Circulation Pumps   Small electric devices inserted into the top of the water reservoirs of the ice block maker. Used to move the water while it freezes, thereby raising the air, minerals, dust and other impurities to the surface and away from the ice block as it hardens.

Clear Ice   Ice blocks that are preferred by sculptors because they are transparent and don't have a cloudy feather running down their centers. Also known as *slick ice* or *crystal clear.*

Clinebell®   Brand name of an ice block-making machine that uses water pumps to produce crystal clear blocks of ice. Named for the freezing method developed by Virgil Clinebell.

CNC   Acronym for *Computerized Numeric Controls.*

Collet   The metal collar through which a drill bit's shaft is passed and then tightened, to secure the drill bit to the power tool.

Composition   The general makeup of a sculpture, the arrangement of parts into proper proportion or order.

Condensation   Process by which water vapor cools and turns to its denser, liquid form (water).

Conductor   A substance, like wire, that transmits heat or electricity.

Contaminated Water   Water containing foreign matter, such as dust or minerals.

Continuation   The perpetual use of a form, such as a primary line, to carry the viewer's eye along a sculpture.

Coroplast®   Brand name for corrugated plastic material.

Cost/Benefit Mix   An evaluation of the costs (time, money, material) expended versus the benefits (profit, publicity, experience) gained by completing an activity.

Cost of Goods Sold   The cost (dollar value) of labor and raw supplies used to create goods (products) that were sold.

Coulomb   A unit of electric charge equal to 6.25×10^{18} electrons passing a point in 1 second.

Crash and Burn   When a sculpture falls (crashes) due to overstepping the limits of balance and fuse strength, resulting in the sculptor's lost entry (burn) from a competition.

Crystallization   The formation of crystals or crystalline shapes. Water, when it freezes, forms a six-pointed crystalline molecular structure.

Current   The flow, or rate of flow, of electricity in a conductor.

Cutting Zone   An imaginary mobile radius of 6' that surrounds a sculptor operating power tools. An area within the *safety zone* for the sculptor to operate power tools without the possibility of endangering another person.

D

Design Elements   Component parts to an overall design or theme.

Dimension   Bodily form or proportion of a sculpture. Can also mean the measurement in one direction.

Display   A setting or presentation of a sculpture.

Display Cart   A custom-built cart for displaying ice sculptures. Usually has through lighting and drainage system.

Disturbed Water   Moving water.

Dremmel®   Brand name for a die grinder manufacturer commonly used by ice sculptors.

Drill   An electric or hand-cranked tool used to bore holes or etch designs into the ice.

Dry Ice®   Brand name for a refrigerant consisting of solidified carbon dioxide.

E

Electromotive   Producing an electric current through differences in potential.

Entrepreneur   An individual who organizes a business and assumes risks in order to create a market for profit.

Ephemeral   Short-lived object, usually lasting only one day.

Erosive Force   Wind, water, ice, or grit that wears down an object when applied forcefully.

Etch   The action or effect of making a design on the surface of the ice, usually with a pick, scribe, chain saw, or die grinder and bit.

Ethafoam®   The brand name for dense sponge-like sheets made from polyethylene, used by ice sculptors to insulate and protect their sculptures.

F

Fahrenheit   A U.S. unit of measurement for temperature. To convert degrees Fahrenheit to degrees Celsius, subtract 32 from the Fahrenheit temperature and multiply the result by $\frac{5}{9}$. At sea level, water boils at 212° Fahrenheit or 100° Celsius.

Feather   Trapped impurities, such as air or minerals, that are forced to the center of the block during the freezing action causing a cloudy, white appearance. Often a softer part of the block due to the trapped air.

Fixed Costs   Costs that do not vary with sales and that are generally known in advance of sales. These include loan payments, rent, salaries, and insurance.

Flat Fusing   The process of attaching two flat surfaces to each other.

Flowing   The rhythm and lifelike quality of a sculpture.

Foam-in-Place   A method of securing a packaged item or sculpture by injecting a polyurethane foam around the item, filling the air void.

Foot   A U.S. unit for measurement of length, equivalent to 0.305 meters.

Form   A three-dimensional object such as a cube, cylinder, or ball. Forms are derived from *shapes*, which are two-dimensional.

Functionality   The use of a sculpture for a particular purpose.

Fuse   The joining or attaching of two or more pieces of ice (see Flat, Natural and/or Peg Fusing).

G

Gauge   A standard measure or criterion. Can also mean the thickness of wire or sheet metal.

Gels   Colored, transparent sheets of plastic-like material mounted over theatrical lighting. Used to illuminate sculptures in various colors.

GFCI   Acronym for *Ground Fault Circuit Interrupter*.

Gouging   Scooping out a cavity or channel in the ice using a saw or power tool.

Gram   A metric unit for measurement of weight. One gram equals 0.035 oz.; 28 grams equals 1 oz.

Graph Paper   Paper ruled for drawing designs. Commonly used by sculptors to design their sculpture templates.

Greenhouse Effect   Extended exposure to sunlight, especially the ultraviolet rays, will melt ice from the inside.

Gross Margin   Sales minus the cost of goods sold equals gross margin. The money remaining before other deductions are taken.

Gross Profit   Sales minus variable costs equals gross profit. The money remaining before fixed costs are deducted.

H

Hair Dryer   Used instead of a heat gun or blow-torch to polish the surface of the ice by melting it.

Hand Saw   Tool with larger teeth than the wood saw, used for splitting blocks, fusing, and marking the base.

Harvesting   Retrieving hardened ice blocks from a frozen pond or ice block making machine.

Hassle Factor   Work requested that is beyond the scope of that ordinarily requested or provided. An additional charge is often applied for such services.

Hatching   Hollowing out an area in the ice that will later be filled with snow to create definition of that area.

Horizon Level   The view at eye level.

Horizontal   Parallel to the horizon, at right angles to a vertical line.

Hot Water Bag   Plastic bag filled with warm water, used to smooth and polish the surface of the ice in a controlled and uniform manner.

I

Ice   Solid form of many substances. For this text, we refer to ice as frozen water molecules.

Iceculture 5200®   Brand name of a CNC router machine developed by Julian Bayley. Precisely cuts ice by the operator programming the dimensions of the ice and the design pattern into its computerized control panel. The ice is then cut using an end mill.

Ice-Friendly   Tools that are adapted to lower their destructive impact when used on ice. Can also mean any object or environment that does not damage ice through its contact.

Ice Knives   Tools primarily used to clean rough edges and perform delicate shaping.

Ice Pick   A single pointed steel-tipped tool used for breaking, scribing, or chipping the ice. Also known as a *one-point chipper*.

Ice Point   The point at which ice begins to melt at 0° Celsius under standard atmospheric pressure.

Ice Sculptures, Ltd.®   Brand name of a style of ice sculptures produced by Ice Sculptures, Ltd., co-authors of this text.

Icework   Ice sculptures done for pay.

Inch   A U.S. unit of measurement for length, equivalent to 2.54 cm.

Income Statement   A financial report that shows the amount of profit or loss a business has made or lost over a given time period. Also known as a *profit and loss statement.*

J

Jig   A device used to guide a tool.

K

Kick Back   The action of a chain saw when its blade chain hits a resistant surface, causing the saw to bounce backwards away from the item being cut. Although common when cutting wood, ice rarely causes kick back.

Kilogram   A metric unit for measurement of mass, equivalent to 2.2 lbs.

Kilometer   A metric unit for measurement of distance, equivalent to 0.62137 miles.

Kinetic   Having movement of its own.

L

LED   Acronym for *Light Emitting Diode.*

Liabilities   The amount of money owed by a company to its creditors. These include loans, debts, and accounts payable.

Lost Opportunity   A situation that arises when a person is unable to take advantage of an opportunity because of a conflict, usually because they are unavailable or do not have the necessary resources.

Lubricate   Oiling the chain saw, usually with clear, food-grade oil that keeps the chain from seizing.

M

Makita®   Brand name for a manufacturer that produces electric chain saws commonly used by ice sculptors.

Marcottage   The artistic design process of blending or mixing sculptures or fragments of sculptures to create a layered effect on a final, larger work.

Mass   A quantity of matter of indefinite shape or size. Can also mean the bulk of a sculpture.

Master Template   Original and primary full-scale drawing that is updated and footnoted as revisions occur during practice sessions.

Mats   Usually made from rubber, floor mats are used to reduce the stress and shock of standing on hard surfaces over an extended period of time. Mats are also used under the ice sculptures to prevent them from "wandering" and to protect the tools while sculpting.

Maxfield Color Method   Process by which colors are suspended in 65° F liquid gelatin and distributed evenly within a pattern on an ice sculpture. Used to create colored designs for logos, pictures, and other patterns. Named for its inventor, Derek Maxfield.

Medium   Material or technical means of artistic expression. Commonly refers to the ice that is being sculpted.

Meter   A metric unit for measurement of distance, equivalent to 3.2808'.

Metric System   A decimal system based on the number 10. Provides standard rules for unit amounts through prefixes.

Mise en place   French for "things in place." Implies the orderly and complete organization of needed tools and/or ingredients.

Models   Representations of a subject used for practice sculpting. Often made from another medium, such as clay, porous concrete, or soap.

Modernist   An artist who thinks and works in the present time using the technology available.

Montage   A composite picture or sculpture that includes a variety of designs or elements.

Movement   In the visual sense, to represent action or activity. Can also mean the flow or order of associated elements in a sculpture.

Multi-Block   A sculpture made using more than one block of ice, usually fused together.

N

Nail Board   A board with the pointed ends of many nails protruding from one side, used for roughing ice.

Nail Board Fusing   A method of joining ice. Two facing sides of ice pieces are roughed up with a nail board then welded with freezing water sprayed between the blocks.

Natural Peg Fusing   A fuse that is made along a natural seam or line in the sculpture, such as a belt, muscle, or fletching of a feather.

Negative Space   Unwanted ice occupying an area of the original block which must be removed to reveal the desired finished piece.

Net Profit/Loss   The money available after all goods and operating expenses are satisfied. Generally calculated monthly and annually.

O

Ohms   A unit of electrical resistance, equal to the resistance of a conductor carrying a current of 1 ampere at a potential difference of 1 volt between the terminals.

Ohm's Law   A formula that relates the voltage, current, and resistance of a circuit, hence allowing the calculation of these values at any point in a circuit. Expressed as $V = I \times R$.

Opaque Ice   Ice that is cloudy due to impurities in it.

Originality Myth   The concept that suggests that nothing is truly original and all designs come from pre-existing elements.

OSHA   Acronym for the *Occupational Safety and Health Administration*, an office of the U.S. Department of Labor that oversees the workplace environment for the protection of the laborers.

Owner's Equity   Equal to the owner's assets minus liabilities. The amount of financial interest the owner has in the assets of the company.

P

Peg Fusing   The creation of a system of tapered ice pegs on one ice piece that fit into corresponding holes on another ice piece for the purpose of joining the two pieces. Also known as *pegging*.

Percival®   A brand of power saw with two shaft lengths, it is used to undercut, trim, and detail sculptures.

Perspective   The conceptual ability to understand or visualize in a balanced manner.

Physical Shock   Damage to an ice block or sculpture when it is bumped against a hard surface, such as a concrete floor or truck bed.

Pick   A small wooden-handled tool with a needle-like steel end used to etch or roughly chop ice.

Picture Plane   The frontal side of a canvas or drawing paper on which the picture is located.

Plotter   Originally associated with mapmaking, oversized printers used in graphic design and CAD offices.

Polish   To smooth, soften, and refine a surface, often to produce a gloss finish.

Pond-Cut   Ice that is cut and harvested from frozen ponds.

Potential   The relative voltage at a point in an electric circuit with respect to some other reference point in that same circuit.

Pounce   The application of powders, such as charcoal dust, to a template. Involves dabbing a bag of powder over the holes in the template to transfer the design.

Pound   A U.S. unit of measurement for mass, equivalent to 0.45 kg.

Power Cords   Heavy-duty, rubber-coated extension cords for power tools.

Power Strips   Insulated receptacles for plugging in multiple power cords.

Power Tools   Electrically powered hand tools used to etch, cut, shape, sand, and drill. Used instead of hand saws and chisels to sculpt ice.

Press Kit   A collection of photographs, fact sheets, and biographies that businesses and professionals compile. These are given to the media to promote publicity about a business or artist.

Primary Lines   Identifies the fundamental shape and outline of the sculpture or its major parts. Also known as *strong lines*.

Primary Sculpture   The first and most important sculpture derived from an ice block.

Primary View   The main direction from which a sculpture is to be viewed. Also known as the *face* of the sculpture.

Production Template   Working templates that are destroyed during the sculpting process.

Professionalism   An attitude and behavior that demonstrates excellence in a profession.

Profit & Loss Statement   A financial report that shows the amount of money a business has earned (net income or profit) or lost (net loss) over a given period (usually a month, a quarter, or a year). Also known as an *income statement*.

Proportion   To make the parts of the sculpture harmonious or symmetrical.

Propylene Glycol   A food grade antifreeze added to edible products to prevent freezing or separation. Also used in mold-making machines to facilitate the even distribution of temperature during the freezing process.

Proximity   Several elements in a sculpture that are close together. Can also mean organizing a work area with elements closely arranged.

Punch Marks   Deep cuts, usually made with a chain saw, to provide guiding marks for removing negative space.

Pure Water   Water without impurities, such as minerals or dust.

Pyrotechnics   A dazzling display of fireworks or fire-related exhibition.

R

Raw Blocks   Whole, uncut blocks of ice. Also known as *raw ice*.

Repetition   The repeated use of a form or shape.

Resistance   Opposition of some force to another, as to the flow of electrical current.

Rhythm   Measured repetition of a shape, form, or feature.

Risk   In business, unknown variables that may negatively affect the outcome of a decision.

Roughing-In   The act of cutting away at ice to reveal a rough likeness or silhouette of the final sculpture. Also known as *making rough cuts* or *blocking-in*.

Rounding   Making every part of the surface or circumference equidistant from the center. In ice sculpting, can also mean continuously removing corners to eventually transform a few larger straight edges into numerous smaller edges until the surface appears rounded.

Rubber Mats   Heavy-duty floor mats, such as the rubber fatigue mats used in commercial kitchens. Used under ice blocks to protect the floor and ice tools while sculpting. Reduces shock fractures and melting at the sculpture's base.

Rust   The reddish-brown coating formed on metal after prolonged exposure to moisture and air.

S

Safety Zone   An area established by cordoning off a perimeter, allowing a sculptor to work without interruption within its boundaries.

Sales   Money coming in from the sale of goods and services. Also known as *sales revenue*.

Sales Revenue   Money coming in from the sale of goods and services. Also known as *sales*.

Sanding   Using a chainsaw blade or sander to shave and smooth ice by running it back and forth over the uneven ice surface.

Scope   The range or extent of the design.

Score   A line made in the ice with a sharp tool, such as an ice pick. Often used to trace a template pattern onto the ice.

Scrap Ice   Unwanted ice from the negative space of the primary sculpture. Often used as packing snow or to make secondary or support pieces.

Scribe   A tool for etching, or the act of etching ice. The sculptor would *scribe* his template design into the ice with a pick.

Sculpture   A three-dimensional work of art formed from solid material, such as ice.

Secondary Lines   Not as strong as the *primary lines* of the sculpture, the secondary lines add depth and definition.

Service Contract   A form that clearly defines and details client expectations and sculptor obligations.

Setting-Up   Ice freezing to a state of hardness. Can also mean the act of putting together a display.

Shape   A two-dimensional object such as a circle or square. Shapes are the foundation of *forms*, which are three-dimensional.

Shaping   Altering the appearance or form of a sculpture by cutting and sanding its exterior.

Silhouette   The outline of an object viewed as circumscribing a mass.

Slick Ice   Another name for clear ice. Produced by circulating water while it freezes to separate out the air, minerals, and other impurities and form transparent ice.

Slush   Partly melted or watery snow. Often packed around a crack or seam to fuse or repair.

Snow   Opaque water/ice molecules. Also used to describe soft, cloudy ice.

Squaring   Standing the ice block so that it is perfectly horizontal, or leveling it prior to sculpting. A safety practice to prevent tipping and uneven cutting.

Static   Having no movement of its own.

Steam Wand   An old-style method of cutting ice by directing steam through a narrow metal wand towards the ice. The wand must be connected to a boiler using rubber hoses and valves.

String   Rope used to measure and draw straight lines.

Strong Lines   Identifies the essential form and outline of a sculpture or its major parts. Also known as *primary lines*.

Styrofoam   Material used as insulation and shock-resistant padding for transporting and storing ice pieces.

Sublimation   The evaporation of solid ice (frozen water molecules) into vapor that occurs when ice blocks are left uncovered in a frozen environment, such as a walk-in freezer.

Sub Templates   Smaller templates used to etch new areas of the inner block that are revealed after preliminary rough cuts.

Sub-Zero Art   A nickname for ice sculpting or ice sculptures due to the fact that its temporary existence is dependent upon being kept in freezing temperatures.

Suggestive Selling   The process of suggesting or recommending products to a customer with the intention of increasing sales.

Symbolism   To represent something in an abstract manner, such as artistic imitation as a means of expression.

Symmetry   The balance or beauty of the art form resulting from corresponding opposite parts.

T

Table   Normally 6–8 feet in length, a useful place to keep tools organized and closely available.

Techno-Artists   Expression applied to individuals who use technology such as power tools and computers to create, design, and produce their artwork.

Temper   Adjusting the internal temperature of an ice block to that of the surrounding environment prior to being sculpted. Often means slowly warming a block by letting it sit for a few hours in the carving room or overnight in a walk-in cooler. Can also be used to describe the slow cooling or reduction of temperature of an ice block when placed in a sub-freezing environment.

Temperature   The amount of heat or coldness of an object. Also used as a measurement of kinetic energy. Usually measured in degrees of *Celsius* or *Fahrenheit*.

Template   The outline of a design that can be placed directly onto an ice block for tracing and guiding the sculptor's tools. May be made from wood, plastic, or metal but is usually made from paper.

Texture   The visual or tactile surface characteristics and appearance of an ice block or sculpture.

Theme   A topic used as a focal point of a buffet, party, or sculpture. Sculptures are often created in support of, or to reflect, event themes.

Thermo-Shock   Weakening and cracking of the ice block caused by an extreme inconsistency between the internal temperature of the ice and the temperature outside the block. Occurs when the surface of the ice is subjected to a change in temperature.

Three-Dimensional Vision   The ability to visualize a sculpture's height, width, and depth.

Tongs   Large, sturdy metal hand tool with pincer ends used to grip and move ice.

Total Operating Expenses   The total of all other expenses, other than the cost of goods, incurred by a company to operate its business.

Tracing Paper   Thin, semi-transparent paper. When placed over a pattern, allows the pattern to be seen and copied by the artist.

Traditionalist   A person who believes in philosophies or who practices methods that have been handed down through generations, despite current trends, practices, or modern technology.

Translucent   Allowing light to pass through, but not transparent.

Transparent   Visually clear; allowing objects to be seen through the material, such as glass or clear ice.

Trays   Used to hold ice sculptures for display. Often outfitted with drainage tubes and underlights.

Two-Wheel Handcart   A labor-saving metal device with two tires used to transport blocks of ice and finished sculptures. Also known as a *two-wheel dolly*.

U

Unity   The presentation of a unified or single image.

V

Vapor   A gaseous form of any substance, normally of a liquid. Visible moisture particles suspended in the air.

Vapor Barrier   A boundary of separation, either natural or man-made, between vapor and other items to prevent moisture contact.

Variable Costs   Those expenses that change as sales change and are not known in advance of sales. Usually includes hourly labor, raw goods, and supplies.

Vectorized (Artwork)   A line drawing composed of only primary lines with no color or shading, such as a template.

Vertical   Straight up and down, at right angles to a horizontal line.

Visualization   The ability to see the finished sculpture within the ice.

Volt   A unit of electromotive force.

Voltage   An electromotive force expressed in volts.

Voltage Drop   The loss of voltage in an extension cord due to the resistance created by extended cord length and narrow wire diameter.

Volume   The amount of space occupied in three dimensions.

W

Watt   A unit of electrical power, equal to the power developed in a circuit by a current of 1 ampere flowing through a potential difference of 1 volt.

Wattage   The amount of electrical power.

Weight to Mass Ratio   The measurement of the force exerted on a mass by gravity in relation to its size and quantity of matter.

Wellingtons   Large rubber boots worn by sculptors to keep their feet dry and grounded from electrical shock. Also known as "Wellies."

Working Templates   Templates or patterns that are used during the sculpting process. Usually copied from the *master template*. Also known as *production templates*.

Work Order   A document used to communicate the customer's design requests. Used by the production staff to create the finished product.

Z

"Z"-Cut   A vertical and horizontal cutting of a new block of ice to form two thinner L-shaped blocks, each with its own base.

Index